YANKEE EMPIRE

YANKEE EMPIRE

Aggressive Abroad and Despotic At Home

James Ronald and Walter Donald

KENNEDY

SHOTWELL PUBLISHING
Columbia, South Carolina

Yankee Empire: Aggressive Abroad and Despotic at Home
Copyright © 2018, 2021 by James R. and Walter D. Kennedy

ALL RIGHTS RESERVED. No part of this publication may be reproduced, distributed, or transmitted in any form or by any means, including photocopying, recording, or other electronic or mechanical methods, or by any information storage and retrieval system without the prior written permission of the publisher, except in the case of very brief quotations embodied in critical reviews and certain other non-commercial uses permitted by copyright law.

Produced in the Republic of South Carolina by

Shotwell Publishing, LLC
Post Office Box 2592
Columbia, South Carolina 29202

www.ShotwellPublishing.com

Cover Design: Hazel's Dream

ISBN-13: 978-1-947660-87-8

10 9 8 7 6 5 4 3 2

Contents

Introduction ix

Chapter One: Southerners are Not Yankees 1

Chapter Two: Modern Day Examples of Worldwide
Yankee Empire in Action 15

    CIA Coup in Iran—1953 18

    Yankee Empire supports dictator in Indonesia—1971-1998 25

    Libya 26

    Iraq 29

    The Boxer Rebellion—China's Century of Humiliation 33

    Teaching the World To Be Second-Class Yankees 39

    The Republic of Colombia 40

    Honduras 42

    Guatemala 44

    Summary: Yankee Empire's major interventions
    into Latin America 46

    The Origins of "Yankee Go Home!" 49

Chapter 3: Hawaii the Yankee Empire's First
International Conquest 51

  Queen Lili'uokalani of Hawaii 51

Chapter 4: From American Republic to Yankee Empire 75

  Is the United States an Empire? 85

  Yankee Empire Reconstructs the Philippines—1899-1947 90

  Yankee Empire Reconstructs Cuba—1898-1959 97

  Reconstructing Native Americans 102

  Reconstructing the South 1865—Present 109

  Pretext for Invasion 118

  Retaliation Against Civilians 122

  Installing Puppet Governments 122

  Divide and Rule 124

  Cultural Genocide 125

  Extermination and Repopulation 127

  The Dangers of Empire 128

Chapter 5: Republics Avoid Foreign Interventions 133

Chapter 6: An Evil Empire's First Invasion 147

  North and South—Not just Different but Antagonistic 149

  Early Warnings of the Danger of Maintaining a Close Union With Yankeedom 156

  North-South Trade Imbalance 158

  Northern Opposition to Lincoln's Illegal War 159

Lincoln the Tyrant 163

The Yankee Empire's War of Extermination 170

The South Suffered First but the World Would Follow 174

Chapter 7: Southern Efforts to End Slavery 179

Chapter 8: Constitutional Republic or Commercial Empire 201

Alexander Hamilton's High Federalist Curse on Liberty 205

Empires Impose Death, Destruction, and Misery 214

Chapter 9: U.S. Army Invades the Confederate States of America .. 219

Fort Sumter 229

Andersonville - Major Wirz 231

General Forrest Massacred Black Soldiers at Fort Pillow 236

The War was Fought Over Slavery 241

Chapter 10: Yankee Empire Plunders a Conquered South 251

The Southern People—From Riches to Rags 252

The Yankee Empire's Destructive Reign of Terror 254

Attempts to Exterminate Black and White Southerners 257

Financial Loss Due to Yankee-imposed Emancipation
of Southern Slaves 260

The Yankee Empire's Exploitation of its Captive Nation 265

Exploitation Under the South's Bayonet Constitutions 266

Sharecropping—a New Form of Slavery 270

Chapter 11: Occupation of a Once Free People..................................273

    The Sovereign States in 1776 273

    A strategic failure—the South's Refusal to Maintain
    its Right to be Free..279

Chapter 12: Cultural Genocide—the Destruction of a Proud Heritage 283

Chapter 13: Globalism—Yankee International Crony Capitalism... 297

Chapter 14: Do Slave-owners or Their Descendants Deserve Freedom?
....311

    The Altar of Freedom is Bathed in Southern Blood 319

Chapter 15: The Will to be Free?...323

    What Price for the South's Soul? 328

    Defining Southern Freedom 332

    Summary—If the South had Won..333

    International Consequences of an Independent
    Confederate States of America 339

Terms and Phrases..343

Select Bibliography 353

About the Authors 361

Index 363

INTRODUCTION

General Robert E. Lee, C.S.A.
Courtesy Library of Congress (LOC)

IN A LETTER TO LORD ACTON written in 1866, former Confederate General Robert E. Lee noted his concern that if the United States used its victory over the Confederate States of America to destroy the American principle of States' Rights, then the United States would morph into a country that would become "aggressive abroad and despotic at home."[1] Unfortunately for the people of the South and the world, General Lee's prediction has become our reality. America's original Constitutionally limited Republic of Sovereign States has been replaced with a supreme federal government controlled by ruling political and financial elites. The supreme federal government assumed unto itself the sole discretion as to the Constitutional limits (if any) to its powers. The former free and prosperous people of the Confederate States of America became the Yankee Empire's first captive nation—we would not be its last.

---

[1] Lee's letter to John Emerich E. Dalberg-Acton (1834-1902), British author, historian, and political philosopher. Available at www.oll.libertyfund.org/titles/acton-selections-from-the-correspondence-of-the-first-lord-acton-vol-i#lf1480_head_058 (Accessed 09/18/2017).

This book is written with the intention of having it initially translated into the Spanish and Russian languages. Therefore, the authors have taken care to explain ideas and topics that are "common" knowledge for most Southerners who have studied the War for Southern Independence—a war incorrectly referred to by the Yankee victor as the "Civil War." A glossary of common words and phrases used in the South is included after the end of the last chapter for the benefit of foreign readers. The central theme of this work is that the current federal government is, in fact, an international (global) commercial, financial, and military empire. The original Constitutionally limited Republic of Republics as established by America's Founding Fathers in 1776 no longer exists! It was destroyed by Lincoln, the Republican Party, and their crony capitalist co-conspirators in 1861-1865. The current federal and state governments were imposed upon the people of the Confederate States of America at the point of bloody bayonets and never let it be forgotten that the blood on those Yankee bayonets is Southern blood. The Yankee Empire and its puppet governments in Southern states are governments founded upon aggressive military and political compulsion. These governments are in violation of the American principle of "consent of the governed" and as such are *illegitimate* governments. As will be demonstrated, the people of the South today are citizens of a captive nation (the Confederate States of America) and subjects of the Yankee Empire.

Few "conservative" scholars or writers will dare to look into the radical change in the governance of the United States that occurred as a result of the Yankee victory in the War for Southern Independence—for Yankees it was the War to *Prevent* Southern Independence. Most conservative "scholars and writers" are abject Lincoln worshippers. Although liberal "scholars and writers" have taken notice of the growth of the American Empire, they never associate the origins of that Empire with the United States' invasion of the peaceful, democratically elected, Sovereign nation—the Confederate States of America. If the Lincoln worshipers dare to admit that the United States is now an empire, they will refer to it as a "Benevolent Empire" doing "missionary" good around the world. The concept that the United States is a "Benevolent Empire" originated in New

England and was taken up by pre-War Whigs[2] and then the Republicans of the High Federalist school. But "Benevolent Empires" bring their "benevolence" only to those with close connections with the Empire's ruling elite. The benefits of empire flow to the empire's ruling elite and those benefits are paid for by the empire's subjects. This book demonstrates what American liberal and conservative intellectuals and writers carefully ignore—the initial imperial acts that produced the current global Yankee Empire occurred with the invasion, conquest, occupation, and deliberate impoverishment of "we the people" of the Confederate States of America.

By the end of the "Civil War," the United States had become an empire—a nation that uses its commercial, financial, and military might to project its power beyond its borders. In recounting the growth of the Yankee Empire, the authors have liberally cited the works of numerous left-wing "scholars and writers." These "scholars and writers" span time and ideology from V. I. Lenin to Noam Chomsky and others. The authors hold no misconception regarding the fact that these left-wing "scholars and writers" would not endorse the South's past or contemporary claim to home rule, local self-government, real States' Rights, and freedom. But the views of these left-of-center "scholars" and "writers" give ample support to our claim that the current global Yankee Empire had its origin in the United States' first (1861-1865) act of invasion, regime change, and eventual incorporation of its Southern occupied territory into the newly created Yankee Empire.

---

[2] Hummel, Jeffery, Rogers, *Emancipating Slaves, Enslaving Free Men* (Chicago: Open Court, 1996), 22, 206, 315; also see "The Benevolent Empire," US History I (AY Collection), Empirecourses.lumenlearning.com/ushistory1ay/chapter/the-benevolent-empire (Accessed 11/06/2017).

For "conservative" Southerners, the recounting of the Yankee Empire's numerous international invasions, "regime changes," and the ensuing bloodletting (euphemistically referred to today as "collateral damage") may prove to be painful.³ Politically conservative, Bible-belt Southerners like to think of "our" country as being generous, compassionate, and always seeking to help the downtrodden, especially by advancing "democracy." But international reality does not support this vision of "our" country. The truth that this book demonstrates to our fellow Southerners and to the people of the world is that the current Yankee Empire is not "our" country. "We the people" of the South are citizens of a captive nation, the Confederate States of America, and subjects of the Yankee Empire.

> The lust of *empire* impelled them [Yankees] to wage against their weaker neighbors [the South] a war of subjugation.
> —President Jefferson Davis, CSA

THIS BOOK IS A CAPTIVE NATION'S PLEA FOR FREEDOM!

---

³ One contemporary commentator noted that conservatives, as opposed to neo-conservatives and globalists, recognize the fact that most foreigners are motivated to fight the "imposition of American values." We point out that it is Yankee values that are being imposed upon people who simply want to be left alone. See Yoram Hazony, "Is 'Classical Liberalism' Conservative?" at www.wsj.com/articles/is-classical-liberalism-conservative-1507931462 (Accessed 10/31/2017).

CHAPTER ONE: SOUTHERNERS ARE NOT YANKEES

New England—where people get together to change the world![4]

PEOPLE LIVING OUTSIDE of the United States of America (U.S.A.) often view *all* U.S.A. citizens as Americans. While this is accurate, it is *equally true* that not all Americans are the same. This is especially true for those citizens residing in the Southern portion of the U.S.A., known as "The South." The South is also referred to as "The Confederate States of America" (C.S.A.), the "Confederacy," "Dixie" or the "Bible-Belt." Americans living in this section of the United States are collectively known as "Southerners." This is true regardless of the racial background of the individual—all are Southerners.

Unfortunately for Southerners, when people from other countries hear the term "American" they immediately think "Yank" or "Yankee."[5] A Southerner traveling in South or Central America may well be met with

---

[4] Heard on PBS (American government sponsored Public Broadcasting Service). Cited in Wilson, Clyde, *The Yankee Problem: An American Dilemma* (Columbia, SC: Shotwell Publishing, 2016), 18.

[5] "Prior to the War Between the States [1861-1865], 'Yankee' was a particular ethnic designation. In fact, the very term may have arisen among Hudson Valley [New York] Dutchmen to designate their disagreeable neighbors to the east [New England]," Wilson, *The Yankee Problem*, 18.

the insult "Yankee go home."⁶ It is an unintentional insult that Southerners have been forced to bear for generations. The insult is similar to branding all Irish, prior to Irish independence in 1922, as being English. The Irish have never been English despite hundreds of years of being held as a captive nation in the English Empire. The same is true for Southerners—we have never been "Yankees" despite being invaded, conquered, occupied, and exploited by the Yankee Empire. The South has been a captive nation ever since the surrender of the Confederate military—*as opposed to the Confederate government*—in 1865. Yankee Imperialism and gunboat diplomacy had its beginning in 1861 when United States President Abraham Lincoln, in conjunction with the Republican Party and its crony capitalist allies, invaded the democratically elected, peaceful, sovereign nation, the Confederate States of America (C.S.A.).

Even though most modern-day Southerners could not explain why they love or have a fond affinity for the South, the feeling of attachment to place and people still exists—even though for many Southerners it is at a subconscious level. There is an almost subconscious drive to defend the place of their home, their family, and their people. Recent research has confirmed what most Southerners have always known; Southerners tend to see themselves as distinct from folks in other areas of the United States and they tend to view their homeland, the South, in a positive light. This

---

⁶ The term "Damn-Yankee" is a common Southern term used to describe Northerners who come down South and, instead of enjoying the diverse and different culture, they attempt to destroy that culture and impose the Yankee's materialistic world view on the subjugated Southern people. The term has its origins in the post-War period during Yankee military occupation of the South but remains even today. It should be noted that *not all Northerners* are "Damn-Yankees," but the vast majority of those who control the media, education, political and financial institutions certainly meet the definition. It is the South's way of saying "Yankee go home!"

strong attachment to place, to "kith and kin"[7] remains even after generations of slanderous anti-South Yankee propaganda. The research also noted that Southerners tend to prefer the slower-paced Southern lifestyle as opposed to the fast-paced lifestyle of Northerners. Even black Southerners tend to identify themselves, by over 70%, as Southerners, while over 60% of white Southerners view the Confederate flag as a symbol of Southern heritage—and do not associate it with racism or the era of racial segregation.[8] Despite over 150 years of Yankee rule and vicious anti-South slander issuing from Yankee controlled media, educational and political establishments, Southerners still love their home, their people, their community, and their captive society. Yankee imperialism may control the physical South, but it has yet to conquer the spirit of the South.

Worldwide Yankee Imperialism has its origin in the North's invasion, conquest, and occupation of The Confederate States of America. Yankee Imperialists set the stage for justifying the invasion of the Confederacy (C.S.A.) by the skillful use of propaganda falsely claiming (1) the South (C.S.A.) fired the first shot of the so-called "Civil War"[9] and thus initiated

---

[7] "Kith and kin" is an old term brought over from the Celtic areas of Britain during the Colonial era. It refers to relatives, friends, and neighbors who are allied by blood and/or neighborly association.

[8] Potts, Michael, "Go Figure: Progressive Academics Misinterpret Southern Identity," *The Abbeville Blog*, www.abbevilleinstitute.org/review/go-figure-progressive-academics-misinterpret-southern-identity (Accessed 7/26/2017). Article cites research done by Christopher A. Cooper and H. Gibbs Knotts—neither professor is friendly toward the South.

[9] The term "Civil War" used to describe the United States' invasion of the Confederate States is an incorrect use of the term. A civil war takes place when two factions are fighting for the control of the same government. The War for Southern Independence (1861-1865) was not an attempt by the South to take over the United States. The South

war and (2) falsely claiming the South (C.S.A.) was fighting to maintain and expand the institution of chattel slavery while the North (U.S.A.) was fighting to free their black brothers from the cruel bonds of chattel slavery.[10] This slanderous anti-South propaganda pattern would be followed throughout the remainder of the 19th, 20th, and into the 21st centuries to justify the invasion, conquest, exploitation and continuing occupation of the Confederate States of America. The same pattern of Yankee propaganda would be used to justify worldwide aggressive military expeditions that always resulted in an expanding military / commercial / financial Yankee Empire. In the century and a half since the end of the so-called "Civil War," the Yankee Empire has followed its "Civil War" practice of using high sounding moral justifications for its aggressive military interventions. Unfortunately for the subjugated people, the asserted moral values used as an excuse to justify foreign military intervention would never be fully, if at all, accomplished—yet, the expansion of the Yankee Empire's military / commercial / financial interests would always be accomplished. The Yankee Empire would always be able to congratulate itself—"mission accomplished," because

---

was fighting for its freedom. The Union (*i.e.*, the United States) would not have been destroyed had the South maintained its independence but would have continued between those states of the North and West that desired to remain in union with each other. Yankee propagandists use the term "civil war" as an effort to imply that "evil" Southerners were attempting to destroy the Union and therefore the United States was fighting for survival. In reality, the United States was fighting to maintain its ability to exploit Southern resources. The Yankee Empire's fight to exploit other people's resources did not end with the surrender of the Confederate military in 1865 but expanded internationally.

[10] A New England, Boston University, historian (and no friend of the South) admitted that claiming that the War was strictly a war to end slavery was an "immense oversimplification." See, Bacevich, Andrew J., *The Limits of Power* (New York: Metropolitan Books, 2008), 19. Bacevich was born in Lincoln's home state of Illinois.

the Yankee Empire's financial and commercial interests are "too big to fail!"

While the Yankee Empire's financial/commercial interests prospered post-war,[11] the people of the United States' first captive nation (the Confederate States of America or simply the South) sunk into dreadful poverty. This is to be expected; after all, empires do not invade free nations to improve the lot of the conquered and occupied people. Empires invade smaller or weaker nations to extract natural resources, gain tribute in the form of tariffs and taxes, acquire cheap labor, create captive markets for the empire's goods, and tap a vast reservoir of impoverished young people who will seek relief from poverty by joining the Empire's military.[12] Yankee General Sherman noted the superb fighting ability of Southern men and hoped to make use of them when the War was over.[13] Southern blood has been a key factor in every war waged by the Yankee Empire since Appomattox. Yet such unquestioned "patriotism" has earned the South only the universal contempt of the Yankee Empire's ruling elite and the Yankee Empire's propagandists.

With the Yankee Empire's control of the media, educational, and political institutions, the Empire pacified the subjugated Southern population and repressed their will to resist the Empire. In time, the

---

[11] "Post-war" refers to events occurring after the so-called American "Civil War," 1861-1865.

[12] The fundamental reason why nations invade other nations or seek to depose the leaders of "enemy" nations is that the "stronger one wants what the weaker one has." Kinzer, Stephen, *Overthrow—America's Century of Regime Change From Hawaii to Iraq* (New York: Times Books, 2006), 321.

[13] Sherman as quoted in an old newspaper clipping and recorded in *Confederate Veteran*, Vol. XXI, No. 2, February 1913, 66.

conquered population began to identify with the Empire. The justification for a free government, based upon the free and unfettered consent of the people, was censored or suppressed to the point where only a very few Southerners retained the burning desire to reject the Yankee Empire and reclaim the right to establish a government that puts the cultural, social, and economic interests of the captive nation first. No doubt, this is the main reason for the sudden (2016) explosion of efforts to eradicate the last vestige of traditional Southern heritage. These efforts include the destruction of Confederate monuments, renaming of streets that are named for Confederate heroes, and censoring via threats or actual violence against black and white folk making up the Southern opposition to the Yankee Empire's continuing slanderous assaults against the South.[14] The Yankee Empire understands that these symbols represent the will of the people to resist overwhelming forces; they represent the potential that a new generation of Southerners will yet again demand the right to be free. The Yankee Empire strikes back at Southern heritage in an attempt to prevent the rise of Southern resistance to the Empire's tyranny. The Yankee Empire's efforts have been very effective, but a few Southern nationalists remain and continue to make their argument in

---

[14] The defeated and occupied South has been subjected to Yankee cultural genocide since 1865. The current efforts (2016) of Yankee cultural genocide is not new. The Kennedy Twins warned Southerners about Yankee cultural genocide in 1994. Unfortunately, we were basically ignored—most Southerners thought that such things could not happen in "our America." The truth is that it is not "our" America—it is the Yankee Empire. See Kennedy & Kennedy, *The South Was Right!* (Gretna, LA: Pelican Publishing Co., 1994), 271-303.

favor of reclaiming America's constitutionally limited Republic of Sovereign States or else a free and independent South.[15]

The moral and legal justification for Southern Independence in 1861 is documented in *The South Was Right!*[16] The Post-War (post-1865) Yankee exploitation and *intentional* impoverishment of the Southern people are documented in *Punished With Poverty—the Suffering South*.[17] While Yankee propaganda claims that they fought the "Civil War" to end slavery, the truth is that they fought the war to maintain their ongoing exploitation of the South via abusive tariffs paid by the South.[18] Revenues gained from those abusive tariffs were used for the benefit of Northern (Yankee) commercial and financial interests. While the so-called "Civil War" ended *chattel* slavery, it did not produce true freedom for the approximately 4.5 million former chattel slaves. Under Yankee domination of the South chattel slavery morphed into sharecropping slavery—a system of debt peonage that bound 8.5 million black and white Southerners for almost 100 years after the end of the so-called "Civil War." Confiscatory Yankee imposed tariffs continued after the war. Governor Jones of Louisiana noted that in the "year of 1937 the Southern cotton farmer paid a tribute of $800,000,000 to the Northern

---

[15] Kennedy, James Ronald, *Dixie Rising-Rules for Rebels* (Columbia, SC: Shotwell Publishing, 2017).

[16] Kennedy & Kennedy, *The South Was Right!*.

[17] Kennedy & Kennedy, *Punished With Poverty—The Suffering South* (Columbia, SC: Shotwell Publishing, 2016).

[18] The system of protective tariffs forced Southerners to pay higher prices for foreign goods or to purchase the goods at a higher price from the North. In the end, the South was paying higher prices for foreign goods and the money collected by Federal Custom Officials on foreign goods was going primarily to benefit Northern "internal improvements."

manufacturer."[19] Mississippi Senator James Eastland declared that such extortion was a form of modern day (1940s) slavery:

> This means that one year in four, one week in four, three months in twelve, one year in each four, the cotton farmer works to pay tribute to the manufacturer of the East. He is forced by law to give this additional labor to the protected interests of this country. When a cotton grower reaches the age of sixty, he has contributed fifteen years of free labor to the protected interests of the North and East—one year in four, fifteen years in sixty. This is not only economic slavery but human slavery, just as bad, just as dark, and just as unjust as ever existed on any continent of this earth.[20]

Of the 8.5 million sharecropper-slaves in the South some 60% were white. All Southerners, both black and white, were intentionally impoverished by the Yankee Empire in an attempt to *exterminate* the political power and the people who had for so long stood in the way of the Yankee Empire's commercial / financial expansion.[21]

The South is uniquely different from the Yankee North. These distinctions alone are reason enough to justify a free and independent South. True Southern scholars—as opposed to self-hating Southerners who are rewarded for dancing to the tune of the politically correct Yankee Empire's piper—have noted the radical difference between the spiritual South and the materialistic North. They note that the South is defined by

---

[19] Gov. Sam Houston Jones, "The Plundered South," The Abbeville Blog, www.abbevilleinstitute.org/blog/the-plundered-south (Accessed 01/31/2018). This is a reprint of a speech given in 1943.

[20] Senator James Eastland, *Ibid*.

[21] Kennedy & Kennedy, *Punished With Poverty*, 69-87.

its attitudes that differ from those of the North, and these unique attitudes set the South apart from "other" Americans. They note that Yankees have repeatedly attempted to remake the South into second-class, impoverished Yankees. The South's refusal to willingly accept its assigned role as second-class Yankees has caused Yankees to constantly meddle in Southern affairs. The Yankee is incapable of letting things remain as he finds them but is compelled to remake other people in his own image—or at least remake them into a second-class Yankee because as he sees it, no one, other than the Yankee, can ever be as good as one who is naturally born to rule the world of commerce and finance.[22] As one Southern scholar put it: "Thus Cromwell is the Yankee's prototype: seek the heathen out, give him a chance to save himself by embracing the prevailing truth, and if he rejects the opportunity then run him through with a bayonet."[23] A better description of Lincoln's invasion of the Confederate States of America could not be written.[24] In essence, the Yankee's worldview is one in which man and society are to be subjected to the Yankee's unrestrained ambition for domination and private gain (profits). It envisions a world held together by trade and sustained by commercial gain.[25] A Southerner writing in 1867 (two years after the South's military defeat) described the Yankee commercial empire thusly:

---

[22] Andrew J. Bacevich a, Boston University, New England, historian (and therefore no friend of the South) noted the "American" tendency to "remake the world" in the "American" (we would say "Yankee") image. See, Bacevich, *The Limits of Power*, 7.

[23] McDonald, Forrest, "Why Yankees Won't (and Can't) Leave the South Alone," *The Imaginative Conservative*, www.theimaginativeconservative.org/2015/07/why-yankees-wont-and-cant-leave-the-south-alone.html (Accessed 02/09/2015).

[24] Also see "Teaching Hate" in Kennedy & Kennedy, *Punished With Poverty*, 51-68.

[25] Bradford, M. E., *Against the Barbarians* (University of Missouri Press, 1992), 19.

The great defect of Northern civilization is in its materiality. It is of the earth earthy and ignores the spirituality of our nature. Its grand motive and object is the accumulation of money, and its prime boast is of the things money can buy—"the lust of the eye, the lust of the flesh, and the pride of life." Mammon is its god, and nowhere has he a more devout or abject worshipper, or has he set up a more polluted civilization than in the North. The whole spirit of Christianity is opposed to this sort of civilization.[26]

The effects on modern-day Southerners of generations of "one nation indivisible"[27] Yankee propaganda and ongoing anti-Southern cultural genocide are evidenced by the willingness of many Southerners to obediently accept their second-class cultural, social, political, and economic status within the current Yankee Empire. The Yankee Empire rattles its war sabers announcing some new international adventure, and pacified Southerners immediately "rally around the flag." They willingly offer their sons and daughters upon the altar of Yankee imperialism. All the while they think they are being patriotic toward America's Constitutional Republic. They never give a thought to the fact that

---

[26] Bledsoe, Albert Taylor, cited in Weaver, Richard, *The Southern Tradition at Bay* (New York: Arlington House, 1968), 154.

[27] The term "one nation indivisible" is taken from the "Pledge of Allegiance" that all Americans are taught to recite. It was crafted after the unfortunate ending of the War for Southern Independence at the insistence of Union Army veterans to complete Lincoln's revolution. The phrase "one nation indivisible" cannot be found in any of the U.S.A.'s founding documents. It is an abject rejection of the Ninth and Tenth Amendments, but pacified Southerners have dutifully engaged in the "vain repetition" for generations and become angry when challenged.

America's original Republic died at Appomattox[28] and was replaced by the Yankee Empire. Southerners, on the other hand, who understand their position as *citizens of a captive nation* and *subjects* of the Yankee Empire will readily understand the similarity between the exploitation of the South and the rapid international expansion of the post "Civil War" Yankee Empire.

Often modern-day Yankee conservatives, when viewing foreign demonstrators with signs proclaiming "Yankee go home," will ask the question, "Why do they hate us?" For a Southerner who understands the toll of blood extracted in human life and suffering by the Yankee invader of the South, it is much easier to understand the rage an invaded, occupied, or exploited people feel. As one Southerner declared, "An invaded country never forgets." The enormous growth of the Yankee Empire's commercial/financial and military-industrial complex has been a windfall for Wall Street's crony capitalists and the federal government's ruling elite[29] in Washington, D.C. This enormous Empire began in 1861 and continues today. It rules the world of finance and commerce with an iron rod while pretending to be the champion of "democracy" and "human rights." Most of the world thinks that while America offers gifts with one hand, it ends up taking with both hands.[30] The only Americans truly

---

[28] Appomattox, Virginia, 1865, when General Robert E. Lee, CSA, surrendered the Army of Northern Virginia ending, for all practical purposes, the military phase of the War for Southern Independence. It must be remembered, however, that while the Confederate military was forced to surrender—the Confederate government never surrendered!

[29] The term "ruling elite" includes not only the politically well-connected but the "donor-class" and other commercial/financial allies of the political elite in Washington, D.C. of both national (Yankee) political parties.

[30] As described by Chappell, Paul K., *The Art of Waging Peace* (Westport, CT: Prospecta Press, 2013), 273.

capable of understanding the truth about the arrogant and oppressive Yankee Empire are those Southerners who understand their reality as *citizens of a captive nation and subjects* of the Yankee Empire. In the following three chapters, we will see this evil empire in action around the world—an Empire that has become "aggressive abroad and despotic at home."

Yankee Empire

How the Yankees See Themselves | Illustration by Charles Hayes

How the World Sees Yankees | Illustration by Charles Hayes

Chapter Two: Modern Day Examples of Worldwide Yankee Empire in Action

SOUTHERNERS TEND TO BE politically "conservative" meaning that they believe in limited government, low taxation, personal responsibility, Biblical morality, local self-government, and a federal government constrained by a strict interpretation of the limits imposed upon the *Federal* government by a written constitution. Americans who grew up during the Cold War were taught to always defend the U.S.A. when it was threatened (actual or alleged) by Communist expansion anywhere in the world.[31] Unfortunately, this super-patriotism directed toward the federal government and its military industrial complex has been used by the Yankee Empire's ruling elite to discourage people from questioning the wisdom of numerous worldwide military and quasi-military interventions. The following examples will demonstrate numerous cases in which there were clear reasons to question these interventions. It provides evidence of an unbridled Yankee Empire seeking to "reconstruct" the world in a manner similar to the way it "reconstructed"[32] the defeated and occupied South—always with an eye toward

---

[31] This Cold War mentality became a windfall for the military/industrial complex as it demanded ever greater portions of tax payer resources to finance the policing of the world. The unacknowledged part of such "world policing" is that it always managed to expand or protect the Yankee Empire's financial/commercial interests.

[32] Active Reconstruction in the post-war South occurred from 1866-1876. It was followed by Passive Reconstruction which continues today. A detailed explanation of the Yankee

advancing the Yankee Empire's commercial, financial, and military interests.

Yankee Americans and pacified Southerners find it hard to believe that "their" America would engage in a secret plot to overthrow a democratic government and replace the legitimate government [33] with a puppet government—all for the sake of preserving or advancing specific financial / commercial interests. Non-pacified Southerners who understand the truth about the so-called "Civil War" (generally referred to by the more appropriate title of "War for Southern Independence") will recognize the Yankee pattern that was used against our nation—the Confederate States of America—as it has been and continues to be played out on an international stage. It was and continues to be a pattern of false justification for aggressive war and empire building.

At the beginning of the so-called American "Civil War," the newly elected president of the United States, Abraham Lincoln, was asked, "Why not let the South go?" He replied, "Where then shall we get our revenues?"[34] Lincoln, his Republican co-conspirators, and their crony

---

Empire's exploitation of Southern resources, labor, and political liberty can be found in Kennedy & Kennedy, *Punished With Poverty*.

[33] A "legitimate government" in the American tradition would be one based upon the free and unfettered consent of the people governed. This theory works well for Americans, but other peoples have the right to determine what they consider "legitimate government" even if it does not agree with the American theory of government.

[34] Well over 75% of U.S.A. revenues in 1860 came from Southern ports. The majority of said revenues, paid for directly and indirectly by Southerners, were used for Northern "internal improvements" and to protect Northern industry from foreign competition—which resulted in Southerners being forced to pay higher prices.

capitalist allies were determined that they would "not let the South go."[35] After the election of Lincoln, the Southern States withdrew from their union with the Northern States and formed a new government—The Confederate States of America. The Confederate government was democratically elected, using voting qualifications similar to those used in the North.[36] Each Sovereign Southern State freely voted to leave (secede) the oppressive Union (U.S.A.) and join (accede) to the new government—the Confederate States of America. Former U.S. Senator Jefferson Davis, from Mississippi, was elected as the South's President. The Confederate government and the various Sovereign States composing the Confederate States of America (C.S.A.) were all organized and based upon the American principle of the "consent of the governed." This American principle (the consent of the governed) was proclaimed in the 1776 Joint Declaration of Independence when the Thirteen American Colonies seceded from their "indivisible" union with Great Britain.[37] After the conquest of the Confederate States by the United States, a new

---

[35] Johnson, Ludwell H., *North Against the South* (Columbia, SC: Foundation for American Education, 1978), 76-77.

[36] Apologists for Yankee invasion of the Confederacy complain that the Southern States were not true democracies, because they did not allow free blacks and slaves to vote. But this argument fails the test of logic, because the Northern States also did not allow free blacks or slaves to vote. Yes, the North (U.S.A.) still had slaves when it invaded the Confederate States of America. The first legislation passed by the U.S. Congress after the South seceded was not legislation to free their slaves but legislation to radically increase tariffs. Yankee profits, not human slavery, was their motive for invading the South and subjecting the Southern people to aggressive war.

[37] "That the union that has hitherto subsisted between Great Britain and the American colonies is thereby totally dissolved..." from Virginia's act of secession from Great Britain; See Kennedy & Kennedy, *Was Jefferson Davis Right?* (Gretna, LA: Pelican Publishing Co., 1998), 258.

system of government, both in the Southern States and the federal government was imposed upon the South. These post-war governments which were imposed upon the South, both federal and state, were created not with the consent of the governed but by the compulsion of the occupying imperialistic power—the victorious Yankee Empire. These "new" governments were, both then and now, *illegitimate* governments. All governments exercising power in the South, subsequent to the conquest of the Confederate States of America, were and still are illegitimate. These governments that rule the Southern people today have no more moral or legal authority to rule the people of the South than the pro-Nazi Vichy or Quisling governments had to rule the people of France or Norway during World War II. Having no moral principles, other than the usual Yankee principle of protecting or expanding their commercial / financial profits, the federal government under Lincoln engaged in a secret plot [38] to initiate a war with their peaceful, smaller, democratic neighbor, the Confederate States of America. Understanding the Yankee Empire's 1861-1865 aggressive military history makes it easy to understand the past 152 years (as of 2017) of the Yankee Empire's worldwide military interventions. Let us review just a few examples of such international interventions.

CIA Coup in Iran—1953

Shortly after the end of World War II, the people of Iran elected an "anti-colonial" figure who was committed to making sure that the British Anglo-Iranian Oil Company, renamed British Petroleum Company (BP), gave the people of Iran a fair deal for the right to extract Iranian oil

---

[38] For a detailed timeline of Lincoln's war plot see Kennedy, James Ronald, *Uncle Seth Fought the Yankees* (Gretna, LA: Pelican Publishing Co., 2015), 348-351.

resources. The Iranian anti-colonialism cause was championed by Mohammad Mosaddeq. His policies toward foreign oil companies were not that different from those of Louisiana Governor Huey Long who, in the 1920s, fought to force Standard Oil to pay a fair share back to the people of Louisiana for the right to extract the State's natural resources. Mosaddeq's efforts to help the Iranian people brought him to world attention. In 1951 *Time* magazine named him "Man of the Year." But his efforts to extract more money from foreign oil companies made him major international enemies. In the U. S., stories began appearing in the media alleging Mosaddeq's connections with Communists in the Soviet Union. Looking back, now that the Cold War is over, it seems that any nation's leader who refused to cooperate with the Yankee Empire's commercial / financial interests always tended to be Communist, or so it would be alleged. It makes one wonder if there were stories behind the "communist threat" story that the Yankee Empire sought to keep hidden from the American people. This "secret story behind the *acknowledged* story" is not that dissimilar from the Yankee Empire's claim in 1861 that the Confederates fired the first shots at Fort Sumter and therefore were the aggressors "firing on the flag." In 1861 Yankee propagandists in the media rattled the war sabers and the Northern people—not realizing that there was another side to the story—rallied around the flag. This artificially created popular support gave Lincoln cover to "cry 'havoc' and let slip the dogs of war" upon a peaceful democratically elected republic—the Confederate States of America.

The details of the plot to remove Mosaddeq were published in an article in the August 19, 2013, issue of *the Guardian*.[39] The article is titled "CIA admits role in 1953 Iranian coup," and it outlines the role the CIA and British MI6 played in the coup that ousted Mosaddeq and replaced the democratically elected prime minister with Shah Mohammad Reza Pahlavi (what could possibly go wrong with such a well-thought-out plan?). The Shah would become one of the Yankee Empire's dictators / authoritarian leaders that the Yankee Empire would support with massive outlays of military equipment and training. Such tyrants were known as "our kind of guy"[40] because they danced to the tune called by the Yankee Empire regardless of the negative impact it had on the local population.

The rule of "our kind of guys" in foreign nations is not that dissimilar from the way scalawags and carpetbaggers [41] ruled the defeated and militarily occupied South on behalf of the Yankee Empire during active Reconstruction. Today, during passive Reconstruction, the vast majority of the South's elected officials are actually the Yankee Empire's "our kind of guys" responsible for maintaining the political status quo in the

---

[39] Saeed Kamali Dehghan & Richard Nortan-Taylor, "CIA admits role in 1953 Iranian coup," *The Guardian*, www.theguardian.com/world/2013/aug/19/cia-admits-role-1953-iranian-coup (Accessed 06/17/2017).

[40] One of the worst examples of such tyrants supported by the Yankee Empire was Indonesian President Suharto whose army, with indirect support from Republican and Democratic Presidents, killed some 200,000 people and displaced 750,000 native inhabitants in an attempt to take over East Timor. President Clinton welcomed Suharto to Washington, D.C., calling him "our kind of guy." See, Chomsky, Noam, *Rouge States* (Chicago: Haymarket Books, 2000), xvii, 3, 29, & 31.

[41] Scalawags: Post-war Southerners who sold out their country (the South) and did the bidding of the occupied South's Yankee masters. Carpetbaggers: Northerners who came down South to take advantage of the chaotic political situation in the occupied post-war South.

occupied South. This is true regardless of which national political party these elected Southern officials represent. Their job is to assure that the people of the South remain pacified. In Iran, the Yankee Empire expected the Shah to keep "his" people pacified.

The Shah immediately agreed to terms that were acceptable to foreign oil interests. The Shah's dictatorial rule of Iran lasted for the next 26 years until a popular revolt, the 1979 Islamic Revolution, removed the Shah. The new leader of Iran and the people who fought to bring him to power for some reason did not trust the Yankee Empire (note: sarcasm!). This is but one of many examples of the unforeseen consequences of the Yankee Empire's meddling in the affairs of foreign nations.

The United States' thrifty Yankee merchants and politicians who orchestrated the CIA-initiated coup did not miss the opportunity to cash in on the results. Prior to the coup, the British had a monopoly on the right to extract oil from Iran. As a result of the Yankee Empire's work to overthrow the elected Iranian prime minister, the British were forced to give access of Iranian oil reserves to five American petroleum companies, plus Royal Dutch Shell and a French petroleum company. President Eisenhower's diary contains an admission that the U.S. was the leader in the Iranian coup. In his journal, Eisenhower expressed concern that if the facts were allowed to become public, it would prevent *other such operations*.[42] The CIA was also concerned. They immediately changed their action plan, not to prevent other such coups but to make sure that

---

[42] Arash Norouzi, "'The Things We Did Were Covert' President Eisenhower's Diary Confessions—Oct. 8, 1953," *The Mossadegh Project*, www.mohammadmossadegh.com/biography/dwight-d-eisenhower/diary/october-8-1953 (Accessed 06/17/2017); also see Johnson, Chalmers, *The Sorrows of Empire* (New York: Henry Holt and Company, 2004), 220; & Kinzer, *Overthrow—America's Century of Regime Change from Hawaii to Iraq*, 117-128.

the CIA would not have their "fingerprints" on other such coups. Enter the economic hit men (EHM).

One of the key men in the Iranian coup was CIA agent Kermit Roosevelt—President Theodore "Teddy" Roosevelt's grandson. Had he been caught, it would have been a disaster for the CIA. After the Iranian coup, the CIA never again used one of their *direct* agents to overthrow a government, but they came up with a system that gave them "plausible deniability" should a future quasi-agent get caught.

To avoid being caught "red-handed," the Yankee Empire set up a system that used hundreds of contracted individuals working for various consulting firms and private corporations. These "private" corporations and individuals would do the Yankee Empire's "dirty work" around the world. These individuals were not government employees and would never receive any money directly from the Yankee government. Even though they were working for non-government corporations and firms they none-the-less "were serving the interests of empire."[43] The system, in a most simplistic description, consisted of Economic Hit Men (EHM) who were backed by financial groups such as the International Monetary Fund (IMF) and the World Bank (both essentially controlled by Wall Street financial interests and the U. S. Federal Reserve). The EHM would target a country that had resources or markets that the Yankee Empire desired and would attempt to corrupt the nation's leaders with offers of loans for various types of "internal improvements." The primary task was to make sure the targeted country assumed more debt than it would ever be able to repay. The country's leaders and those close to the leader would become rich in the process, but the country would approach bankruptcy.

---

[43] Perkins, John, *The New Confessions of an Economic Hit Man*, (Oakland, CA: Berrett-Koehler Publishers, Inc., 2016), 21.

Then the leader, bound by an enormous debt, would become one of "our guys." The Yankee Empire could then rely on the leader to support the Yankee Empire in the UN or other international groups such as the Organization of American States and to allow special access to the targeted country's natural resources or markets for the Yankee Empire's commercial interests.

If the EHM failed to corrupt the targeted country, then the Jackals would be sent in. Jackals are specialty groups who organize coups against the leader or if necessary, take the leader out via assassination—usually an unexplained plane crash or other such "accident." If the Jackals failed, then and only then would a pretext be created to send in the U.S. military. Just like the invasion of the Confederate States of America, the Yankee Empire never tells its citizens or the world the real reason for the use of the American military in foreign interventions. During the Cold War, the excuse was to limit Communist expansion, then it was to fight Drug Cartels, or to prevent a rogue "madman" (usually "one of our guys" who refused to comply with the Yankee Empire's commands) from developing weapons of mass destruction. Plausible pretexts are always advanced for the use of the Yankee Empire's military—in 1861 the pretexts were that the South fired the first shot, and the North was fighting to free slaves. The Yankee pattern used so successfully against the Confederacy has been repeated worldwide for the last 152 years (and counting).[44]

---

[44] Liberal historians and writers have noted that empires willingly use force to gain access to foreign resources but what distinguishes Americans [Yankees] is that they must first persuade themselves that they are doing it out of humanitarian motives. See Kinzer, 316. But liberals are blind to the fact that Lincoln and company initiated the process to keep Southern tariffs flowing into Yankee coffers. "Slavery" is a Yankee talisman or magic wand that allows liberals to ignore or justify their crimes against the formerly free and prosperous people of the South.

Unfortunately, for Southern conservatives, information about the international clandestine activities of the Yankee Empire is not easy to find. Such information is never found in neo-conservative journals or commentary from Yankee conservative talking heads on radio or TV. Most such journals and talking heads will "rally around the flag" at the slightest hint of military intervention. Failure to support Yankee America's military intervention will cause individuals to be chastised for failing to "support our troops." Even today neo-conservative (New England-based) journals still defend the Shah of Iran and ridicule those who question America's involvement in the 1953 coup.[45]

Of all Americans, Southern Americans should understand the ability of the Yankee Empire to find a plausible excuse to invade a non-threatening country if that country has resources that the Yankee Empire covets. Even if the Yankee Empire does not use its CIA to overthrow leaders who resist Yankee corruption, most of the people of the world believe that the CIA is in the business of doing such things. Even if the Yankee Empire is completely innocent of all such charges, it has failed to conduct itself internationally in a manner that would preclude such suspicion. Most of the world views the United States as untrustworthy because its actions leave the impression that the United States has hidden and ulterior motives for its actions. Southern mothers teach their children that "it is not enough to avoid evil—you must avoid the appearance of evil!" Why do they hate us? To many people around the world, the Yankee Empire appears to be evil. They hate the arrogant Yankee who assumes he has the right to dominate those to whom he has

---

[45] John Gellernter, "Iran: The Truth about the CIA and the Shah," *National Review*, www.nationalreview.com/article/421595/what-really-happened-shahs-iran (Accessed 06/17/2017).

assigned a position of less value than himself. After the War for Southern Independence, the Yankee Empire assigned the rising generations of Southerners to their permanent place upon the "stools of everlasting repentance." This same Yankee Empire has subsequently spent over 150 years seeking other nations to forcefully convert to the Yankee religion of money-worshiping materialism.

Yankee Empire supports dictator in Indonesia—1971-1998

The effort to turn General Suharto, President for Life of Indonesia, into "one of our guys" began in 1971 when he was targeted by EHM.[46] Suharto enjoyed the support of Yankee America's presidents from both Republican and Democrat parties. Until the end of his rule, he enjoyed bipartisan support from the Yankee Empire's ruling elite. It has been estimated that, under Suharto's leadership, 729,000 people were killed in Indonesia including some 200,000 in East Timor.[47] Approximately 80% of the population of East Timor became refugees in an attempt by "our kind of guy" to prevent East Timor's secession from Indonesia,[48] all done with the aid of Yankee America's military equipment and training. Some have claimed that "our guy" Suharto's atrocities in East Timor were far

---

[46] Perkins, *New Confessions of an Economic Hit Man*, 33.

[47] Rummel, R. J., *Death By Government* (New Brunswick, NJ: Transaction Publishers, 1994), 94.

[48] In 1999 East Timor voted to secede from Indonesia and became an independent nation—secession in action! It should be noted that East Timor and the Republic of the Philippines are the only two predominantly Christian nations in Asia. Yet, Yankee America's presidents from both political parties supported predominantly Muslim Indonesia's efforts to deny the people of East Timor the right of self-determination and a government based upon the consent of the governed.

worse than anything that Saddam Hussein is said to have done in Kuwait. Perhaps the Yankee Empire ignored these atrocities because American oil companies wanted to maintain their access to oil reserves that would fall under an independent East Timor's rule.[49] Others have stated that "our guy" Suharto was given the "go ahead" to invade East Timor by Henry Kissinger, provided it could be done quickly and without a prolonged guerrilla war.[50] Suharto invaded independent East Timor December 7, 1975. By 1978, his military had incorporated East Timor into Indonesia,[51] but a long and bloody guerrilla war ensued. East Timor seceded from Indonesia in 1999 and was recognized as an independent sovereign nation. "Our guy," Suharto, became such an international embarrassment that the U.S. Congress prohibited any American aid from going to him, but President Clinton (Democrat) found creative ways to go around the Congressional prohibition.[52] Suharto's undoing appears to have occurred after he failed to "toe the line" according to directives from the International Monetary Fund (IMF). He was forced to resign and was replaced with another one of "our kind of guys."[53]

Libya

The story of the Yankee Empire's use, misuse, and contribution to the ultimate death of Libya's dictator, Muammar Gaddafi, typifies the Yankee

---

[49] Chomsky, *The Rogue States*, 29.

[50] Johnson, *The Sorrows of Empire*, 75-76.

[51] "Indonesia invades East Timor," History.com, www.history.com/this-day-in-history/indonesia-invades-east-timor (Accessed 06/19/2017).

[52] Chomsky, *Rouge States*, 53.

[53] *Ibid.*, 48.

Empire's willingness to "hate" or "love" a tyrant, depending upon his usefulness or threat to the Yankee Empire. During the Cold War, Gaddafi sided with the Soviet Union. His relationship with the Soviets assured him a degree of protection, but the "protection" evaporated with the demise of the Soviet Union. The Yankee Empire had targeted Gaddafi during the Cold War. Efforts to overthrow Gaddafi included the training of several hundred Libyans in one of the Yankee Empire's worldwide secret bases. The U.S. sponsored training took place in Iraq—at that time Saddam Hussein was the Yankee Empire's "kind of guy."[54] The Yankee Empire also rescued a high-ranking Libyan officer, Khalifa Haftar, from a prisoner-of-war camp in Chad and brought him to a safe house in Virginia, located close to the CIA's Washington headquarters. Haftar was not trusted in Libya because of his close connections to the CIA.[55] Perhaps the Yankee Empire was grooming him to one day be "our kind of guy" in Libya?

With the Soviet Union no longer providing "protection," Gaddafi tried to normalize relations with the West, particularly the U.S. He admitted Libya's role in terrorism, paid millions of dollars to settle the Lockerbie, Scotland, airline bombing claims, and removed his weapons of mass destruction. In the process, the British released the mastermind of the Lockerbie bombing on "humanitarian" grounds. But a later report indicated the release was tied to secret arms deal between Great Britain and Libya worth £400 million. Shortly after the arms deal was worked out, British Petroleum (BP) announced it would be investing about £545

---

[54] *Ibid.*, 35.

[55] "Profile: Libya's military strongman Khalifa Haftar," *BBC News*, www.bbc.com/news/world-africa-27492354 (Accessed 6/19/2017).

million to search for £13 billion of oil in Libya.⁵⁶ Things seemed to be working out for Gaddafi, and in 2006, Libya was removed from the U.S. list of terrorist nations. Then came the Obama Administration and the Arab Spring.

For reasons we mere mortals will most likely never know, Gaddafi fell out of favor with the Yankee Empire—he was no longer "our kind of guy." The Obama Administration and its Secretary of State, Hillary Clinton, praised the street revolts in the Muslim world known in the West as the Arab Spring. According to Obama, this uprising represented the beginning of the era of democratic rule as Arab and other Middle Eastern dictators were replaced with popular governments. Gaddafi was once again targeted by the Yankee Empire. He proved to be more resilient than Obama and Clinton had imagined. He was close to destroying the Arab Spring revolt in Libya until the UN, at the insistence of the United States, authorized military intervention. NATO forces conducted destructive aerial attacks against Gaddafi's forces.⁵⁷ The Arab Spring in Libya turned out to be a great benefit for extremists who wanted to capture Libya's oil resources to fund their campaigns. It also allowed Muslim extremists to create a hostile local environment that would send waves of Libyan Muslim refugees into Europe—especially Italy.

The mystery remains as to why Gaddafi fell out of favor once he renounced his ties to terrorism and gave up his weapons of mass

---

⁵⁶ Ian Drury, "Lockerbie bomber 'was released by Britain because of £400 million arms deal with Libya,'" *Daily Mail*, www.dailymail.co.uk/news/article-2380333/Lockerbie-bomber-released-Britain-400million-arms-deal-Libya.html (Accessed 06/20/2017).

⁵⁷ "Terrorism in Libya: Causes and Effects," USMilitary.com, www.usmilitary.com/35021/terrorism-in-libya-causes-and-effects (Accessed 6/20/2017).

destruction. He gave the appearance of becoming—and in fact for a short time was—one of "our kind of guys." There is a claim that Gaddafi had been encouraging Arab countries to demand payment for their oil in Libya's gold-based currency.[58] A widely accepted gold-based currency would cause major problems for the Yankee Empire's economic system based upon a dollar backed up by nothing other than the Yankee Empire's "good word." Recall that "our kind of guy" in Indonesia was ousted, at least in part, because he ran afoul of the directives from the International Monetary Fund. Those who have dealt with the financial centers on Wall Street have noted that "Washington and Wall Street view attacks on the dollar and the Federal Reserve practically as acts of war."[59] Southerners know only too well that the only principle thrifty Yankee merchants and political rulers consistently uphold is the principle of unlimited Yankee profits.[60]

Iraq

The story of Saddam Hussein, the former unquestioned dictator of Iraq, is something fit for a Greek Tragedy. Saddam lived a life encompassing significant themes such as abuse of power, pride, great loss, and a protagonist (Saddam in the case of Iraq) who commits a terrible crime without realizing how foolish and arrogant he has been. In addition to foolish and arrogant, we would add "cruel and evil." But of his many errors in judgment, trusting the Yankee Empire was the one that resulted in his ultimate destruction. The chaos that is now Iraq is

---

[58] Perkins, *New Confessions of an Economic Hit Man*, 252.
[59] *Ibid*.
[60] Kennedy & Kennedy, *Punished With Poverty*, 89, 97.

Saddam's revenge—a revenge made possible by the misguided, even inept, intervention of the Yankee Empire.

Saddam was known to the CIA long before he took over as Iraq's dictator. In 1973, prior to seizing power in 1979, he helped develop the country's initial chemical weapons program.[61] The CIA was aware that Iraq's military and secret service used torture, rape, and assassination to maintain their control over Iraq. Within a month of seizing power, hundreds of his political enemies were killed.[62] Saddam's primary usefulness to the Yankee Empire, other than Iraq's rich oil reserves, was that he came to power the same year the Islamic revolution in Iran deposed the Shah—the Yankee Empire's "guy" in Iran—and installed the Ayatollah Khomeini. The Yankee Empire, therefore, lost their "guy" in Iran and was eager to find a replacement. Saddam was their man. In 1980, he invaded an oil-rich section of Iran adjacent to Iraq. During this time, the Yankee Empire and its Western allies backed Saddam. They did this even though the invasion was a clear violation of international law, and it also required the Yankee Empire to turn a blind eye to Saddam's use of chemical weapons (weapons of mass destruction) in genocidal attacks against Kurds and Shiite populations in Iraq.[63]

The Yankee Empire's EHM[64] made efforts to bring Saddam into the Yankee Empire's fold of "our kind of guy." The Yankee Empire's support of their "guy" in Iraq included the administrations of Presidents Reagan,

---

[61] "Saddam Hussein," *Biography*, www.biography.com/people/saddam-hussein-9347918 (Accessed 06/21/2017).

[62] *Ibid.*

[63] Ibid.

[64] Economic Hit Men.

Clinton, and Bush. But by the late 1980s, it was apparent that Saddam could not be controlled by EHM methods.[65] When he invaded the oil-rich Kingdom of Kuwait, he gave the Yankee Empire the excuse needed to send in the U.S. military. It has been pointed out that prior to Saddam's invasion of Kuwait, Iraq was one of the Yankee Empire's "favored friends and trading partners." In all probability, this "favored friend" or "our kind of guy" was double-crossed or mislead regarding the willingness of the U.S. to "look the other way" if he invaded Kuwait.[66] After all, the Yankee Empire has an international reputation for "looking the other way" when a dictator friendly to the Yankee Empire invades a neighboring country—such as Indonesia's Suharto's invasion of East Timor. Did Saddam think he had a similar "agreement" with the Yankee Empire? Pacified Southerners would vehemently deny such a thing could happen with "their" government. But if one understands the willingness of the Yankee Empire to engage in "double-talk," obfuscation, lies, and secret plots to initiate its desired invasion of the Confederacy—it certainly gives one reason to doubt the veracity of the Yankee Empire's contemporary international dealings.

One of the Bush Administration's main concerns was that once Saddam's forces took control of Kuwait, they would immediately install a puppet government and quickly withdraw leaving Saddam's illegitimate government in control of Iraq's new province of Kuwait.[67] This illegitimate government would be a puppet government controlled by Iraq. This pattern is not new, nor is it unfamiliar to the ruling elite of the

---

[65] Perkins, *New Confessions of an Economic Hit Man*, 194.

[66] Chomsky, *Rogue States*, 27; Kinzer, *Overthrow*, 287.

[67] Chomsky, *Rogue States*, 27.

Yankee Empire. The same method of control was used by the Yankee Empire after it occupied the Confederate States of America in 1865. The Yankee Empire installed their puppet governments in each Southern state and withdrew leaving their *illegitimate* governments to control the conquered territories. This scenario was played out in the 1903 invasion of Panama and again in the 1989 invasion of Panama when the Yankee Empire installed its puppet governments and quickly withdrew its military while maintaining invisible control. The 1989 invasion of Panama created great anger in Central and South America and set the stage for two United Nations Security Council resolutions condemning the Yankee Empire's "flagrant violation of international law and of the independence, sovereignty, and territorial integrity of states."[68] The invasion was also denounced by the OAS (Organization of American States) and the European Union Parliament. Both denounced the invasion as a brazen violation of international law.[69] But as has been pointed out, the Yankee Empire's only moral code is unlimited profit for its international commercial and financial empire.[70] International law is no more of a barrier to the profit-seeking Yankee than the Constitution was to Lincoln as he launched his illegal, immoral and unconstitutional invasion of the Confederate States of America.

Few knowledgeable people would mourn the removal of a cruel dictator such as Saddam Hussein. But, like so many unforeseen consequences of the Yankee Empire's military interventions, the social chaos left in the wake of the U.S. invasion of Iraq and Saddam's removal

---

[68] *Ibid.*

[69] "The U.S. invades Panama," History.com, www.history.com/this-day-in-history/the-u-s-invades-panama (Accessed 6/21/2017).

[70] Kennedy & Kennedy, *Punished With Poverty*, 89, 97.

created problems far greater than those that were given as an "excuse" for Saddam's removal. The "collateral damages," primarily the death of thousands of innocent Iraqi citizens, will remain forever as yet another stain on the Yankee Empire's inglorious history. The Yankee Empire has produced rivers of blood from nations worldwide—blood that mixes with the blood of thousands of Southerners who fought, bled, and died fighting against a cruel and evil empire's invasion of their home and country—the Confederate States of America.

The Boxer Rebellion—China's Century of Humiliation

After the capture of the Philippines during the Spanish-American War (1898), Yankee imperialists were quick to note the importance of maintaining foreign bases to protect America's future trade with China. As Republican Senator Beveridge of Indiana proclaimed, "The Philippines are ours forever ... and just beyond ... China ... the Pacific Ocean is ours."[71] With naval bases and troops stationed in the American-controlled Philippines, it was easy for the Yankee Empire to "protect American interests" in China during the so-called "Boxer Rebellion" in 1900. Few Americans know the history of China's "Century of Humiliation." It all began with China's attempt to prevent foreigners from bringing illicit drugs into their country. The British Empire demanded the "right" to provide opium to the Chinese drug market. British merchants had

---

[71] Senator Beveridge, cited in Johnson, *The Sorrows of Empire*, 43.

Boxer prisoners being guarded by elements of the U.S. Sixth Cavalry | Illustration by Charles Hays

already begun bringing opium from India into China—a flagrant violation of Chinese law! British merchants wanted their illicit "trade" protected by the British Empire.[72] Naturally, from the Chinese point of view, this was an unwanted product, but the British insisted upon the right to sell opium in China. The Chinese refusal to submit to this British demand resulted in the Opium Wars (1839-1842) which ended in disaster for China and its ill-equipped military. (A humiliating lesson that the Chinese people vividly remember today—more unforeseen consequences arising from imperialistic interventions.)

In the years following the Opium Wars, various parts of China fell under the occupation of no less than seven imperial powers. The Chinese naturally resented this foreign occupation by people far different in language, dress, religion, and manners. They logically viewed the foreigners as trespassers. In the late 1890s, a group of militant defenders of Chinese sovereignty established the Society of Righteous and Harmonious Fists, known in the West as the Boxers. By 1900, the ruling

---

[72] "Boxer Rebellion: The Chinese React to Imperialism," *United States History*, www.u-s-history.com/pages/h902.html (Accessed 10/6/2017).

Qing Dynasty allied itself with the Boxers, and another war to expel foreigners broke out. Not wanting to be left out of the spoils of victory in China, the Yankee Empire used its bases in the newly conquered Philippines to send troops to China to "protect American interests."

In 1899, American Secretary of State John Hay encouraged the United States to take a more active part in maintaining an "open door policy" in China.[73] The so-called "open door policy" was a euphemism for not allowing the Yankee Empire to be left out of its imperial share of China. The United States was one of seven imperial powers that sent troops to maintain their hold on China. The Commander of the United States troops during the Boxer Rebellion was an Ohio (Yankee state) native and Union Veteran of the War for Southern Independence, General Adna R. Chaffee. The United States sent a battalion of Marines, two battalions from the Fourteenth U. S. Army Infantry and the Sixth Cavalry, and one battery from the Fifth Artillery or just over 3000 men. It was during the Boxer Rebellion that Lieutenant Smedley D. Butler, author of *War is a Racket*, won special attention for his personal bravery and was promoted to Captain. In looking back over his service in the Yankee Empire's military, Butler declared that he was a "high class muscle man for big business, Wall Street, and Bankers.... in China I helped to see to it that Standard Oil went on its way unmolested."[74] The overall commander of American Troops, General Chaffee, began his military career by helping to subdue the Confederate States of America. Following that action, he fought against the American Plains Indians, the Spanish (Spanish-

---

[73] Trevor K. Plante, "U. S. Marines in the Boxer Rebellion," *National Archives,* www.archives.gov/publications/prologue/1999/winter/boxer-rebellion-1.html (Accessed 10/10/2017).

[74] Butler, cited by Johnson, *The Sorrows of Empire,* 169.

American War) where America took possession of the Spanish Empire's foreign territory, commander of the American forces in the Boxer Rebellion, and commanding the occupying forces in the Philippines. During Chaffee's last years of service to the Yankee Empire, he was advanced to Chief of the U. S. Army.

With the defeat of the Boxer Rebellion, the government of China was forced to sign the Treaty of Boxer Protocol. This was a major national humiliation that China was forced to endure. China's subjugation in the Boxer Rebellion resulted in China losing control of a large area of its territory. The surrender terms contained in the Boxer Protocol of September 7, 1901, required China to destroy forts protecting Beijing; numerous Chinese officials involved in the "rebellion"[75] were to be executed; foreign powers were to be allowed to station troops in Beijing; China was not allowed to modernize its military; and China was required to pay foreign governments involved in putting down the "rebellion" $330,000,000.[76] For all practical purposes, China was no longer a sovereign nation. Even in matters dealing with foreigners who were accused of breaking Chinese law, its laws and courts would not have final jurisdiction. It was a century (1839-1949)[77] in which China was divided

---

[75] Note how empires always brand resistance to their occupation as a "rebellion" and the patriots protecting their homes as "rebels." The "official" history of the War for Southern Independence, written by the United States, is titled *Official Records War of the Rebellion*.

[76] Yohuru Williams, "Boxer Rebellion," History.com, www.history.com/topics/boxer-rebellion (Accessed 10/05/2017). The United States also forced the defeated Confederacy to pay for the cost of subduing the Confederacy. See, Kennedy & Kennedy, *Punished With Poverty*, 179-180; also see Fleming, Walter Lynwood, *The Sequel of Appomattox* (Yale University Press, 1970), 9.

[77] Alison A. Kaufman, "The 'Century of Humiliation' and China's National Narratives," www.uscc.gov/sites/default/files/3.10.11Kaufman.pdf (Accessed 10/02/2017). This

between the Imperial powers of Europe, an emerging Japan and eventually the Yankee Empire. The Yankee Empire was the last Western empire to arrive in China. But by the time of the Boxer Rebellion (1900) there were already significant American "interests" in China that required U.S. military intervention to "protect." There is an old saying or truism that non-pacified Southerners understand: "The story of a successful tiger hunt is profoundly different when written, not by the successful hunter, but by the dead tiger's cubs." The story of the Boxer Rebellion, just like the story of the War for Southern Independence, demonstrates that old truism.

In China today, much of its history is told with reference to "before the Opium War and after the Opium War."[78] Very similar to the way many Southerners review Southern history as "before the War" and "after the War." The "long century" of Chinese humiliation lasted for 110 years from 1839 (the British Empire's Opium Wars) to 1949 when the Red Army (backed by the Soviet Union) won its war against Chinese Nationalists (backed primarily by the Yankee Empire). The People's Republic of China was established on October 1, 1949.[79] Even though China is today (2017) a growing commercial and military power, its century of humiliation still exerts a major influence on how its leaders view the outside world. As one U.S. military analyst noted, China's leaders "still present China as the perpetual and innocent victim of Western nations' continued

---

Testimony was given before the U.S.-China Economic and Security Review Commission Hearing on "China's Narratives Regarding National Security Policy" on March 10, 2011. The Chinese refer to this 110 years as "the long century."

[78] *Ibid.*

[79] *Ibid.*

determination to subjugate it."⁸⁰ Imperialism has unforeseen consequences, and the world today is living with the results of the humiliation of China by Western imperial powers.

Even though the Chinese had over 140,000 "Boxers"⁸¹ and thousands of Chinese soldiers fighting against the foreign powers, they were ultimately no match for the imperial powers' modern armies. The foreign powers assembled a force of approximately 54,000 troops. The national breakdown of troops committed was: Japan 20,840; Russia 13,150; Great Britain 12,020; France 3,520; United States 3,420; Germany 900; Italy 80; and Austro-Hungary 75.⁸² The Yankee Empire's troop commitment included the U.S. Sixth Cavalry. This unit was originally organized by the Yankee Empire during the War for Southern Independence. It was the only *regular* army cavalry regiment *raised* by the North during the War for Southern Independence. The other Yankee cavalry units were Northern state units.⁸³ During the War for Southern Independence, the Sixth U.S. Cavalry suffered a causality rate of 61% in an action in Virginia against Confederate units and was forced to withdraw.⁸⁴ The U.S. Library of Congress has an old grainy photograph of the Sixth U.S. Cavalry

---

⁸⁰ *Ibid.*

⁸¹ "Boxer Rebellion: The Chinese React to Imperialism," *United States History*, www.u-s-history.com/pages/h902.html (Accessed 10/06/2017).

⁸² "Boxer Rebellion," *New World Encyclopedia*, www.newworldencyclopedia.org/entry/Boxer_Rebellion (Accessed 10/06/2017).

⁸³ See Caugney, Donald C. & Jones, Jimmy J., *The 6th United States Cavalry in the Civil War: A History and Roster*, (Jefferson, NC: McFarland, 2013)

⁸⁴ "6th United States Cavalry," *The Battle of Gettysburg*, gettysburg.stonesentinels.com/us-regulars/us-cavalry/6th-us-cavalry (Accessed 10/06/2017).

guarding Boxer prisoners at the end of the Boxer Rebellion. The Sixth U.S. Cavalry, just like all Yankee Empire military units, learned the lessons of invasion, conquest, and occupation of a free people during its service in the Yankee Empire's invasion, destruction, and occupation of the Confederate States of America.

TEACHING THE WORLD TO BE SECOND CLASS YANKEES

The note on the blackboard reads "The consent of the governed is a good thing in theory, but rare in fact...the U.S. must govern its new territories with or without their consent." The Poster above and to the left of the door reads "The Confederate States refused their consent to be governed; But the Union was preserved without their consent." Notice on the front row Philippines, Hawaii, Puerto Rico, and Cuba; the black child washing the window; Indian child holding a book upside down just inside the door; with a Chinese child standing outside looking in. First published in *Puck* magazine January 1899. (Image courtesy LOC)

The Republic of Colombia

In 1903 the South American nation of Colombia became a victim of Yankee imperialism. President Theodore "Teddy" Roosevelt wanted to construct a canal across the Isthmus of Panama. Panama at the time was a province of Colombia. Colombia refused Roosevelt's demand for permission to construct a canal across Panama. The Yankee President then engineered and supported the secession of Panama from Colombia.[85] In 1903, Roosevelt dispatched the *USS Nashville* to Panama and landed U.S. troops who killed the local military commander and declared the province of Panama to be an independent nation. They then set in place a puppet government that would dance to the tune called by the Yankee Empire. When it came time for the "new" nation of Panama to sign a treaty with the U.S. allowing the construction of the canal, not a single Panamanian signed the treaty! The Yankee Empire's President engineered the secession of Panama in order to allow for the construction of "his" canal. This is the same Yankee American President who arrogantly refused to have any correspondence with Jefferson Davis, the deposed president of the Confederate States of America. Teddy Roosevelt's reason for refusing to communicate with Davis was because Roosevelt claimed that Davis represented Southern secession.[86] Yankees find secession convenient only if it aids their commercial / industrial /

---

[85] Boston University historian and former colonel in the U.S. Army, Andrew Bacevich described Teddy Roosevelt's actions against Columbia as an "outrageous swindle" orchestrated by American politicians "unburdened by excessive scruples." Bacevich, *The Limits of Power*, 22.

[86] Kennedy & Kennedy, *Was Jefferson Davis Right?*, 41.

financial empire.[87]   In 1921, the Yankee Empire paid Colombia $25,000,000 ($322,000,000 in 2017 dollars) as payment for the Yankee Empire's role in Panama's secession from Colombia. The payment is a de facto admission of the Yankee Empire's guilt. After the unfortunate ending of the War for Southern Independence, the Yankee Empire repaid the people of the Confederate States of America by punishing them with poverty! It should be noted that this intentional impoverishment was inflicted upon all Southerners, former slave owners—who were a minority of the population—and whites who never had owned slaves—who were the majority of white Southerners. "All Southerners" also includes black Southerners. Indeed, the newly freed slaves and their descendants suffered the most from the Yankee Empire's punishment of poverty.[88]

Honduras

In December of 1904, Yankee President Theodore Roosevelt declared the Roosevelt Doctrine. The Yankee Empire used this doctrine to justify intervening in any Central American or South American nation that failed to pay debts owed to U.S. financial interests. Roosevelt's doctrine, a modification of the Monroe Doctrine, justified the Yankee Empire's claim to having "international police power."[89]   Roosevelt's successor as president of the Yankee Empire, William Howard Taft, called it "dollar

---

[87] In 1815, New England States planned to secede from the United States because the ongoing War of 1812 was harming its commerce. See Kennedy & Kennedy, *Was Jefferson Davis Right?*, 261-262.

[88] See Kennedy & Kennedy, *Punished With Poverty*.

[89] Johnson, *The Sorrows of Empire*, 192.

diplomacy" which meant the Yankee Empire had the right to "promote and *protect* American business interests overseas."[90] [Emphasis added]

Between 1898 and 1934, the Yankee Empire sent troops to Honduras seven times in order to "protect" the Yankee Empire's business interests.[91] In more recent times Central and South American countries have been burdened with massive debt. Much of this debt was assumed by national leaders under the direct or indirect influence of Yankee EHM (economic hit men) whose purpose is to make sure the nation assumes more debt than it could ever repay. A meeting of 17 Central and South American countries in 1999 was held in Tegucigalpa, Honduras. The topic was the debt problem facing many Central and South American countries. In the meeting, the Archbishop of Tegucigalpa and president of the Latin American Conference of Bishops described debt as "the problem" facing Latin America.[92] The effectiveness of the Yankee Empire's EHM is demonstrated by the fact that in 1970 Central American debt was $60 billion, but by 1980 it had increased to $200 billion.[93] While this increased debt was a windfall for "our kind of guys" and to those associated with "our kind of guys" as well as the Yankee Empire's financial / commercial establishment, it did nothing to lift the unrepresented people of those countries out of poverty.[94] A conservative Honduran

---

[90] *Ibid.*

[91] For a sad commentary on the Yankee Empire's encroachment upon Honduran Sovereignty in 1911, see Kinzer, *Overthrow*, 71-77.

[92] Chomsky, Noam, *Rouge States*, 124-5.

[93] *Ibid.*, 125.

[94] These puppet governments established by the Yankee Empire never benefit the people but always benefit the ruling elite, their cronies or donor class, and the Yankee Empire's commercial interests. The same is true for the puppet governments that have ruled the

Bishop noted that the U.S. investments actually increased a "high level of poverty and favoritism towards the minority while the majority [had] just the minimum to survive."[95] Even if only a small portion of this account is true, it represents a massive failure of "American democracy." The failure of Yankee democracy is understandable because such rhetoric (democracy, peace, freedom, etc.) is merely a smokescreen hiding the unquenchable thirst of Yankee crony capitalists for more and more profits—regardless of how crooked the pathway to ultimate Yankee victory. And it must be pointed out that debt was also used against the occupied people of the post-war South. Sharecropping slavery in the post-war South was also referred to as "debt peonage."[96]

Guatemala

The Yankee Empire used the "threat" of Communist expansion into Guatemala as a justification (pretext) for orchestrating the 1954 coup that overthrew Jacobo Arbenz.[97] According to some reports, U.S. planes bombed the capital city in support of the coup.[98] The United Fruit Company had a major interest in ridding Guatemala of Arbenz, because he was pushing for land reform. At the time 2-3% of the population

---

former Confederate States of America! As documented in *Punished With Poverty*, the Southern people remain the poorest people in the United States. Southern puppet governments merely maintain Yankee control of a conquered people, while masquerading as a "representative government."

[95] Chomsky, *Rouge States*, 138-139.

[96] Kennedy & Kennedy, *Punished With Poverty*, 108-109.

[97] Johnson, *The Sorrows of Empire*, 34; also see Kinzer, *Overthrow*, 136.

[98] Perkins, *New Confessions of an Economic Hit Man*, 79.

owned 70% of the land leaving landless peasants in the same position as the Yankees left the landless newly freed slaves and white sharecroppers in the post-war South. United Fruit Company was a major landowner not only in Guatemala but also in Colombia, Costa Rica, Cuba, Jamaica, Nicaragua, Santo Domingo, and Panama.[99] If Arbenz had been successful in Guatemala, it would serve as a model for these other nations. According to John Perkins, a former Economic Hit Man, the United Fruit Company is owned by "Zapata Oil, George Bush's company."[100] In the following 40 years over 200,000 people in Guatemala were killed[101] by various regimes. During this time, the military of these regimes were supplied and/or trained by the Yankee Empire. The 1954 coup that overthrew Jacobo Arbenz occurred during Eisenhower's presidency, but every subsequent Yankee president, Republican and Democrat, supported their version of "our kind of guy" ruling Guatemala. Puppet governments, whether in the former Confederate States of America or Guatemala, never serve the interest of the common man—the ruling elite and those with close connection with the ruling elite (donor class/crony capitalist) prosper while the common man suffers.

---

[99] *Ibid.*, 79.

[100] *Ibid.* See also footnote 101. (Below)

[101] Elisabeth Malkin, "An Apology for a Guatemalan Coup, 57 Years Later," *New York Times*, www.nytimes.com/2011/10/21/world/americas/an-apology-for-a-guatemalan-coup-57-years-later.html (Accessed 6/19/2017).

Summary: Yankee Empire's major interventions into Latin America

- **1885:** Yankee Empire initiated its Latin American version of Yankee gunboat diplomacy when it dispatched the *USS Wachusett* to Guatemala to defend American (Yankee) interests
- **1898:** Yankee Empire defeated Spain and incorporated Cuba and Puerto Rico into the Yankee Empire's sphere of commercial and financial interests. One can only wonder why the Yankee Empire did not call its new empire in the Caribbean, Central and South America "The Greater Caribbean, Central and South American co-prosperity sphere."[102]
- **1903:** The Hay-Bunau-Varilla Treaty gave the Yankee Empire "sovereignty" over the Panama Canal Zone—said treaty did not have the free and unfettered consent of the people of Panama but was achieved via the compulsion of the Yankee Empire's bayonets.
- **1903:** The Yankee Empire required Cuba to ratify the Platt Amendment which turned Cuba into a virtual protectorate of the Yankee Empire. The Amendment was named after Yankee Senator Orville Platt from the New England state of Connecticut.
- **1904:** Yankee Empire's President "Teddy" Roosevelt assumes customs control of the Dominican Republic

---

[102] With reference to the Imperial Japanese Greater East Asia Co-Prosperity Sphere see Gordon, Bill, "Greater East Asia Co-Prosperity Sphere," wgordon.web.wesleyan.edu/papers/coprospr.htm (Accessed 6/19/2017).

- **1905:** Yankee Empire sends its Marines into Honduras to protect Yankee American interests
- **1906-1909:** Yankee Empire sent troops to reoccupy Cuba
- **1910:** Yankee Empire sent troops to Nicaragua and assumed indirect control of the nation's finances for the next 38 years
- **1912:** The Yankee Empire's commercial interest, the United Fruit Company, began operations in Honduras
- **1914-1934:** Yankee Empire's military took control of Haiti
- **1916-1924:** Yankee Empire sent in the Marines to occupy the Dominican Republic
- **1918:** Yankee Empire dispatched its military to Panama to protect its commercial interests—primarily the interests of the United Fruit Company
- **1920-1921:** Yankee Empire dispatched military to support a coup in Guatemala
- **1926-1933:** Yankee Empire sent Marines to take over Nicaragua and help defeat peasant uprising.
- **1936-1979:** Yankee Empire involved in various means of support for the Somoza García dynasty of Nicaragua
- **1954:** Yankee Empire used its CIA to engineer a coup in Guatemala to overthrow government hostile to the interests of the United Fruit Company
- **1961:** Yankee Empire planned and executed invasion of the Bay of Pigs in Cuba
- **1966:** Yankee Empire's Special Forces participated in "Operation Guatemala" in which approximately 8,000 Guatemalans were killed—collateral damage.
- **1981-1990:** Yankee Empire provides funding for *contra* war in Nicaragua
- **1983:** Yankee Empire invaded Granada
- **1989:** Yankee Empire invaded Panama to remove one of its "guys" gone rogue. Between 500 (U.S. sources) to 5000 (international sources) Panamanians killed—collateral damage.

Yankee Americans as well as pacified Southerners, wonder "Why do they hate us?" "Why do they chant "Yankee go home?" The answer is simple, and it was pointed out recently by a Pakistan national when he observed that the American people do not understand the evil "their" government is doing in other peoples' countries.[103] There are reasons for the Central and South American cry of "Yankee go home!" Of all people, Southerners who have "enjoyed" the pleasure of entertaining Yankee bayonets in their homeland should understand. Collateral damage inflicted by the forces of the Yankee Empire assure that "Invaded countries never forget."

---

[103] See Chappell, *The Art of Waging Peace*, 265.

YANKEE EMPIRE

THE ORIGINS OF "YANKEE GO HOME!"

The Yankee Empire's Anaconda Plan (1861-5) starving those who resist its rule | Courtesy LOC

The Yankee Empire, circa 1900, threatening those who resist its rule. Note gunboat close to Mexico and Cuba labeled "Debt Collector." | Courtesy LOC

Chapter 3: Hawaii the Yankee Empire's First International Conquest

But if we manifested any incompetency, it was in not foreseeing that THEY would be bound by no obligations, by honor, or by oath of allegiance, should an opportunity arise for seizing our country, and bring it under the authority of the United States.[104]

Queen Lili'uokalani of Hawaii

ALTHOUGH THERE WERE A FEW Hawaiians who fought for the South during the War for Southern Independence,[105] the real connection between the people of Hawaii and the people of the Confederate States of America is through their mutual history with the Yankee Empire. As already stated, Yankee Imperialism began in earnest with the invasion, conquest, and occupation of the Confederate States of America. In Queen Lili'uokalani's quotation cited above, the Queen complained about a group of people bound by "no obligations, by honor, or by oath of allegiance, should an opportunity arise for seizing our country." Who was this group of people she is referring to? They were the same people who Confederate General Robert E. Lee often referred to as "those people." In

---

[104] Queen Lili'uokalani, *Hawaii's Story by Hawaii's Queen* (1898, Honolulu, HI: Hui Hanai, 2013), 210.

[105] As sailors on the *CSS Shenandoah*. See Brock, Steve, "Hawai'i in the War Between the States," *Confederate Veteran*, Frank Powell, ed., Vol. 76, No. 1, January-February 2018, 22-23.

both their war against the Confederate States of American and the Kingdom of Hawaii, the ruling elite of the Yankee Empire displayed callous and self-serving characteristics of a people who were determined to bring the invaded people under the rule of the United States—now the Yankee Empire.

Reviewing the history of the Kingdom of Hawaii will demonstrate the remarkably similar features in the Hawaiian and the Southern historical experience. For example: (1) Both nations were invaded and their governments forcefully changed; (2) in both nations, the Yankee Empire totally disregarded its foundational document, the Declaration of Independence, in order to advance its commercial interests; (3) in both nations military force was used to overthrow a legitimate government and nullify the will of the people; (4) in both nations the leaders of the resistance to the Yankee Empire's military force were imprisoned after the conquest of their nation was completed; and, (5) both the Native Hawaiians and Southerners were portrayed by the invaders as less than civilized and surely less worthy than the Yankee invader.

The kingdom of Hawaii was first organized in 1795 when King Kamehameha the Great united all the Hawaiian Islands under his rule. His dynasty would last until the overthrow of Queen Lili'uokalani in 1893, thereby ending the Hawaiian kingdom. By the end of the reign of Kamehameha III, 1854, the Kingdom of Hawaii was governed as a constitutional parliamentary monarchy similar to that of Great Britain. The natural question to ask is why and how was the kingdom's constitutional monarchy overthrown? As with all aggressors of a sovereign nation, the invader always attempts to hide his unlawful actions behind praiseworthy excuses—bringing civilization to a savage people, freeing slaves, defending the rights of its citizens, defending the homeland, protecting democracy, or when nothing else works, protecting the empire's property and/or tax revenues.

In the case of Hawaii, the United States used two excuses to invade and conquer the Kingdom of Hawaii: protect American property and protect the "rights" of Americans. Another technique to hide the raw fact of invasion and conquest is to demonize the invaded people as backward, barbarian, and subhuman. The Yankee invader of Hawaii had honed his skills in demonizing the people to be subjugated during the War for Southern Independence. In 1862, upon the floor of the United States House of Representatives, Ohio Congressman Clement L. Vallandigham noted how Radicals in the North had "taught the people of the North and West not only to hate but to despise"[106] Southerners. This "teaching" of hate and/or loathing of a soon-to-be invaded and conquered people is always indispensable in paving the way for one people to psychologically prepare themselves to engage in immoral and criminal acts against "the others," those who do not deserve the usual respect given to "normal" people. Before the War for Southern Independence, none other than Massachusetts native, Ralph Waldo Emerson, had already pronounced Southerners as a subhuman species. Emerson displayed his anti-South bigotry when he proclaimed the South to be a "troublesome, crime-infested area ... [where] man is an animal, given to pleasure, frivolous, irritable, spending his days in hunting and practicing with deadly weapons.... Such people live for the moment, they have properly no future."[107] The fact is there was and is a great gulf between Yankee society and the culture and society of the South. Southerners understood the differences and were amused at said difference, whereas, Yankees viewed any deviation from the Yankee model of society as corrupt, wasteful, evidence of slothfulness and therefore, "evil." This deviation from the Yankee concept of normal is labeled as evil, and for Yankees, this form of evil must be destroyed.

Hawaiians also had to deal with "those people" (Lee's term for Yankees) from the very beginning of their contact with Yankees. On

---

[106] Clement L. Vallandigham cited in Kennedy & Kennedy, *Punished with Poverty*, 53.
[107] Kennedy & Kennedy, *Punished with Poverty*, 57.

March 30, 1820, a group of Boston, Massachusetts, missionaries caught their first sight of Native Hawaiians whom they viewed as savages and sinners. These Bostonian missionaries were shocked at the sight of the tropically dressed natives who met them. One missionary described the effect this meeting had on him and his fellow Yankees:

> the appearance of destitution, degradation, and barbarism, among the chattering, and almost naked savages ... was appalling. Some of our number, with gushing tears, turned away from the spectacle. Others with firmer nerve continued their gaze, but were ready to exclaim, 'Can these be human beings!'[108]

Notice how these Yankees questioned the humanity of the Hawaiian people simply because they were so different from the self-congratulatory perfection of the Yankee. This description of Hawaiians is virtually the same description Yankees, such as Emerson, gave of Southerners—remember Emerson's description of Southerners as "animals."

In her defense of her peoples' right to rule themselves, Queen Lili'uokalani noted the sharp distinction between the culture of the Yankee and the Hawaiian: "... the habits and prejudices of New England Puritanism were not well adapted to the genius of a tropical people, nor capable of being thoroughly ingrafted upon them."[109] As the Queen noted, "Although settled among us, and drawing their wealth from our resources, they were alien to us in their customs and ideas respecting government, and desired above all things the extension of their power ... and to secure their own personal benefit."[110] As pointed out in *Punished with Poverty-*

---

[108] Rev. Hiram Bingham, cited in Wisniewski, Richard A., *The Rise and Fall of the Hawaiian Kingdom* (Honolulu, HI: Pacific Basin Enterprise, 1979), 27.

[109] Lili'uokalani, *Hawaii's Story*, 401.

[110] *Ibid.*, 210.

the Suffering South, it was this driving desire on the part of the Yankee "to secure their own personal benefit" which drove the South to secede from the Union. A union with such a self-centered, self-righteous, and bigoted people would lead to everlasting conflict and ultimate subjugation of the "subhuman" subjects of Yankeedom. This concept of life under the rule of the Yankee Empire is not something that grew out of the bitterness of Southern defeat by the Yankee Empire in 1865; it existed before the War. In 1854, a North Carolina newspaper warned the world about the meddling Yankee: "A meddling Yankee is God's worst creation; he cannot run his own affairs correctly, but is constantly interfering in the affairs of others, and he is always ready to repent of everyone's sins, but his own."[111]

Just as the Yankees were incorrect in their assumptions about Southerners being lazy, slothful, dangerously violent, and ignorant, they equally misjudged the Native Hawaiians. By the time of the arrival of Americans to the Islands, the Kingdom of Hawaii was already speedily moving into the modern world. By the time of Lili'uokalani's birth in 1838, the Kingdom of Hawaii was a Christian nation, with a written language, and a government patterned after the great monarchs of Europe and Asia. The Kingdom received ambassadors from Asia, Europe, and America. Simply put it was a *real* kingdom. Although it had adopted many modern and western ideas in religion, government, and dress, it still had its own customs, laws, and unique social order. As a modern kingdom, its trade put it in contact with many nations. The Aloha spirit (love, affection, pity) infused Hawaiian society and government in the Kingdom. While many foreigners returned this greeting in kind, others saw in it a means of taking advantage of these "simple" people—remember the Queen's comments about "those people" who were eager,

---

[111] North Carolina newspaper cited in Wilson, *The Yankee Problem*, 55.

"to secure their own personal benefit." The taking advantage of Hawaiian people by foreign-born and foreign residents of Hawaii progressed from shady land and water deals to the ultimate overthrow of the Native Hawaiian's government and adding it to the imperial possessions of the Yankee Empire.

With the rapid growth of Hawaiian agriculture, especially the sugar industry, immigrants began to flood into the Kingdom. Large capital investments were made by Americans and Europeans and with this investment came a sizable influx of white settlers. The white settlers were usually the owners and overseers of large plantations, while the stoop labor was done by imported Asian laborers. A very large segment of this stoop labor force came from Japan and China. Soon a combination of men emerged eager to "secure their own benefit." The purpose of this combination was to depose the monarch or at least reduce Royal power to such an extent that it would not stand in the way of their lust for power and wealth.

In 1887, a group known as the Missionary Party (chiefly composed of descendants of New England missionaries who no longer held to the religious faith of their fathers) in association with The Hawaiian League, "a secret revolutionary society formed in 1887 by individuals associated with the missionary party to achieve annexation of Hawaii to the United States,"[112] emerged upon the political landscape. This group, composed of mostly non-native Hawaiians, secured a new constitution for Hawaii. This new constitution stripped the reigning monarch, King David Kalakaua, of most of his Royal authority, transferring it into the hands of cabinet ministers. This cabinet did not exist to serve the people of Hawaii but to advance the cause of union with the United States: "The policy of

---

[112] Lili'uokalani, *Hawai's Story*, 213.

the new cabinet was distinctively American, in opposition to that which may properly be called Hawaiian ... seeking to render the Islands a mere dependency ... on the government of the United States."[113] The new constitution became known as the "Bayonet Constitution" because it was backed by the power of militias composed of mostly non-Hawaiian citizens and foreigners. According to the Queen, the Bayonet Constitution, "practically took away the franchise from the Hawaiian race." It is acknowledged that voting rights were extended exclusively to only literate males of Hawaiian, American, and European descent. The Bayonet Constitution also imposed income and wealth requirements to be eligible to vote for the House of Nobles, thereby, consolidating power among only the elite (white) residents of the island. The Bayonet Constitution was drafted by Stanford B. Dole and other Americans, not the native people of Hawaii.[114] Dole noted how the Bayonet Constitution was forced upon the King and people of Hawaii: "If he [King Kalakaua] doesn't accept it, he will be promptly attacked, and a republic probably declared."[115]

It was under the government of the Bayonet Constitution that an agreement was reached with the United States for harbor rights in Pearl Harbor.[116] As the Queen noted, with the efforts of foreigners and foreign-born Hawaiians, a treaty was made with the United States. The Native

---

[113] *Ibid.*, 53.

[114] Forbes, David W., *Hawaiian national bibliography, 1780-1900* (University of Hawaii Press: 2003), 232–233. Although born in Hawaii, S. B. Dole's parents were from Maine and both were white. He is the second cousin once removed of James Dole, of the Dole pineapple empire.

[115] Dole, cited in Wisniewski, *Rise and Fall of the Hawaiian Kingdom*, 84

[116] *Ibid.*, 85.

Hawaiians had always feared that such an act would "become the entering wedge for the loss of our independence."[117] King Kalakaua continued his struggle to maintain the ancestral government of the Hawaiian people and safeguard the sovereignty of the Kingdom against the ever-growing efforts of the annexation party. From the time of the Bayonet Constitution until the King's death in 1891, the power and influence of Americans and the Yankee Empire's military dramatically increased in Hawaii.

Upon the death of the King Kalakaua,[118] his sister, Lili'uokalani, became Queen[119] of the Kingdom of Hawaii. Shortly after the death of King Kalakaua, the Queen received a petition bearing the names of two-thirds of the voters asking her to nullify the bogus Bayonet Constitution and return the government of the Kingdom back to the people of Hawaii.[120] Desiring to protect the ancestral rights of the Hawaiian people and inspired by her people's desire for home rule, the Queen set about working for the restoration of the sovereignty of her Kingdom. On January 14, 1893, the Queen informed "her" cabinet of her intent of repealing and replacing the Bayonet Constitution, thereby, securing the sovereignty of the Kingdom of Hawaii and the ancestral rights of the people of Hawaii. It should be noted that under the Bayonet Constitution "her" cabinet was composed of Americans (Yankees) and those favoring annexation of Hawaii to the United States. The Missionary Party and

---

[117] Lili'uokalani, *Hawaii's Story*, 211.

[118] King David Kalakaua died January 20, 1891, having reigned 17 years.

[119] Queen Lili'uokalani was crowned Queen of the Kingdom of Hawaii on January 20, 1891. Her reign was overthrown on January 17, 1893.

[120] Denoon, Donald, *The Cambridge History of The Pacific Islanders* (Cambridge University Press, 1997), 233.

other radical advocates of annexation quickly rallied their forces to resist the Queen's moves. Lorrin A. Thurston, a prime mover in the annexation movement, quickly went to American diplomatic minister John L. Stevens, who was also a radical advocate of annexation, for help. Ambassador Stevens came to Hawaii in 1889 fully supporting the idea of taking Hawaii for the United States, by peaceful or other means if necessary. In a letter to Secretary of State James G. Blaine, Stevens noted that "the golden hour is at hand" for the annexation of Hawaii. He warns the Secretary of State about the danger of other foreign powers, such as Great Britain or Japan, obtaining rights in Hawaii if the Kingdom of Hawaii remained independent. But as he pointed out to Blaine, "Annexation excludes all dangers of this kind."[121]

From the time of her coronation, the Queen struggled with forces who continued to agitate for ending the Hawaiian Kingdom and uniting it with the United States. These forces were led by American immigrants (wealthy planters and merchants) and first-generation Americans born in Hawaii. The Native Hawaiians remained loyal to the Queen and desired to be left alone to live their lives in their peaceful kingdom. On January 12, 1893, a "no confidence" vote was passed by the Hawaiian Legislature causing the pro-annexation leaning cabinet to resign. The next day the Queen named new ministers to her cabinet who were in favor of maintaining the Kingdom's sovereignty. This move and the news that the Queen would follow through with her intention of "repealing and replacing" the Bayonet Constitution caused great concern among the Missionary Party (those supporting union with the U.S.) who quickly took action. The first action taken by those desiring union with the U.S. was not to go to the people to encourage them to support keeping the Bayonet

---

[121] *Ibid.*, 223.

Constitution but to go to the United States military seeking help.[122] Word was quickly passed to Captain G. C. Wiltse of the *USS Boston*[123] stationed in Pearl Harbor to land United States troops. Under the pretext of "protecting American lives," and with a written request from John L. Stevens, American Diplomatic Minister, "162 Marines and bluejackets descended upon the city."[124] These troops were quartered in a building alongside Aliiolana Hale, the Hawaiian government building, near the Royal Palace. The message was clear—cooperate or else!

With foreign troops invading the kingdom, the big guns of a United States naval vessel in Pearl Harbor, and rallies being held seeking union with the United States (these demonstrations were composed almost entirely of Americans or their descendants, representing only a small minority of the Hawaiian people), a union of pro-annexation groups was formed calling itself, the Committee of Safety. The "Committee" was composed of thirteen Caucasians, six Americans born in Hawaii, five Americans born in the North, one German, and one British citizen. Conspicuously absent from membership in the Committee were Native Hawaiians, Pacific Islanders, or Asians (there were more Japanese and Chinese than Americans living there at that time). The Committee of Safety denounced the Queen stating that "responsible government was impossible under the monarchy," removed the Queen from power and proclaimed itself the government of the Republic of Hawaii.[125] This

---

[122] Wisniewski, *Rise and Fall of the Hawaiian Kingdom*, 95-96.

[123] The *USS Boston* also saw imperial service in the Philippines and China. See "USS Boston," *Revolvy*, www.revolvy.com/main/index.php?s=USS%20Boston%20 (1884) (Accessed 10/10/2017).

[124] Wisniewski, *Rise and Fall of the Hawaiian Kingdom*, 97.

[125] *Ibid.*

provisional government proposed to hold power until a union with the United States could be achieved. The Committee selected Stanford B. Dole as the acting president of the republic. Unsure about taking this office, Dole sought advice from the American Diplomat John L. Stevens. Stevens, as already noted, was a firm advocate for the annexation of Hawaii by the United States as was Dole. Stevens advised Dole, "I think you have a great opportunity."[126] Within hours of the Committee of Safety proclaiming a republic, American Diplomatic Minister Stevens "recognized" the Republic of Hawaii—of course, this action by a mere diplomatic minister is totally unconstitutional, but when have Yankees, bent upon self-aggrandizement, ever let the plain language of a written Constitution stop them? Soon other nations' delegations followed, sealing the fate of the Kingdom of Hawaii. In her account of this revolution, Queen Lili'uokalani stated that the Kingdom was:

> overawed by the United States to the extent that they can neither ... throw off the usurpers, nor obtain assistance from other friendly states, the people of the Islands have no voice in determining their future but are virtually relegated to the condition of the aborigines of the American continent.[127]

The one paramount reason the Kingdom of Hawaii did not resist the overthrow of the Queen's government and the establishment of a rogue republic is the threat of United States military power: "If we did not by force resist their final outrage, it was because we could not do so without striking at the military force of the United States."[128]

---

[126] *Ibid.*

[127] Lili'uokalani, *Hawaii's Story*, 403.

[128] *Ibid.*

On the 17th day of January 1893, under protest, Queen Lili'uokalani issued a statement which announced she could not resist the combination assembled against her government. The Queen stated:

> Now, to avoid any collision of armed forces, and perhaps the loss of life, I do, under this protest and impelled by said forces, yield my authority until such time as the United States shall ... reinstate me in the authority which I claim as the constitutional sovereign of the Hawaiian Islands.[129]

From the day of this declaration, the Kingdom of Hawaii ended, and the Republic of Hawaii commenced. This rogue republic did not have the support of the majority of the people residing in the Islands, but it did have the support of the planter/business class and the United States military. The sole purpose of the republic was to serve as a temporary government until such time as a treaty with the United States could seal the union between the United States and Hawaii. Without widespread support from the general populace, the government feared for its safety. On January 27, 1893, for the second time, American troops were landed, and on February 1, 1893, the United States Flag was raised over the Hawaiian government building, and U. S. Ambassador Stevens announced placing the "Government of Hawaii under the United States protection."[130] To secure the "peace," a company of Marines was stationed in the Hawaiian government building. The "protection" given by the United States did not prevent American interference in the government of Hawaii, but it did put all foreign nations on notice that, "intervention in the political affairs of the islands would be considered as an act

---

[129] *Ibid.*, 422.

[130] Wisniewski, *Rise and Fall of the Hawaiian Kingdom*, 98.

unfriendly to the United States."[131] This resolution is a somewhat ironic display of the old adage, "Do as I say, not as I do!"

The newly established "republic" wasted no time in adopting a treaty of annexation with the United States. This treaty was sent to the Congress of the United States for its approval. President Benjamin Harrison, Republican from Ohio and Union War Veteran, was an advocate of Hawaiian annexation. Unfortunately for the Hawaiian Republic, when the treaty was submitted, a new president, Grover Cleveland, a Democrat from New Jersey and *not* a veteran of the Union Army, was opposed to the actions of John L. Stevens, the American diplomatic minister in Hawaii. Upon examining the facts around the overthrow of the Queen's government, President Cleveland stated:

> By an act of war, committed with the participation of a diplomatic representative of the United States and without authority of Congress, the Government of a feeble but friendly and confiding people has been overthrown.[132]

Unable to get its treaty ratified by the United States Senate, the Republic of Hawaii governed Hawaii while waiting for a time when an annexation treaty could be successfully presented to the Senate. With the election of William McKinley, a Republican from Ohio and a Union Army veteran, the annexation effort was once again pushed forward. With the initiation of the Spanish-American War, it became obvious to many that a permanent naval station in Hawaii would help to extend American

---

[131] Resolution of the Senate and House of Representatives, United States of America, 1894, *Ibid.*, 101.

[132] Grover Cleveland, message to Congress, December 18, 1893. See Sai, Keanu, "The 1893 Attempted Overthrow of the Hawaiian Kingdom," *Mauna Kea*, www.mauna-a-wakea.info/maunakea/K_link4.html (Accessed 6/24/2017).

power into the Pacific. Nevertheless, enough Democratic Senators opposed the obvious imperialistic act of this territorial acquisition, thereby denying the Republican President the needed two-thirds vote to ratify the treaty of annexation of the former Kingdom of Hawaii into the Yankee Empire's union. Not to be outdone, the supporters of Hawaiian annexation in the Senate proposed adding Hawaii as an American territory via a Joint Resolution of Congress, as was done when admitting Texas in 1845. By a simple majority vote in both Houses of Congress, the issue of Hawaii was settled. The question of its legality is unclear, but the question of its morality is clear—it was an immoral act of imperialistic aggression. One thing was for certain, with the overthrow and invasion of the Kingdom of Hawaii and foreign territory gained as a result of American victory in the Spanish American War, the United States was now clearly and without doubt a full-fledged empire.

It should be pointed out that it was not just Southerners, people of the Confederate States of America, who were opposed to the creation of the Yankee Empire. For example, United States Senator Joseph Lane of Oregon[133] warned Americans what could happen to the United States if it followed the Republicans' attack upon sovereign states:

> A province of an empire ... is held by the oppressor as an integral part of his dominions. The yoke once fastened on the neck of the subject, is expected, to be worn with patience and entire submission to the tyrant's will. *This is the theory of despotism.* [Emphasis added] [134]

---

[133] Oregon is a state in the Northwest portion of the U.S., far from the American South.

[134] Joseph Lane, cited in Kennedy, Walter D., *Rekilling Lincoln* (Gretna, LA: Pelican Publishing Co., 2015), 287-288.

As Senator Lane, a Democrat from Oregon noted, Republicans were exchanging sovereign American States for an empire where the "states" would become mere provinces of an empire.

General Robert E. Lee was the most prominent military leader produced by the South during the War for Southern Independence. Lee displayed his concern about the danger of the loss of States' Rights and the making of the United States government into an all-powerful empire. In a letter to famous British historian and political philosopher, Lord Acton, Lee (1866) informed Lord Acton of his fear of what would become of the United States as a result of the defeat of the Confederate States of America and the loss of States' Rights:

> I consider it [States' Rights] as the chief source of stability to our political system, whereas the consolidation of the states into one vast republic, sure to be *aggressive abroad* and despotic at home."[135]

Acton's high regard for the South's struggle for independence and General Lee is noted by Acton's comment that he believed that "you [Lee] were fighting battles for our liberty, our progress, and our civilization."[136]

Just before the outbreak of hostilities known by Southern patriots as the War for Southern Independence, a Northern Senator warned Americans of the danger of allowing Lincoln's Republican Party to subvert and transform America's Republic of Republics into an empire. As Senator Lane (a Democrat from a Northern state) noted in 1861, an empire exists for the benefit of those closely associated with the empire.

---

[135] Nov. 4, 1866, letter to Lord Action from Robert E. Lee, Online Library of Liberty, www.oll.libertyfund.org/titles/acton-selections-from-the-correspondence-of-the-first-lord-acton-vol-i#lf1480_head_058 (Access 09/18/2017).

[136] *Ibid.*

The original American system of Federalism (Republic of Republics, Republic of Sovereign States or a Compound Republic) limited the power of the central government and protected the people at the local level. Following the defeat of the Confederate States of America, General Lee, in a letter to Lord Acton noted that with all power transferred to Washington and away from the states, America would become "aggressive abroad and despotic at home." Here a Southerner, General Lee, in 1866 is describing the actions of an empire—like Senator Lane (Democrat Oregon) had warned America about in 1861.

As harsh as it may sound, Imperial America was born with the death of the Confederate States of America. With the death of REAL States' Rights, the federal government became an authority unto itself—just like all other empires. If the empire desired something or coveted another nation's resources, it simply took it—wealth from the South or the Kingdom of Hawaii. All that was needed was the will of the federal government to do so—ask any Southerner who lived along the line of march of the invading Federal army about the power of an empire. The unconstitutional acts of the Federal government during the War for Southern Independence are too numerous to mention here but are fully documented by those suffering under its unlimited power. The greed of "those people" for power, wealth, and territory became insatiable as they invaded the nation to its south, the democratically elected and peaceful Confederate States of America. Why would anyone think it odd that these same people or the descendants of "those people" would have no qualms about overthrowing the monarchy of the Kingdom of Hawaii?

During this examination of the conquest of the Kingdom of Hawaii, the term "Yankee" has often been used as synonymous with the term "American." Remember the people of the defeated and occupied Confederate States of America, also referred to as the South, had been impoverished by its Yankee conquerors. These Yankee conquerors impoverished and relegated Southerners to the status of second-class citizens within the new all-powerful Yankee Empire. Impoverished Southerners had little means or desire to get involved in the affairs of the Kingdom of Hawaii. A quick look at those Americans who were some of the prime advocates for the invasion and conquest of the Kingdom of

Hawaii will dispel any notions of "over-statement" of the Yankee involvement in the takeover of Hawaii:

- **Dr. John S. McGrew**, Republican, a Union Army veteran from Ohio, arrived in Hawaii in 1866 and established a prosperous medical practice. He was a vociferous advocate for union with the United States to the extent that King Kalakaua referred to him as "Annexation McGrew."[137]
- **John L. Stevens**, United States diplomatic minister to the Republic of Hawaii, Republican from Maine, very active in Republican presidential politics from 1856 until his death. Although censured for his action in having troops landed in the Kingdom of Hawaii and declaring the "recognition" by the United States of the Republic of Hawaii, his actions more than anyone helped secure the downfall of the Hawaiian Monarchy.
- **Lorrin A. Thurston**, born in the Kingdom of Hawaii in 1858, his family came to Hawaii from Massachusetts and Connecticut as missionaries. Although born in the Kingdom of Hawaii, his affection and loyalty were strictly Yankee. Thurston was the virtual author of Hawaii's infamous Bayonet Constitution.
- **Stanford B. Dole**, Republican, was born in the Kingdom of Hawaii in 1844 to missionary parents from Maine. As with other Americans born in the Kingdom, Dole's loyalty was to the United States as seen by his action in promoting the overturning of the monarchy and union of Hawaii with the United States. He served as president of the rogue republic until it was annexed by the United States, at which time he was appointed Territorial Governor of Hawaii and in 1903 was appointed Federal District

---

[137] Lili'uokalani, *Hawaii's Story*, 53.

Judge—the empire always rewards its faithful agents. Dole, acting as President of the Republic of Hawaii, presided over the transfer of the Republic of Hawaii to the United States. During the transfer ceremony, Dole gleefully proclaimed that he was yielding "... up to you as the representative of the Government of the United States, the sovereignty and public property of the Hawaiian Islands."[138]

- **Chester A. Arthur,** born in Fairfield, Vermont, Quartermaster during the War and United States President 1881-1885, Republican. His Secretary of State, Benjamin Harrison was active in encouraging the American agents in Hawaii in their annexation efforts.
- **James G. Blaine,** born in Pennsylvania, moved to Maine, Republican, Secretary of State, and Congressman from Maine. During the War for Southern Independence, Congressman Blaine was an enthusiastic supporter of Lincoln and his war against the Confederate States of America. It was through the efforts of Blaine that John L. Stevens was appointed chief diplomat in Hawaii—this is the man who "recognized" Dole's rogue republic, thereby destroying the Kingdom of Hawaii.
- **Benjamin Harrison,** born in Indiana, Union Army veteran, United States President 1889-93, Republican. Harrison was an eager supporter of the annexation of Hawaii. Upon receiving the treaty of annexation from Dole's rogue republic, Harrison quickly forwarded it to the Senate for ratification. Harrison's term in office expired before the Senate could act upon the treaty, and with the election of Democrat Grover Cleveland as president (1893-1897), the treaty was not acted upon. As already noted,

---

[138] Wisniewski, *Rise and Fall of the Hawaiian Kingdom*, 108.

Cleveland condemned the actions of the United States during the Hawaiian Revolution of 1893.

- **William McKinley,** born in Ohio, Union Army veteran, Republican, United States President 1897-1901. McKinley, a vociferous advocate of American imperialism, reintroduced the Hawaiian annexation treaty which his Democratic predecessor had denounced but could not obtain the two-thirds majority in the Senate to ratify the treaty. Deterred in the Senate, the annexation forces proposed annexation of Hawaii via a Joint Resolution of Congress which only required a simple majority vote of Congress. This Joint Resolution was passed, and Hawaii became a possession of the United States. During the McKinley presidency, the United States became a worldwide imperial power; therefore, it is often said that McKinley was the "innovator of the United States interventionist policy." McKinley oversaw the largest colonial expansion of the Yankee Empire since the defeat and occupation of the Confederate States of America.

The lives and actions of the men just listed offers proof positive that Robert E. Lee's famous statement about the adverse consequences of the defeat of the Confederate States of American was the correct analysis. Lee warned that the United States of America would become "aggressive abroad and despotic at home." The colonial possessions of the new Yankee Empire, beginning with the Confederate States of America, and followed by Cuba, Puerto Rico, Guam, the Philippines, and the Kingdom of Hawaii, all stand witness to General Lee's insight and wisdom. Like a big pink elephant that everyone pretends is not there, colonialism, is in the room!

Americans should remember that colonialism is the very thing these United States fought against in 1776 and declared immoral, unjust, and illegal in the Declaration of Independence. How can a nation that claims to believe that a *just* government is based upon "the consent of the governed"[139] justify its aggressive actions against the people and nations just mentioned? The United States in its founding document, the Joint Declaration of Independence, declared that just governments are based upon the consent of the governed and that people have a right to alter or abolish *any* government that no longer governs by the consent of the people. How can such a nation force nations and people, at the point of a bayonet, to never attempt to "alter or abolish"[140] a government they do not desire to live under? How could a nation that alleges to be a Christian nation be so complacent in the rape, murder, and plunder of the rights and property of so many sovereign nations?

These questions weighed heavy on Queen Lili'uokalani's mind as she, much like President Jefferson Davis,[141] became a prisoner of the despoilers of her country. In the closing of her book, *Hawaii's Story by Hawaii's Queen,* she warned Americans about the abandonment of the *principles* that had made America such a free, prosperous, and Christian nation. She noted that America could become just like the European Empires with many colonial possessions, and America could create a "vast military and naval power."[142] The Queen then poses the question: "Is such a departure from its established principles patriotic or politic?"[143] Senator Lane from Oregon did not think it was a good idea and in 1861 strongly warned against the United States following the Republican Party's agenda

---

[139] Joint Declaration of Independence of America's Thirteen Colonies 1776.

[140] *Ibid.*

[141] Jefferson Davis was president of the Confederate States of America. At the downfall of the Confederate Armies, Davis was captured, shackled, and imprisoned by the Yankee Empire. See Kennedy and Kennedy, *Was Jefferson Davis Right?*, 97-110.

[142] Lili'uokalani, *Hawaii's Story*, 406.

[143] *Ibid.*

of transforming the United States into an empire—the Yankee Empire. As he noted, it would lead to an empire—"This is the theory of despotism." Likewise, General Lee in 1866 did not think it a good idea either. He predicted what would happen to America if Americans allowed Lincoln's victory over the Confederate States of America to create a federal government with the power of an empire, because such an empire would surely be—"aggressive abroad and despotic at home."

After failing to receive justice from the United States government, Queen Lili'uokalani addressed an appeal to the American people:

> Oh, honest Americans, as Christians hear me for my downtrodden People! Their form of government is as dear to them as yours is precious to you. Quite as warmly as you love your country, so they love theirs. With all your goodly possessions, covering a territory so immense that there yet remains parts unexplored ... do not covet the little vineyard of Naboth's so far from your shores, lest the punishment of Ahab fall upon you, if not in your day, in that of your children, for 'be not deceived, God is not mocked'.... He will keep his promise and will listen to the voices of His Hawaiian children *lamenting for their homes.*"[144] [Emphasis added]

"Children lamenting for their homes" could have been said of the children of the defeated and occupied nation, the Confederate States of America. Building an empire has many costs not just for the subjugated nations. As Senator Lane pointed out, the liberty of the people of the empire as well as those conquered are reduced or lost. Hawaii's ordeal, while not as bloody as the subjugation of the Confederacy, was just as deadly. After the overthrow of the Hawaiian Monarchy, the rogue

---

[144] *Ibid.*, 406-407.

government prohibited the display of any emblems of the Royal family or government. The press was controlled so as to limit information to only that which favored the rogue republic.[145] Today, throughout the South, emblems of the Confederate States of America are being destroyed, moved, or "reinterpreted," while the media twists and distorts facts in such a manner as to condemn all things Southern. Whether in Hawaii or the South, the conquered people are warned to never question the wisdom, veracity, or morality of their conquering Yankee master. No one, and surely not a conquered subject of the empire, should ever dare state that "the Emperor has no clothes!"[146] Unfortunately for the Kingdom of Hawaii and the Confederate States of America, the wondrous robes of liberty which once clothed these United States of America have been stripped away—is there anyone who will dare declare "the Emperor has no clothes"?

---

[145] *Ibid.*, 409.

[146] In Hans Christian Anderson's story, "The Emperor's New Clothes," a foolish emperor is swindled into thinking he has on a fine suit of clothes that anyone that is *unfit for his station in life* cannot see. Therefore, he struts about his kingdom naked, because no one is brave enough to say that the emperor has no clothes on until an innocent child shouts out, "The emperor has no clothes!"

Yankee Empire Troops Invade the Kingdom of Hawaii | Courtesy LOC

Chapter 4: From American Republic to Yankee Empire

WHEN YANKEE-AMERICANS, Southerners, or people of the world look upon the current government of the United States of America, that which is seen is NOT the government as established by the founders of the original American Republic.[147] The American Leviathan of power viewed today is the very opposite of the Republic of Republics established by the Sovereign States when they acceded to the U. S. Constitution in 1787-1789.[148] The original American Union of Sovereign States was established as a limited federal system in which the federal government was the creature and therefore the servant of the people of the states. The states in the original American Republic were NOT mere provinces answering to a supreme central government holding ultimate power over all Americans. The states, in league together but each acting independently of the others, delegated—not surrendered—certain and specific powers to their newly created agent, the federal government. The term "Sovereign State" meant exactly that! The people within their specific state would be

---

[147] The original American Republic was established circa 1776 and lasted until 1861. The second American Republic was established circa 1861, the Confederate States of America—the C.S.A. government never surrendered its right to exist, just like occupied Ireland prior to 1922; the C.S.A. government merely awaits its people's call.

[148] The current United States government is the very antithesis of the original and therefore, legitimate government of the U.S.A. See, chapter 13, "The Federal Government Rejected by the Founding Fathers," in Kennedy, James Ronald, *Nullification! Why and How*, 75-92; [Free pdf download available at: www.kennedytwins.com/Nullification_Book_2012.pdf]

the ultimate judge as to whether or not their agent—the federal government—was acting in accordance to the limitations placed upon it by the specific wording of the original Constitution.[149] The people of a state had the ultimate authority to nullify onerous, oppressive, or unconstitutional acts of their agent, the federal government. If necessary, the people, acting through their specific sovereign state, could withdraw their consent from the federal government via an act of secession.[150]

America's constitutionally limited Republic of Republics[151] died when the major Confederate Army was surrendered at Appomattox Courthouse in 1865. It was replaced with a supreme federal government having the ultimate power to determine the extent of its own powers. After Appomattox, the government of the United States became a consolidated government, and the once sovereign states became mere provinces within the Federal Empire. Even though they retained the title of "states" their function was limited to that of a mere province that answers to a supreme central authority. The Republic of Sovereign States established by

---

[149] See Thomas Jefferson and James Madison's 1798 Virginia and Kentucky Resolves in Kennedy & Kennedy, *Was Jefferson Davis Right?*, 281-285.

[150] Those encumbered with a "liberal" education will deny the State's Right of secession because it is not enumerated or declared in the Constitution. But the Constitution was designed as a limit to federal actions, NOT state actions, unless clearly specified in the written Constitution. Secession and nullification are among a whole host of rights that are "unenumerated" rights as described in the Ninth Amendment and not delegated to the federal government as plainly declared in the Tenth Amendment of the United States' Constitution.

[151] The United States was also referred to as a "compound republic" in the *Federalist Papers,* 50 & 62; William Rawle's textbook on the Constitution used at West Point Military Academy (circa 1825) referred to the Union as "an association of people of republics." Rawle, William, *A View of the Constitution*, Kennedy & Kennedy, eds. (1825, Baton Rouge, LA: Land & Land Publishing, 1993), 234. Also referred to as a Republic of Sovereign States.

America's founding fathers was turned into an empire that would serve the political, commercial and financial elites in Washington and Wall Street. This had been the "dream" of big government advocates, especially those of the North, from the beginning of the United States.[152]

A key to the victory of the Federal Empire over the Confederacy was the support of Northern crony capitalists. The seeds of the Yankee commercial and financial empire were planted by Lincoln and watered with the blood of thousands of Southern men, women, and children—both black and white—during the invasion, conquest, and occupation of the Confederate States of America. Northern crony capitalists understood that the commercial/financial empire they desired was impossible to achieve as long as the United States remained a constitutionally limited Republic of Sovereign States.

Prior to the War for Southern Independence, Senator John C. Calhoun of South Carolina warned Americans that a consolidated federal government would result in "despotism."[153] Calhoun understood that allowing the federal government to become the judge of its own powers, as opposed to the Sovereign States being the final judge, would result in a consolidated, all-powerful, central government that would destroy the rights and liberties of the people. He understood that "in the reserved

---

[152] The "dream" of a big all powerful supreme federal government was held by High Federalists, such as Alexander Hamilton, political supporters of crony capitalism and subsequently by big government men such as Senators Henry Clay, Daniel Webster, and Whig/Republicans such as Abraham Lincoln.

[153] John C. Calhoun in Wilson, Clyde N., *The Essential Calhoun* (New Brunswick, NJ: Transaction Publishers, 1992), 282.

rights of the States will be found, in the end, the only true conservative principle in the American system." [154]

By 1861, the numerical majority of the North controlled the federal government. Realizing that this majority would use its position in the federal Congress to continue and expand their oppression and exploitation of the South, the people of the South decided, via state secession conventions, to withdraw their consent to be governed by a Union controlled by anti-Southern Republicans. It had become clear to Southerners that the only recourse to Northern tyranny was to withdraw their consent (secede) and to "institute new Government ... laying its Foundations on such Principles, and organizing its Powers in such Form, as to them shall seem most likely to affect their Safety and Happiness." [155] To remain in a Union with such people who now controlled the federal government would only allow the commercial interests of the North to continue extracting Southern resources for the benefit of Northern commerce. Southern statesman, John C. Calhoun, understood that an American ruling elite established by the numerical majority would eventually result in the destruction of the Republic and the establishment of an empire.[156] To remain in such a Union would assure the South's position as an oppressed minority resulting in the eventual impoverishment of the Southern people. This is the reason the South seceded in 1861. Understanding this basic truth explains why Yankee

---

[154] *Ibid.*, 274-275.

[155] The Joint Declaration of Independence of the Thirteen American Colonies. Such language is strikingly similar to the wording of the 1581 Dutch Declaration of Independence; see, Berendse & Lucas, *The Act of Abjuration, the Dutch Declaration of Independence (1581)* (Amsterdam: Elsevier-Boeken, 2014), 38-39.

[156] Wilson, *The Essential Calhoun*, 283.

propagandists labor so hard to slander the South by falsely accusing the Confederacy of "fighting for slavery."

The financial interests of Wall Street were major advocates of a national bank—controlled of course by and for the financial elites on Wall Street. The South, under Calhoun's leadership, was an early opponent of such schemes. Calhoun followed Virginian Thomas Jefferson who also saw the danger to liberty inherent in the rule of Wall Street's financial and commercial elites. Jefferson warned that Northern political, commercial, and financial elites wanted to create:

> A single and splendid government of an aristocracy, founded on banking institutions, and moneyed incorporations under the guise and cloak of their favored branches of manufactures, commerce and navigation, riding and ruling over the plundered ploughman and beggared yeomanry.[157]

Southerners, such as Thomas Jefferson and John C. Calhoun, were early defenders of the common man against financial elites on Wall Street and New England's commercial interests. New England's favorite son, Daniel Webster from Massachusetts, in 1837 urged the acceptance of a Constitutional theory that allowed the federal government to engage in printing paper money and other banking actives.[158] Calhoun had already taken the position that a national banking system—today it is referred to as the Federal Reserve—would be detrimental to the country when he declared that it "will certainly ruin the country."[159] It was the same type of Hamiltonian banking scheme that Thomas Jefferson also contended

---

[157] Jefferson as cited in Kennedy & Kennedy, *Was Jefferson Davis Right?*, 219.

[158] Wilson, *The Essential Calhoun*, 259.

[159] *Ibid.*, 269.

against. Calhoun saw the danger in allowing the federal government to print paper money:

> It had been justly stated by a British writer that the power to make a small piece of paper, not worth one cent, by the inscribing of a few names, to be worth a thousand dollars, was a power too high to be entrusted to the hands of mortal man.[160]

The financial elites on Wall Street and the commercial interests in the North won a major victory at Appomattox—they had finally *exterminated* the South's political power in their federal government. It was a victory that would eventually result in the establishment of Robber Baron Monopolists, the Federal Reserve, the World Bank, and the International Monetary Fund—all controlled by the elites of Wall Street and Washington, D.C. They would eventually become "too big to fail" while the common, taxpaying men and women, living in "fly-over country"[161] would be too small to count.

Calhoun also foresaw the dangers posed to the American Republic by military adventures. Calhoun was not an enthusiastic supporter of the Mexican-American War—he defended his position even though his opinion ran against popular opinion. In a speech delivered in the Senate January 4, 1848, he warned that the war would have a "disastrous" effect on the "liberty of the people."[162] In an earlier speech, he declared, "I hold this war to have been a great departure from our true line of policy, and, therefore, deeply to be deplored ... we shall take a step which, I fear, we

---

[160] *Ibid.*, 271.

[161] "Fly-over country" is a derogatory term used by elites living in Hollywood and the Washington, D.C.-Boston northeast corridor to refer to the vast "unwashed rabble" who live in the rest of the United States.

[162] Wilson, *The Essential Calhoun*, 114.

Colonel Ambrosio Jose Gonzales, a Cuban revolutionary who served on Confederate General Pierre Gustave Toutant Beauregard's staff during the War for Southern Independence. | Illustration by Charles Hayes

shall long have to rue."[163] Calhoun saw America—especially the South—as having a close connection with Mexico[164] and Central America.[165] This close connection was demonstrated during the War for Southern Independence as numerous Hispanic people became officers in the Confederate army in charge of white and Hispanic soldiers.[166]

Unfortunately, after Appomattox Calhoun's and Jefferson's warnings would be ignored as Lincoln's newly created Yankee Empire began to look around the world for new nations to incorporate into its empire—an empire built upon the ashes of the formerly free and prosperous people of the Confederate States of America and

---

[163] *Ibid.*, 133.

[164] *Ibid.*, 132.

[165] *Ibid.*, 121.

[166] Kennedy, *Uncle Seth Fought the Yankees*, 180-182; Examples described include Colonel Santos Benavides, & Captain Cristobal Benavides who served in Texas and photo in center section of Colonel Ambrosio Jose Gonzales, a Cuban revolutionary who served on General Beauregard's staff.

America's original, constitutionally limited Republic of Republics—the legitimate United States of America. The Republic was dead, and an *illegitimate*, aggressive, commercial / financial / military empire was loosed upon an unsuspecting world.

Yankee nationalists and their sycophants saw the War for Southern Independence, often referred to by Southerners simply as the "War," as an opportunity to create a new nation that would dominate the world. After the ejection of Yankee forces from Fort Sumter, Reverend Bellows of New England saw a vision of a new America, one in which "The state [the national government, i.e., the federal government of the U.S.A.] is indeed divine, as being the great incarnation of a nation's rights, privileges, honor, and life...."[167] Reverend Horace Bushnell saw the war against the Confederate States of American as a means to change the United States from a mere compact among states into a Godly creation of a nation with a "sense of nationality [that] becomes even a kind of religion." [168] Reverend Bellows preached a sermon in which he admonished the congregation on the virtues of "Unconditional Loyalty" and the "divine right" of government.[169] Reverend Henry Ward Beecher from Connecticut, speaking in Charleston, South Carolina, February 14, 1865, celebrated the death of the Sovereign states and the birth of the

---

[167] As cited by Stromberg, Joseph R., "Blood on the Pulpit: Northern Clergymen, the Kingdom of God on Earth, and the Abolition of the South," *Northern Opposition to Mr. Lincoln's War*, Jonathan D. White, ed. (Waynesboro, VA: Abbeville Institute Press, 2014), 57.

[168] Ibid., 59-60.

[169] Ibid., 61.

supreme Federal Empire when he declared "The nation, not the States, is sovereign.... The only condition of submission is to submit."[170]

The August 1865 edition of the Presbyterian *Observer* noted that the North's victory over the Confederate States produced "a great field for Northern energy and capital...."[171] Here we see the ultimate union of government, commerce / finance, and ideologically driven aggression. Yankee theologians and political leaders saw the nation that emerged from the War as a mystical American nation, divinely appointed to impose Yankee order on an otherwise barbaric world. This new "American" mindset[172] was a merger of Yankee commercial / financial nationalism and Yankee secularized religion that produced a new Manifest Destiny— as God's elect—the Yankee Empire would reconstruct the world. Yankee ministers declared that "our national deliverance has been wrought out for us, as a world-historical act, by God himself;"[173] "a singular destiny a divinely chosen people;"[174] "the free North ... must one day carry liberty all over the world ... We are its divinely appointed representatives and defenders.... Our influence will renew and unite the world."[175] The emerging visionary mission of the Yankee Empire to conquer the world

---

[170] *Ibid.*, 66.

[171] *Ibid.*, 67.

[172] Today this American "mindset" has been described as a unique combination of "arrogance and narcissism" and a view of America as the "universal" and "providentially" appointed nation. See, Bacevich, *The Limits of Power*, 7. [The authors would substitute "Yankee" for "American" and "Yankee Empire" for "America."]

[173] Citing John Williamson Nevin of the German Reformed Church, Stromberg, Joseph R., "Blood on the Pulpit," *Northern Opposition to Mr. Lincoln's War*, 70.

[174] Citing Noll, *Ibid.*, 70.

[175] Citing Reverend Gilbert Haven, *Ibid.*, 72.

was demonstrated in the third year of the War when the New York *Herald* put the world on notice by declaring:

> With a restored Union, prosperity would once more bless the land. If any bad blood remained on either side, it would soon disappear, or *be purged by a foreign war*. With a combined veteran army of over a million of men, and a fleet more powerful than that of any European power, we could order France from Mexico, England from Canada, and Spain from Cuba, and enforce our orders if they do not obey. The American continent would then govern the New World. The President at Washington would govern the New World.[176] [Emphasis added].

Empowered by this new American (actually Yankee) mindset, the Yankee Empire had a new, dynamic, and profit laden mission. This new mission would distort international relations and domestic policies giving the world the fulfillment of Confederate General Robert E. Lee's 1866 prediction—a centralized American nation that had become "aggressive abroad and despotic at home."[177]

The overt military phase of the expanding Yankee Empire began in 1861 with the invasion and destruction of the Confederacy and ended in 1898 with the occupation of the Philippines. During this time, the Yankee Empire attempted to duplicate in other nations its success in its "reconstruction" of the South from an independent and prosperous nation into an impoverished dependency of the Yankee Empire. After the turn of the 19th century, the Yankee Empire used less overt military intervention, opting for covert or limited military intrusions in Central

---

[176] Pollard, E. A., *Southern History of the War*, Vol. II (1866, New York: The Fairfax Press, 1977), 291-292.

[177] General Robert E. Lee, CSA, as cited in, Kennedy & Kennedy, *The South Was Right!*, 41.

and South America and limited military intervention in China during the Boxer Rebellion. As we have already documented, in more recent times, the Yankee Empire opted to use economic pressure via economic hit men (EHM) and save any direct U.S. military action as a last resort, if needed, to command obedience to the Yankee Empire.

Is the United States an Empire?

Yankee-American conservatives and pacified Southerners will object to the idea of calling "their" government an empire. But what else could you call a nation that has acknowledged having military bases on every inhabited continent on earth? In 2005, the U.S. Department of Defense admitted to having over 737 foreign military bases of all sizes with over 2.5 million people[178] foreign and American engaged in servicing these bases. This number includes 196,975 troops. The United States' overseas bases are estimated by the U. S. government to be worth $127,000,000,000! [179] Looking at only the large to medium-sized bases, used mainly to support Army, Air Force and Naval activities, the U.S. has 38 such bases worldwide. The British Empire at its height had 36 naval and army bases and the Roman Empire at its height had 37.[180] The U.S. military spending is equal to the total military budgets of the next seven highest-spending countries in the world! For every dollar China spends on its military (the world's second largest military spender), the U.S.

---

[178] Johnson, Chalmers, "737 U.S. Military Bases = Global Empire," Alternet, www.alternet.org/story/47998/737_u.s._military_bases_%3D_global_empire (Accessed 06/22/2017). Article cites Johnson's new book, *Nemesis: The Last Days of the American Republic.*

[179] *Ibid.*

[180] *Ibid.*

spends $2.77.[181] There is an old saying down South that "if it looks like a duck, acts like a duck and quacks like a duck, it most likely is a duck." The United States worldwide military footprint looks, acts, and sounds like an empire. As will be seen in the following examples, it is not now, nor has it ever been a benevolent empire. As with all empires, it serves to enrich the empire's elites by extracting resources from subjugated people who are forced to pledge allegiance (in one form or another) to the very empire that is enriching itself at their expense. The Yankee Empire would never have reached this level of international power and dominance had it not been successful in its original imperial adventure—the invasion of the democratically elected Republic, the Confederate States of America. Postwar, it did not take long for the aggressive Yankee spirit to seize control of the newly created supreme federal government and create a worldwide Yankee Empire.

In 1890, a mere twenty-five years after the end of the so-called "Civil War" Alfred T. Mahan wrote a book which became a major textbook for those seeking to expand and use the United States' military for foreign adventures. The book was titled *The Influence of Sea Power Upon History*. Mahan was born in New York, educated at the prestigious Columbia University and the U.S. Naval Academy. Mahan served in the Union navy during the War for Southern Independence. He was an early proponent of acquiring Hawaii as a naval base for the United States. He proclaimed that a shipping nation[182] must have a strong navy to protect

---

[181] "U.S. Military Spending vs. the World," National Priorities Project, www.nationalpriorities.org/campaigns/us-military-spending-vs-world (Accessed 06/21/2017).

[182] From the very beginning of the United States, the New England states were "shipping" states whereas the Southern states were agricultural states. This major

its commerce and that it was the "duty" of the government to develop these "foreign bases" so necessary to supply a far-flung navy.[183] He advocated acquiring these bases by "force or favor."[184] He described these American bases as "outpost of power" [185] and a "foothold in foreign lands" that would provide our commercial interests new markets to sell their goods and thereby create new wealth.[186]

In 1890 Mahan published an article in the *Atlantic Monthly* titled "The United States Looking Outward" urging American political leaders to develop aggressive policies that would balance the powers of Europe and an emerging Asia.[187] In 1893 he wrote a letter to the editor published in the *New York Times* urging for national defense purposes the immediate annexation of Hawaii as a "necessary first step to exercise control of the North Pacific."[188] He predicted that if the United States failed to take control of Hawaii, other powers such as an emerging China would take advantage of the opportunity. He concluded that "it would be impossible to exaggerate the momentous issues dependent upon a firm hold of the

---

difference created two peoples with two differing international outlooks. This major difference alone was reason enough to justify two separate nations.

[183] Mahan, A. T., *The Influence of Sea Power Upon History* (1890, Boston, MA: Little, Brown & Co., 1894), 83.

[184] *Ibid.*, 27.

[185] *Ibid.*, 34.

[186] *Ibid.*, 27.

[187] Sempa, Francis P., "The Geopolitical Vision of Alfred Thayer Mahan," *The Diplomat*, thediplomat.com/2014/12/the-geopolitical-vision-of-alfred-thayer-mahan (Accessed 9/02/2017).

[188] *Ibid.*

[Hawaiian] Islands by a great civilized maritime power."[189] In another book, *The Problem of Asia,* (1900), he warned of the potential threat posed by Russia declaring "the vast, uninterrupted mass of the Russian Empire, stretching without a break ... from the meridian of western Asia Minor, until to the eastward it overpasses that of Japan."[190] In other words, American national security (actually its commercial interests) required that the United States become a modern imperial power and of course such international power would provide new markets for America's crony capitalist commercial enterprises. This was the mindset of the emerging international Yankee Empire. President Theodore "Teddy" Roosevelt, formerly Assistant Secretary of the Navy, no doubt was greatly influenced by Mahan's advocacy of an expanding American empire.

During the years from 1866 to the turn of the century (1900), the victorious North was enjoying an expanding economic growth. It was the era of the super-rich Yankees, such as John D. Rockefeller and J. P. Morgan. The victorious states of the Yankee Empire were all receiving the benefits of the Empire. For example, the property value of the Northern state of Ohio in 1860 (the year before Lincoln's invasion of the Confederacy) was $1 billion, and by 1900 it had tripled to $3 billion. But the opposite was true for the South. While the victorious Yankee Empire was enjoying the "fruits" of the empire, the South was suffering impoverishment. In 1860 Virginia's property value was $793 million, but by 1900 it was only $707 million—less than it was in 1860! [191] The point being that while the Yankee Empire was using its military to bring in

---

[189] *Ibid.*

[190] *Ibid.*

[191] Kennedy & Kennedy, *Punished With Poverty*, 189.

"wealth" from its imperial possessions, the South, as the Yankee Empire's first and primary imperial possession, was not "enjoying" part of the Yankee Empire's wealth. Captive nations do not share in imperial glory—nor should they desire to be part of an evil empire that uses its military to exploit others.

The hidden role of the Yankee Empire's military as a vehicle for strong-arming weaker nations was vividly described by Lieutenant General Smedley Butler [192] who spent thirty-three years in the U.S. military. During his tenure in the military, he was awarded two Congressional Medals of Honor. He sadly reflected on the time he spent in uniform around the world:

> During that period, I spent most of my time as a high-class muscle-man for big business, for Wall Street, and the bankers ... Thus, I helped make Mexico and especially Tampico safe for American oil interests in 1914. I helped make Haiti and Cuba a decent place for the National City Bank boys to collect revenues in. I helped in the raping of half a dozen Central American Republics for the benefit of Wall Street.... In China I helped to see to it that Standard Oil went its way unmolested.[193]

The attempt of the Yankee Empire to reconstruct its conquered nations temporarily ceased after its experience in the Philippines. After its success in reconstructing the South, the Yankee Empire then reconstructed the American Indians of the West; the natives of Hawaii; the non-white people of Cuba; and the Philippines. With its geographical,

---

[192] Lt. General Butler (1881-1940) was at the time of his death the highest decorated Marine in history. He became an outspoken critic of the U.S. military adventures. One of the books he authored is titled *War is a Racket*.

[193] Butler as cited by Johnson, *The Sorrows of Empire*, 169.

worldwide empire established, the Yankee Empire then focused on expanding its commercial empire. Renewed efforts of the Yankee Empire to directly reconstruct its conquered nations would have to wait until the beginning of the 21st century. During the administration of President George W. Bush (the younger President Bush), his administration declared to the world that it was the duty of the U.S.A. to bring democracy to the middle east—whether they wanted it or not! [194] Iraq and Afghanistan would enjoy Yankee reconstruction under Republican and Democratic administrations while Libya would enjoy reconstruction under Obama's Democratic administration. Yankee economic imperialism or "dollar diplomacy" [195] was the rule subsequent to the pacification / reconstruction of the Philippines. From 1902 to 2002 the world was spared direct Yankee reconstruction (for the most part), while the Yankee Empire's commercial and financial empire seized control of vast portions of the world's economy via "dollar diplomacy" and the work of its economic hit men (EHM).[196]

Yankee Empire Reconstructs the Philippines—1899-1947

The Spanish-American War (April 1898—August 1898) was termed by Yankee-American politicians as "a splendid little war." This "splendid little war" gave the Yankee Empire unquestioned dominance of the Caribbean, Central and South America. Although the "excuse" for the war was based in Cuba, the war also gave the Yankee Empire an opportunity

---

[194] Chalmers, *The Sorrows of Empire,* 233; also see, Bacevich, *The Limits of Power*, 7. Noting American "hubris" thinking we can "reshape global order." [Bacevich blames "Americans" but actually it is "Yankees."]

[195] Chalmers, *The Sorrows of Empire*, 192.

[196] Perkins, *New Confessions of an Economic Hit Man*, 190-191.

to seize Spanish possessions in the Pacific—the most important being the Philippines. Theodore "Teddy" Roosevelt, then Assistant Secretary of the Navy, made sure Admiral Dewey had orders to move against the Philippines as soon as war was declared. This "unofficial" order was known to Roosevelt's superiors, but the "orders" were not countermanded. The reason is clear to those who understand the workings of the "dollar worshipers" who control the Yankee Empire. Senator Beveridge, Republican of Indiana, saw clearly the opportunity for Yankee commerce that the Philippines offered, "The Philippines are ours forever ... and just beyond the Philippines are China's illimitable markets.... The Pacific Ocean is ours."[197] Those who controlled the Yankee Empire saw the Philippines as "stepping-stones to China."[198]

Prior to the outbreak of the Spanish-American War, the people of the Philippines had been fighting for their independence and initially saw the intervention of the Yankee Empire as a positive development. The Philippine freedom fighters controlled most of the land area and had pushed the Spanish army into isolated compounds in Manila and other large cities. Shortly after Admiral Dewey defeated the Spanish navy, the Spanish commander of the Philippines surrendered to the Americans. The Philippine freedom fighters were not invited to participate in the surrender negotiations and were allowed no input to the surrender agreement. The Yankee Empire's military forces immediately replaced the Spanish military in Manila. The Philippine forces were not allowed to enter their capital city. It soon became apparent that the Spanish colonial power had been replaced not by an independent Philippine government,

---

[197] Senator Beveridge as cited by Chalmers, *The Sorrows of Empire*, 43.
[198] *Ibid.*

but by the Americans who now assumed the role of colonial masters of the Philippines. A war of national liberation ensued.

The war took over 200,000 Philippine lives[199] and imposed great suffering on innocent men, women, and children. At one point, the American military, in response to an ambush, carried out orders to kill every male ten years or older in the district where the ambush occurred. Retaliation against civilians for ambushes or attacks against U.S. military is similar to the response used by the Yankee military against Native Americans on the western plains. This technique was also used by the Yankee Empire against Southern civilians during the War for Southern Independence.[200]

During the Philippine insurrection against the Yankee Empire, General Jacob A. Smith, a former Union (Yankee) Army officer from Ohio, gave Major Walker an order that was strikingly similar to (Yankee) General Sherman's orders during Sherman's destructive march through Georgia during the War for Southern Independence. General Smith told Major Walker, "to make Samar a howling wilderness."[201] During the War for Southern Independence, General Sherman had declared that he would "make Georgia howl." Same song—different verse. Walker later testified that General Smith's orders were:

---

[199] Some estimates are as high as a million deaths due to combat, disease, and starvation. It is difficult to make an accurate determination of civilian deaths in a country that is being invaded. This was also the case in the South where more people, black and white, died as a result of disease and starvation than in direct military action. See Kennedy & Kennedy, *Punished With Poverty*, 111-112, 180.

[200] *Ibid.*, 76-77.

[201] Dumindin, Arnaldo, "Balangiga Massacre, September 28, 1901," Philippine-American War, 1899-1902, www.filipinoamericanwar.com/balangigamassacre1901.htm (Accessed 06/23/2017).

I want no prisoners. I wish you to kill and burn: the more you kill and burn, the better you will please me ... all persons killed who were capable of bearing arms and in actual hostilities against the United States ... an age limit, designate the limit as ten years of age. ... kill and burn and make Samar a howling wilderness ... everybody killed capable of bearing arms ... over ten years of age, as the Samar boys of that age were equally as dangerous as their elders.[202]

The *St. Louis Globe-Democrat* justified the harsh use of United States military against the Philippine people by declaring that the United States had treated Southerners the same way during the "Civil War."[203] The Republican Convention of 1900 agreed, they believed that both Filipinos and Southerners were wrong to resist the federal government.[204] Whether it is a Yankee invader declaring that he intends to "Make Georgia howl" or "Make Samar howl," the result is the same—a free people are punished for supporting the right of their nation to be free of the Yankee Empire.

Southern writer Samuel Clemens (pen name: Mark Twain) from Missouri was among those who lamented the American action in the Philippines. He declared:

We have robbed a trusting friend of his land and his liberty; we have invited clean young men to shoulder a discredited musket and do bandit's work under a flag which bandits have been accustomed to fear, not to

---

[202] *Ibid.*

[203] As cited in Kinzer, Stephen, *Overthrow*, 54.

[204] Masters, Edgar Lee, *Lincoln the Man* (1931, Columbia, SC: The Foundation for American Education, 1997), 449.

follow; we have debauched America's honor and blackened her face before the world.[205]

Once again it is interesting how Southerners who understand their true history as an invaded nation can, not just sympathize but, empathize with other people who have born the burden of invading Yankee armies. Southerners can empathize because even after generations of the Yankee Empire's propaganda being forced upon each successive generation, there still remain a few who understand the reality of being invaded and forced to be the subject of an evil empire. Perhaps this is why the Yankee education and media establishments work so hard to destroy Southern heritage and replace it with the victor's rationale (excuse) for their illegal invasion, conquest, occupation, and exploitation of their first captive nation—the Confederate States of America.

After World War II the Yankee Empire gave the Philippines its independence—almost! As a price for "independence," the Philippine legislature was required to pass an amendment granting "parity" to certain American business interests and granting the Yankee Empire rights to military bases. The required legislation would result in preventing the full development of the Philippine economy. One scholar noted that these requirements prevented the Philippines from joining the other booming Asian economies.[206] Essentially the legislation allowed the Yankee Empire's commercial and financial interest to continue exploiting the Philippines. The Philippine legislature initially refused to pass the legislation. But the Yankee Empire, using divide and rule, used local businessmen to help assure the passage of the legislation. To gain the

---

[205] Extract from "To the Person Sitting in Darkness," February 1901, www.loc.gov/rr/hispanic/1898/twain.html (Accessed 06/23/2017).

[206] Chalmers, *The Sorrows of Empire*, 208.

required number of votes for passage, the Yankee Empire, in conjunction with their local cronies and puppet politicians, had eight Philippine representatives and three senators removed on fabricated charges of fraud and terrorism. With these Philippine representatives and senators removed (all of whom would have voted against the legislation), the legislation passed.[207] Again, it should be recalled that the only principle the Yankee Empire lives by is the principle of profit—profit uninhibited by any inconvenient moral values.

The effort needed to pass a favored piece of legislation even when the people's representatives did not favor it was not new for the Yankee Empire. During the reconstruction of the conquered and occupied Confederate States of America, the Yankee Empire was faced with a similar problem. The Republicans, who controlled the post-war Congress, desired to pass the Fourteenth and Fifteenth Amendments. Democrats in Congress (Northern and Southern) recognized that these amendments would radically change the form of the United States government from a republic to an empire, and therefore, they opposed and blocked these amendments. To resolve the problem, the Republicans expelled all Southern representatives and Senators from Congress and also physically removed key Northern opponents in Congress and Northern State Houses.[208] Problem solved! The Fourteenth and Fifteenth Amendments were then declared "enacted" as opposed to the constitutional term "ratified." The Yankee Empire learned its lessons well while reconstructing the South and applied these harsh lessons to other people and nations around the world.

---

[207] *Ibid.*, 207-9.

[208] Kennedy & Kennedy, *The South Was Right!*, 169-170, 365-367, 375-376, 377-379.

The destructive impact of the illegally enacted Fourteenth Amendment was recognized by U.S. Supreme Court Justice Holmes who had been a Yankee soldier during the War. Justice Holmes in a 1921 dissenting opinion noted the damage done to the Constitutional right of State Sovereignty and the unlimited aggrandizement of federal power that resulted from the Fourteenth Amendment:

> I have not yet adequately expressed the more than anxiety I feel at the ever-increasing scope given to the Fourteenth Amendment in writing down what I believe to be the constitutional rights of the states. As the decisions now stand, I see hardly any limit but the sky to the invalidating of those rights if they happen to strike a majority of this Court as for any reason undesirable.[209]

The admitted similarity between the aggression of the United States against the people of the Philippines and its aggression against the people of the Confederate States of America was demonstrated in the Republican Party's 1900 Convention held in Philadelphia, Pennsylvania. It was noted that all the speakers at that Republican Convention declared that suppressing Philippines resistance to the United States was "exactly what Lincoln did when dealing with the Southern states." [210] From the view of those supporting crony capitalism, both the people of the Philippines and the people of the South were evil because they dared to resist the Yankee Empire's imperial embrace. As General Lee warned, a centralized federal government that rejected the American principle of State Sovereignty would become "aggressive abroad and despotic at home."

---

[209] *Baldwin v. Missouri*, 281 U.S. 312, (1921), 344; Holmes writing in dissent to the majority.

[210] Masters, *Lincoln the Man*, 449.

Yankee Empire Reconstructs Cuba—1898-1959

Cuban freedom fighters, similar to Philippine freedom fighters, had spent generations fighting Spanish colonial rule. By 1898 Cuban freedom fighters had forced the Spanish army into defensive positions in Cuba's major cities. The freedom fighters' struggle to oust the Spanish caused great disorder to Cuban commerce. By the 1890s over 50% of Cuba's trade was with the U.S. The disorder caused by the revolt was harming this lucrative trade. In addition, America's New York-based "Yellow Journalists" were in competition for dramatic headlines which promoted U.S. intervention in Cuba.[211] William Randolph Hearst, owner of the *New York Journal*, dispatched an artist to Cuba. Upon arrival in Cuba, the artist wired back that there was no war in Cuba. Hearst responded, "You furnish the pictures, I'll furnish the war."[212] These are the same type of Yankee newspapers that had constantly fanned the flames of anti-South hatred prior to the War for Southern Independence. These Yankee newspapers eventually demanded, for economic reasons, that the federal government use military force to prevent Southerners from organizing a peaceful, democratic, government of their own.[213]

---

[211] "U.S. Diplomacy and Yellow Journalism, 1895–1898," Office of the Historian, history.state.gov/milestones/1866-1898/yellow-journalism (Accessed 06/23/2017).

[212] Johnson, *The Sorrows of* Empire, 40.

[213] When Yankee newspapers realized the economic impact of allowing the Confederacy to remain as a free and independent nation, they began beating the "war drums" and "rattling war sabers" insisting that Lincoln and company take military action. The *Newark Daily Advertiser* April 2, 1861, deplored the lower tariffs that would be in place in Confederate ports noting that they would "operate to the serious disadvantage of the North" and insisted on immediate military action; *The Boston Transcript* March 18, 1861, also noted the lower tariffs in Confederate ports that would destroy the greatness of the North and warned "The government would be false to its obligations if this state of

The Spanish military commander, General Valeriano Weyler, attempted to do with the local Cuban population, who were supporting the freedom fighters, what the Yankee Empire had done to the Native Americans on the western plains and blacks in the South during the War for Southern Independence. He set up "reconcentration" camps similar to reservations for the Native Americans on the western plains and contraband camps for slaves who were captured by the Union Army during the War for Southern Independence.[214] While General Weyler's counter-insurgency efforts were effective in limiting the ability of the freedom fighters to gain supplies and information from a supporting population, it caused great social disruption and the spread of contagious diseases. It was reported that he learned these techniques by studying General William T. Sherman's "Civil War" campaign while serving as a military attaché in the Spanish Embassy in Washington, D.C.[215] Thousands of Cuban civilians died, and the American President McKinley denounced the practice as an effort to "exterminate" an entire population. As a former Brevet Major in the Ohio Infantry during the War for Southern Independence, he should have been well aware of how an empire uses its power to "exterminate" an unruly population.[216]

The Spanish were quickly forced to surrender to the Americans. It soon became apparent to the Cuban freedom fighters that they had merely

---

things were not provided against." Cited in Kennedy & Kennedy, *Punished With Poverty*, 79.

[214] Kennedy & Kennedy, *Punished With Poverty*, 85, footnote 267, and the "Devil's Punch Bowl," 77.

[215] Gabriel Cardona, Juan Carlos Losada Malvárez, *Weyler, Nuestro Hombre En La Habana*, (Barcelona, Spain: Planeta, 1988), 34-35.

[216] Kennedy & Kennedy, *Punished With Poverty*, 69-87.

exchanged one imperial power in Spain with another from the United States. The Cubans soon realized that the new colonial power (Yankee Empire) did not share the same religion, cultural values or language as did the previous colonial power (Spain). But thanks to a relatively quick war lasting around ten weeks and a widespread contagion of Yellow Fever, the Yankee Empire removed most of its troops by the end of the 1898. But the Cuban nation would remain a virtual protectorate of the Yankee Empire until 1959 when Fidel Castro came to power.

Prior to the "liberation" of Cuba from Spain, the U.S. Congress passed the Teller Amendment April 20, 1898. This Amendment reportedly was meant as an assurance to the people of Cuba that the U.S. would not annex Cuba—as they openly planned to do to the Kingdom of Hawaii, annexing the Kingdom on July 7, 1898. Later, the Teller Amendment was modified by the Platt Amendment which gave the U.S. the right to intervene into Cuba any time U.S. interests were threatened. In other words, Cuba was not a sovereign nation but a virtual colony of the Yankee Empire. The U.S. Marines reoccupied Cuba in 1906, 1912, 1917, and 1920. The Platt Amendment was crafted by a New England Senator, Orville Platt, of Connecticut. And Yankee-Americans and pacified Southerners wonder "Why do they hate us?" As Gandhi told the British "Even a bad government of our own making is better than a good government you force upon us."[217] Consent of the governed (that is, *legitimate* government) cannot be produced by a foreign invader's bloody bayonets.

Cuba remained a virtual dependency of the United States until the arrival of Fidel Castro. The Yankee Empire made numerous attempts to remove Castro, but all attempts failed. The degree of evil that an empire

---

[217] This was stated in the movie *Gandhi*—may not be his exact words but certainly consistent with his sentiments.

will resort to is demonstrated by the efforts of the Yankee Empire to create an excuse to invade Cuba after Castro had ousted "our kind of guy" Fulgencio Batista y Zaldívar in 1959. The U.S. Joint Chiefs of Staff developed a plan titled "Operation Northwoods" in which it was proposed that the American military, in clandestine operations, shoot innocent American civilians on the streets of America and engage in other terrorist attacks in Washington and other cities. The blame for these attacks would be placed on Castro's agents supposedly hiding in the U.S. The Joint Chiefs all endorsed Operation Northwoods.[218] Thankfully, calmer heads vetoed the idea. But it does, once again, demonstrate how the Yankee Empire can "cook up" (fabricate) an excuse to invade a peaceful neighbor.[219] Lincoln, the Republican Party, and their crony capitalist allies "cooked up" an excuse for aggressive war in 1861, and almost a hundred years later, the Yankee Empire was still playing the same game—a game to them but such "games" cost the lives of hundreds of thousands of innocent men, women, and children in the South and eventually worldwide.[220] Today such human cost is euphemistically referred to simply as "collateral damage." [221]

Yankee-Americans and pacified Southerners might question whether "their" government would stoop to such inhuman and uncivilized

---

[218] Johnson, *The Sorrows of Empire*, 301.

[219] The authors are not making judgement on Castro's intentions regarding obtaining and using nuclear weapons against the civilian targets in the U.S.A. But one must wonder "Why would he hate us so much?"

[220] "History taught him that most of the avowed objects of any war proved inevitably, in the event, not to have been the real reason," John D. Wade, "The Life and Death of Cousin Lucius," *I'll Take My Stand*, (1930, Baton Rouge, LA: LSU Press, 1983), 289.

[221] "A single death is a tragedy; a million deaths is a statistic." Attributed to Joseph Stalin.

methods (such as Operation Northwoods) to advance United States' political, economic or military interests. Patriotism has been used by the Yankee Empire to convince "patriotic" Americans to "look the other way" while the federal government (Yankee Empire) violates basic Christian, moral, and ethical values. It has been a common occurrence for the Yankee Empire to simply rattle its war sabers while declaring that patriotic Americans must "rally around the flag." Then patriotic Americans rally to "support our troops" while the Yankee Empire "goes marching on." Pacified Southerners have lost the ability to discern between aggressive nationalism—empire building—and true patriotism.[222]

Between the years of 1932-72, the United States Public Health Services conducted an experiment using human subjects without first gaining their informed consent—the subjects were kept "in the dark" regarding the fact that they were part of an experimental study using human subjects. A review of the Tuskegee Syphilis Experiment might cause "patriots" to rethink their attitude regarding "their" government. Between 300 and 600 black Southern men were victims of this cruel United States government study. They were lured into the study with the promise of free healthcare for their syphilis infection.[223] The study came to an abrupt halt in 1972 after a news reporter broke the story. In another case, the U.S. government from 1948 to 1952 intentionally released radiation into the atmosphere to see how far it would travel. The release sites were all populated: Los Alamos, New Mexico; Dugway, Utah; and

---

[222] For the contrast between "patriotism" and "nationalism," see, Kennedy, *Uncle Seth Fought the Yankees*, 15.

[223] "U.S. Public Health Service Syphilis Study at Tuskegee," Center for Disease Control and Prevention, www.cdc.gov/tuskegee/timeline.htm (Accessed 6/23/2017).

Oak Ridge, Tennessee. In Nashville, Tennessee, 751 pregnant women were secretly exposed to radiation thirty times greater than natural radiation. Follow-up records have been "destroyed," but it is known that a five-year-old child of one of the victims died of lymphatic leukemia, which is associated with radiation exposure.[224] This is the same Yankee Empire that made a determined effort to *exterminate* black and white Southerners during the War for Southern Independence.[225] It was lucky for the South, "those people" (Yankee invaders of the South) in 1861 did not have "the bomb" yet!

Reconstructing Native Americans

One of the primary goals of the Yankee Empire during the War for Southern Independence was to *exterminate* as many black and white Southerners as possible and then repopulate the South with Yankees and other immigrants.[226] But Southerners were not the only North American group the Yankee Empire had targeted for extermination. The aboriginal inhabitants of North America's western plains, Native Americans or American Indians, were also targeted. Even while the Yankee Empire was busy conducting its campaign of genocide down South, it decided to open a second genocide front out west. The Yankee Empire took part of its military forces under Yankee General Pope and sent him to what was then considered the northwest[227] to take care of the "Indian problem." For

---

[224] Kennedy & Kennedy, *Why Not Freedom?*, 235; citing *The USA Today*, December 21, 1993, 1A-2A.

[225] Kennedy & Kennedy, *Punished With Poverty*, 69-87.

[226] *Ibid.*, 69-87.

[227] The State of Minnesota.

Southerners, the solution should be strangely familiar. Yankee General Pope declared, "It is my purpose to utterly *exterminate* the Sioux."[228] Pope planned to use bloody Yankee bayonets to make a "final settlement with all these Indians." The Yankee Empire's plan of genocide would require Pope to kill as many Indians—men, women, children, and infants as possible; deprive them of their land by herding them into government reservations; and then reeducating the survivors to make them obedient, second class Yankees. The reeducation would require the cultural cleansing of all hints of Indian heritage especially their unique language. The Yankee Empire would force them to adopt the English language, as well as the white man's customs and dress. The Yankee Empire attempted to re-make the Indians' world in the image of the materialistic, dollar worshipping, world of Yankeedom. But the Native Americans were not creatures of commerce and materialism. An Indian religious leader of the Nez Perce tribe described the spirit of the American Indian thusly:

> My young men shall never work. Men who work cannot dream; and wisdom comes to us in dreams ... [viewing the earth to be the mother of all he declared] You ask me to plow the ground. Shall I take a knife and tear my mother's bosom? You ask me to cut grass and make hay and sell it and be rich like white men. But can I cut off my mother's hair?[229]

Such non-materialistic reasoning was and still is incomprehensible to the Yankee mind. To a materialistic Yankee, nothing is higher than profit. Their morality is based upon the gaining of material possessions,

---

[228] Kennedy & Kennedy, *The South Was Right!*, 291-292; citing Nichols, *Lincoln and the Indians* (Columbia & London: University of Missouri Press, 1978), 87.

[229] Howard, Helen Addison, *Saga of Chief Joseph* (1941, Lincoln, NE: University of Nebraska Press, 1978), 87.

especially things of financial value. Admiral Raphael Semmes of the *CSS Alabama* described the Yankee as one that held the acquisition of money as the highest if not the only reason for living:

> He [the Yankee] is ambitious, restless, scheming, energetic, and has no inconvenient moral nature to restrain him from the pursuit of his interests, be the path to these never so crooked. In the development of material wealth, he is unsurpassed.... But is like the beaver, he works from instinct, and is so avid of gain, that he has *no time to enjoy the wealth he produces*. Some malicious demon seems to be goading him on.[230] [Emphasis in the original]

The conflict between the Native Americans and the Yankee Empire was a conflict between two different peoples—one determined to gain material possession by whatever means necessary and the other trying to live out a life handed down through the generations—adapting and changing to their surroundings gradually over time. Like Southerners, they merely asked to be left alone to work out their own destiny. But the arrogant and aggressive Yankee would not allow such slothful people to stand in their way. They made it clear that their purpose was to:

> change the disposition of the Indian to one more mercenary and ambitious to obtain riches and teach him to value the position consequent upon the possession of riches.[231]

---

[230] Semmes, Raphael, *Memoirs of Service Afloat* (1868, Secaucus, NJ: The Blue & Grey Press, 1987), 482; Contemporary Boston University New England historian, Bacevich noted that "Americans" (Yankees) are restlessly searching for money and are willing to engineer the "elimination" of those standing in the way of their "gratification." Bacevich, *The Limits of Power*, 17.

[231] Kennedy & Kennedy, *The South Was Right!* 292; citing Nichols, 180.

When the Yankee finds a people with spiritual values—as opposed to the Yankee's materialistic values—the Yankee views such people as backward, barbaric, and in desperate need of Yankee salvation. "Yankee salvation" is usually accomplished by bringing in new converts at the point of massed bloody bayonets.

The Sioux Indians would most likely agree with Confederate Secretary of War, Judah P. Benjamin[232] who, in response to an inquiry from a foreign visitor as to why the Yankees were so cruel, replied:

> If they had behaved differently; if they had come against us observing strict discipline, protecting women and children, respecting private property.... But they could not help showing their cruelty and rapacity, they could not dissemble their true nature, which is the real cause of this war. If they had been capable of acting otherwise, they would not have been Yankees, and we should never have quarreled with them.[233]

The quote above is a great explanation of two differing peoples who should have never been unequally yoked together!

General Pope's campaign of "extermination" against the Sioux was just the beginning. As soon as the Yankee Empire had exhausted the Confederacy's military, they turned their attention to completing the extermination of the Indians on the western plains.

The attempt to exterminate Native Americans was rooted in Lincoln's promise to reserve the western territories for white settlers. He declared

---

[232] After the War, Benjamin's brother, Joseph, fled to Mexico and then moved to Honduras, because he refused to take an oath of allegiance to the United States; Evans, Eli N., *Judah P. Benjamin-the Jewish Confederate* (New York: The Free Press, 1988), 381.

[233] As cited by Weaver, *The Southern Tradition at Bay*, 70.

in his seventh debate with Senator Douglas, "Our new territories being in such condition that white men may find a home ... as an outlet for free white people." It was noted that his remarks received loud applause from the gathering of Northerners.[234] Depopulation was necessary before the Yankee Empire could repopulate it with loyal Northerners—this was true for the lands of Native Americans and Southerners.[235] The repopulated lands would then be admitted to the "Union" as loyal Yankee states—with regard to the former Indian territories—or with regard to the South, pacified into politically fearful / submissive Southern states.

Depopulation of Native Americans occurred by direct methods such as military action and indirectly via creating a social environment in which Native Americans could no longer adequately feed themselves—resulting in malnutrition and death by otherwise "normal" diseases.[236] There are historical records for the direct military action taken by the Yankee Empire, but the record of Native American deaths due to malnutrition do not exist.[237] Once malnutrition became widespread, the Indians were herded into reservations where their conversion to the ways of dollar-

---

[234] Kennedy & Kennedy, *Punished With Poverty*, 96, footnote 299.

[235] *Ibid.*, 69, 77, 157-159, 168.

[236] This also occurred in the South after Yankee occupation. Yankee-imposed malnutrition resulted in a "South-only" disease, Pellagra, that plagued the South up to the 1940s. See Kennedy & Kennedy, *Punished With Poverty*, 111-112, 182.

[237] Similar to the lack of records for the massive number of black Southerners who died due to small pox epidemic after Yankee conquest of the Confederacy. The Yankee authorities made no effort to fight the epidemic because Yankees believed that black Southerners would go extinct once the plantation system was destroyed. See, Downs, Jim, *Sick from Freedom* (Oxford University Press: 2012), 118. (Downs is a Yankee intellectual and no friend of the South, yet his scholarship on this subject certainly collaborates Southern claims regarding the hateful treatment of Southerners by the Yankee Empire).

worshipping Yankeedom could be accomplished or failing that, the Native Americans on reservations would slowly go extinct.

Prior to the War for Southern Independence, in 1851, the Yankee Governor of California, Peter Burnett, called for a "war of extermination" to continue "until the Indian race becomes extinct."[238] The next Governor of California, John McDougal, was equally aggressive most likely because the Native Americans' land was located in an area that contained rich deposits of minerals coveted by Yankee commercial interests. He warned that if the Indians refused to "negotiate" (a euphemism for giving up their ancestral lands), a war would ensue that would result in the "extermination of many of the tribes."[239] The reconstruction of California's Indians saw an almost complete fulfillment of his prediction.

In the Northwestern state of Idaho on January 23, 1863, the Bear River Shoshoni encampment was attacked. The attack resulted in the killing of 400 Shoshoni, many of them unarmed men, women, and children. Some 21 Shoshoni women who survived the attack were raped by the troops.[240] Rape has always been an evil side effect of aggressive war. The troops of the Yankee Empire while invading the South engaged in such cruel and immoral pastime.[241] Another example of Yankee "humanity" is the 1864

---

[238] Rensink, Brenden, "Genocide of Native Americans: Historical Facts and Historiographic Debates," Digital Commons at University of Nebraska, digitalcommons.unl.edu/cgi/viewcontent.cgi?article=1034&context=historydiss (Accessed 06/23/2017).

[239] *Ibid.*

[240] *Ibid.*; also see, Rummel, *Death By Government*, 57-58.

[241] Kennedy & Kennedy, *Punished With Poverty*, 76, 81, 83-84.

Sand Creek Massacre.²⁴² Colonel John Chivington, U.S. Army, was in charge. He was from Ohio, a Methodist minister and an abolitionist.²⁴³

The reconstruction of Native Americans continued at the Battle of Washita River on November 27, 1868, when a group of soldiers attacked Native Americans. In this "Battle" unarmed women and children were targeted and killed. A similar deadly incident occurred in 1890 at the now infamous Battle of Wounded Knee (more appropriately the Massacre at Wounded Knee). Once Indian resistance was extinguished and the Native American people disarmed, Yankee reconstruction in the form of cultural genocide could be completed. But even today the words of Chief Joseph still echo in the ears of all who reject a purely materialistic worldview and cling to the memory and honor of their ancestors: "A man who would not love his father's grave is worse than a wild animal."²⁴⁴

Yankee-Americans and pacified Southerners will object to describing this record of Yankee genocide. They attempt to mitigate the harsh history of Yankee extermination by declaring that Lincoln was a compassionate person who believed in "malice toward none." But the truth is frightfully different. In the 1862 campaign against the Sioux Indians in Minnesota, General Pope defeated the Indians and captured more than 300 warriors. The whites of Minnesota were demanding the

---

²⁴² "Nine of Colonel Chivington's men were killed; 148 of Black Kettle's followers were slaughtered, more than half of them women and children. The Colorado volunteers returned and killed the wounded, mutilated the bodies, and set fire to the village." "Sand Creek massacre," History.com, www.history.com/this-day-in-history/sand-creek-massacre (Accessed 05/23/2018).

²⁴³ "John Chivington Biography," National Park Service, www.nps.gov/sand/learn/historyculture/john-chivington-biography.htm (Accessed 05/23/2018).

²⁴⁴ Howard, *Saga of Chief Joseph*, 89.

execution of all the warriors. Lincoln did not want to anger the whites, after all he needed their votes in the next election. So being a skilled politician he compromised. He personally participated in the selection of thirty-nine Indian prisoners-of-war who would be executed by hanging. Abraham Lincoln is the only U.S. President to personally be involved in the selection and mass execution of prisoners of war captured in battle.[245] Such scandalous "facts" are carefully avoided in standard American history. But Lincoln's foray into the mass execution of prisoners all worked out well for the Yankee Empire. Lincoln carried Minnesota in the next election, and the Yankee Empire was eventually able to find a "final solution" to its American Indian problem.[246]

Reconstructing the South 1865—Present

In every case of the Yankee Empire's intervention or invasion of sovereign nations recorded in previous pages, all have one thing in common—none of these invasions or interventions would have occurred

---

[245] Kennedy & Kennedy, *The South Was Right!* 31; also see, Kennedy, *Rekilling Lincoln*, 174.

[246] The history of the conflict between European settlers and Native Americans is one of the "less than noble" chapters in American history. The "Trail of Tears," in which so many Native Americans died, occurred in the South under the leadership of a Southerner, President Andrew Jackson. However, it is worth noting that the only "nations" to recognize the Confederacy were the five "civilized" tribes indigenous to the South—Cherokee, Choctaw, Seminole, Chickasaw, & Creek nations. Not all Southern Indians were removed, many remained on their native land. For example, many in North Carolina joined Thomas's Legion and fought with the C.S. Army. It was not usual for Native Americans to serve in political post in the South, such as Choctaw Chief Greenwood Leflore who was a member of the Mississippi legislature. The last Confederate land force to surrender was under the command of Brigadier General Stand Watie, a Cherokee officer who commanded both white and Indian soldiers.

had Lincoln and his emerging Yankee Empire failed in their efforts to prevent the establishment of a free and independent Confederate States of America. With the *extermination* of the South's constitutionally conservative political influence in the Yankee Empire's Congress, the North's political and crony capitalist elite were given a free hand to establish crony capitalism[247] as a major, if not the major, power in the Yankee Empire's government. The political, commercial, and financial elites of the Yankee Empire were richly rewarded [248] for violating the American principle of the "consent of the governed" down South. But one victory is never enough for an emerging empire. The Yankee Empire's ruling elite immediately began looking around for other opportunities for commercial and financial aggrandizement. The emerging Yankee Empire (circa 1861) would have died if the Confederate States of America had been successful in defending its independence. The emerging Yankee Empire would have died because Lincoln's Republican Party was a minority party and would have been handed a resounding defeat in the next election if he had lost the War. But, as it turned out, the Yankee Empire's industrial and military power created for the emerging Yankee Empire a golden opportunity to enrich its elites by "reconstructing" the South. After "mission accomplished" in the South, the Yankee Empire

---

[247] Crony Capitalism is often incorrectly viewed or defined as the same as free market capitalism. Crony capitalism depends upon government to give the connected elite a favored position in commerce. It is a "partnership" between financial/commercial elites and the political ruling class. Today the Yankee Empire uses its military to protect crony capitalist foreign investments and uses taxpayers to "bail out" crony banking/financial interests, because "they are too big to fail." This system is not free market capitalism but is closer to national socialism or fascism. True free market capitalism dies as soon as government encroaches into the free market.

[248] Kennedy & Kennedy, *Punished With Poverty*, 99-100, 179-180.

began looking around the world for others to offer the "benefits" of massed Yankee bayonets.

In 1861 the emerging Yankee Empire hid from the world its true intentions for invading the Confederate States of America. It must continue to do so, because to do otherwise would call into international question the right of the Yankee Empire to continue to hold the Confederate States of America as a captive nation—it would brand the Yankee Empire as an *illegitimate* governing power. The Yankee Empire's propagandists falsely claimed the Confederates initiated the war by firing the first shots at Fort Sumter. They warned the world not to recognize the Confederacy or else those doing so would incur the wrath of the Yankee Empire.[249] And they falsely told the people of Europe that the United States was fighting to free blacks from slavery.[250] They did this to conceal the fact that the Yankee Empire was actively engaged in denying the people of the Confederate States of America the right to form a government based upon the free and unfettered consent of the governed—tyranny always hides its true purposes for invading or interfering with peaceful nations.

People the world over have the right to determine how to establish their legitimate government. Some may favor a hereditary Royal House,[251] others may prefer a tribal or clan-based government, while

---

[249] Admiral Semmes of the *CSS Alabama* noted the fear that the Spanish & French had for the Yankee Empire. Semmes, *Memoirs of Service Afloat*, 257, 300.

[250] In Europe, men such as Marx and Engels were used to promote this same slanderous lie about the South's struggle for freedom. Benson & Kennedy, *Lincoln's Marxists*, (Gretna, LA: Pelican Publishing Co., 2011), 64-72.

[251] Libertarian scholar Hans-Hermann Hoppe makes a point that to maintain their dynasty kings must have a long-term view of the impact of their policies whereas democratic leaders only have a short-term view to assure reelection. Therefore, kings

others decide on some form of a representative democracy. The important point is that people of differing cultures and historical experiences will select the form of government that they believe will best suit their unique situation. A system of government good for one group may not be well suited for another. *This is a point that Americans, drunk on Yankee propaganda advocating "democracy for the world," have never understood.* The Yankee mindset has always been to attempt to force the world to accept their way of living—thereby creating a world of second-class Yankees. Americans, under the influence of Yankee leadership, have always fought its wars as a campaign to "free the slaves," to "free oppressed brown people from Spanish colonial rule," to "make the world safe for democracy," or to "establish democracy in the Mideast." These are just a few of the *excuses* used by the ruling elite of the Yankee Empire to marshal the support of the American population for yet another invasion or international policing action. But such wars have always been a "rich man's war and a poor man's fight."

A fundamental principle of America's founding political philosophy is that for any government to be legitimate, it must be founded upon the free and unfettered consent of the governed.[252] Without consent, any

---

tend to select polices that have less long-term negative impact on the common people than politicians in a "democracy;" see Hoppe, Hans-Hermann, *Democracy: The God That Failed* (New Brunswick and London: Transaction Publishers, 2001), xix, xx, 24, 29.

[252] This is an "American" political principle with English and European roots. It is essential for the establishment of legitimate government *for Americans,* but that does not mean that Americans (Yankees) have a right to use military force to compel other people to use a principle of government developed for Americans. Other people have the right to develop their own definitions of legitimate government—regardless of whether or not Americans (Yankees) think such governments are good governments. There have been too many unforeseen and disastrous consequences arising from forcing "good" governments on other people who have different historical and cultural experiences. As Jesus instructed his followers, "Do unto others as you would have them do unto you."

government formed by the Yankee Empire is therefore illegitimate. Reconstruction of the post-war South was the Yankee Empire's first, but not last, time the Yankee Empire would force a government upon a conquered people. The Reconstruction and post-Reconstruction governments did not have the free and unfettered consent of the people of the South. They were and are governments that the conquered people of the Confederate States were forced, at bayonet point, to accept. All such governments, federal and state, were and still are, therefore, *illegitimate*. The mere passage of time does not bestow legitimacy upon an illegitimate government. For example: had the Nazi government lasted for a thousand years, the puppet governments the Nazis installed in Vichy, France, and Quisling, Norway, would still be illegitimate. The same is true for the governments, both federal and state, forced upon the people of the South.

After the surrender of the Confederate military, the Yankee Empire seized control of all Southern governments and established its military as the ultimate authority in its newly conquered territories. Under Yankee domination, the people of the formerly free and prosperous Confederate States of America were reduced to subjects of the Yankee Empire. If a local official offended the Yankee authorities, he would be arrested and held without bail or the benefit of any other Constitutional right. The London *Telegraph* in 1866 noted that the United States "may remain a republic in name, but some eight million of the people [Southerners] are subjects, not citizens."[253] The original and legitimate Constitutional

---

Basically, it means to leave people alone—historically, this seems to be an impossible commandment for most Yankees.

[253] As cited by Bowers, Claude, *The Tragic Era* (New York: Halcyon House, 1929), 146-147.

Republic of Thomas Jefferson had been pushed aside "to make way for the triumphant industrialists and capitalists."[254]

The Yankee Empire's Congress passed the "Reconstruction Act" March 2, 1867,[255] thereby dissolving all Southern state governments—except Tennessee which was already under control of a Yankee puppet government—and divided the states of the Confederacy into five military districts each ruled by a Yankee General. Yankee military officers sat in the state legislatures to make sure nothing was done that would interfere with Yankee rule. Most white Southerners were removed from the voting rolls while mostly illiterate former slaves were registered by the Union army and were told how to vote by various Yankee-controlled "Union Leagues."[256] For the next ten or more years, a system of corruption and fraud would ensue. The massive debt created by the Yankee-controlled state governments during Reconstruction is demonstrated by the fact that South Carolina did not entirely pay off its reconstruction debt until the early 1950s.[257] The horrors of Active Reconstruction convinced most post-war Southerners that they had to do whatever was necessary to convince the Yankee Empire to relent in Active Reconstruction and that Southerners should never again do anything that might cause the Yankee Empire to reinstate Active Reconstruction. Primarily it meant that Southerners must accept their puppet governments as legitimate and never again attempt to assert their right to self-government—thus would begin the current phase of Passive Reconstruction. The prior sentence

---

[254] *Ibid.*, 147.

[255] Kennedy & Kennedy, *The South Was Right!* 169-170, 365-367, 375-376, 377-379.

[256] For a documented account of Reconstruction that avoids the Yankee propagandist's "spin," see Bowers, *The Tragic Era*.

[257] Kennedy & Kennedy, *Punished With Poverty*, 162.

describes the major *strategic failure* on the part of Southerners. It was and continues to be a strategic failure that negates the efforts of Southerners to exercise their right of self-government.

During Active Reconstruction, the Yankee Empire deliberately used the tactic of "divide and rule" by creating racial fear and hatred between black and white Southerners.[258] Divide and rule is an old but effective tactic used by occupying powers to keep the locals under the empire's control.[259] One of the significant efforts of Active Reconstruction was to teach black and white Southerners that they could no longer trust each other and inject the virus of Northern racism into the occupied and powerless South.[260] For the next ten years[261] Southerners were held as a people without a country—essentially Southerners were, and still are, being held as political prisoners of the Yankee Empire.

During Active Reconstruction, the Republican Party used—as in took advantage of or exploited—newly freed slaves[262] to complete Republican designs to radically alter the American constitutional system of States' Rights and limited federalism. After the Republican Party "enacted" the Fourteenth and Fifteenth Amendments it quickly lost interest in black Southerners and eventually abandoned them.[263] The Republican Party's

---

[258] *Ibid.*, 66, 192.

[259] *Ibid.*, 13, 51, 66, 84, 123, 135, 189, 194.

[260] *Ibid.*, 44.

[261] Yankee-imposed Active Reconstruction lasted longer in some Southern States and less in others.

[262] Clark & Kirwan, *The South Since Appomattox* (New York: Oxford University Press, 1961), 67.

[263] Johnson, *North Against the South*, 267.

primary concern was to destroy States' Rights and thereby centralize political power in Washington, D.C. Republicans understood that, "The great stumbling block, the great obstruction in Lincoln's way and in the way of thousands, was the old doctrine of States' Rights."[264] The Republican Party from its very inception was a Northern regional party. It had never expressed a desire to develop the party in the South.[265] The only plan the Republican Party had for the South was to use whatever means necessary to *exterminate* their great opponent—the conservative tradition loving South.

Active Reconstruction ended after the Yankee Empire's politicians in Washington, D.C., using unconstitutional methods, changed (without the consent of the people of the South) the Constitution from an instrument that limited the federal government's power to a new "Constitution" that limited state power. One of the major accomplishments of Active Reconstruction was that the states would no longer be sovereign. The constitutional principle of states' rights, as enunciated by Southerners and former U.S. Presidents Thomas Jefferson and James Madison in the Kentucky and Virginia Resolves of 1798,[266] was dead. In place of states' rights, the once sovereign states now "enjoyed" states' privileges—privileges exercised at the sufferance of the ruling elite of the Yankee Empire. The term "states' rights" was still used by Southern politicians, but its meaning had been covertly changed. As part of the price for

---

[264] Ingersoll, Robert G., as cited in, Benson & Kennedy, *Lincoln's Marxists*, 280. Ingersoll was a socialist, Republican, and former Union Army officer.

[265] Cooper, Jr, William J., *Jefferson Davis—American* (New York: Alfred A. Knopf, 2000), 275.

[266] See, Kentucky & Virginia Resolves of 1798, Kennedy & Kennedy, *Was Jefferson Davis Right?*, 281-285.

relenting Active Reconstruction, it was understood or passively accepted by Southerners, that they could not make this distinction. The political term "states' rights" was used by Southern politicians, but it actually now meant "states' privileges" exercised only with the permission of the supreme federal government. The once sovereign states became no more than mere provinces of the central government in Washington, D.C.—a central government that had morphed into an empire. This change in the federal government assured that the ruling elite in Washington, D.C. and their crony capitalist allies on Wall Street would always maintain ultimate governing authority in their newly created Federal Empire—regardless of which national political party controlled the federal government. This was done by enacting (as opposed to the Constitutional method of ratifying) the Fourteenth and Fifteenth Amendments[267] and by the admission of several new "Union" friendly states carved out of the depopulated territory in the western plains—territories formerly occupied by Native Americans. The Congressional votes from these new "loyal" western states gave the elite rulers a lock on the Yankee Empire and assured them that they would always be able to outvote the Southern delegation in Congress. Active Reconstruction ended in 1877, and Passive Reconstruction began.

Passive Reconstruction was enforced by puppet Southern state governments—the leaders of which knew that if they did anything that appeared to be an attempt to reassert the South's right of self-government—the Yankee Empire would re-impose Active Reconstruction. Despite the best efforts of some of the leaders in these puppet governments, the people of the South, black and white, suffered impoverishment while the industrial North became the center of the

---

[267] Kennedy & Kennedy, *The South Was Right!* 171-176, 369-374, 375-376, 377-379.

world's leading industrialized nation. In the meantime, the South became a colonial appendage of the Yankee Empire—a captive nation populated by pacified second-class and impoverished subjects of the Yankee Empire.

It is interesting to note how the Yankee Empire used similar methods against its international targets as it used against the people of the Confederate States of America. The lessons the Yankee Empire learned in its first foray into imperialism would be put to good use around the world. And with its total control of the history of the War for Southern Independence, the Yankee Empire, its cronies and sycophants, would be able to prevent the truth from becoming known. This "total control" of the history of the War produced "soft censorship"[268] enforced by the Yankee Empire's sycophants in the media, Hollywood, the educational and political systems—"soft" but censorship nonetheless.

Pretext for Invasion

To justify the invasion and conquest of its peaceful, democratic neighbor to the south, the Yankee Empire manufactured a pretext or excuse to initiate a war of conquest. Even before Lincoln had taken office, the Radical Republicans were scheming to initiate a war. The Confederacy was a smaller nation with no standing army, no navy, no international recognition, and therefore, had no incentive to threaten the

---

[268] A recent poll demonstrates the impact of the Empire's soft censorship—the chilling of free speech. In the poll, 71% stated that political correctness has silenced public discussion, and 58% said they were afraid to share their political views. See Ekins, Emily, "Poll: 71% of Americans Say Political Correctness Has Silenced Discussions Society Needs to Have, 58% Have Political Views They're Afraid to Share," Cato Institute, www.cato.org/blog/poll-71-americans-say-political-correctness-has-silenced-discussions-society-needs-have-58-have (Accessed 10/31/2017).

large industrial nation to the north. All the Confederacy wanted was to be left alone.[269]

Peace and friendly trading relations with the United States were all the Confederate States wanted—which would have been an easy thing to accomplish if the United States shared the desire for peace. The Confederate government sent a peace delegation to Washington, D.C. to discuss a peaceful settlement of property belonging to the federal government. Lincoln sent word through a third party that they had no plans for military action but delayed meeting with the Confederate peace delegation. During the delay, Lincoln and company were making secret plans to attack Fort Sumter in Charleston Harbor, South Carolina. The Yankee Empire had occupied Fort Sumter[270] in violation of an armistice that had been agreed to by the authorities on both sides. This violation was, in fact, according to international law, an act of war by the Yankee Empire. But the Confederate authorities did not respond with force, being assured all the while by Lincoln's government that the United States had no intention of keeping Fort Sumter. Lincoln's lies and secret war plans[271] became apparent April 12, 1861 when a Yankee invasion fleet was discovered approaching Charleston Harbor. At this point the South had

---

[269] The Southern desire for peaceful relations was expressed in Senator Jefferson Davis's "Farewell Address to the U.S. Senate" and again in his Inaugural Addresses as President of the Confederate States of America; see Kennedy & Kennedy, *The South Was Right!*, 315-329.

[270] Fort Sumter in Charleston Harbor was unoccupied when South Carolina seceded from the Union on December 20, 1860. An armistice had been agreed upon by the Federal authorities and the State of South Carolina, but Federal troops, in violation of the armistice then in place, moved from their position in Fort Moultrie and occupied the more threatening Fort Sumter, which would be easier to resupply from the sea.

[271] For timeline of Lincoln's secret war plans see Kennedy, *Uncle Seth Fought the Yankees*, 341-351.

no choice but to defend one of its major cities from Yankee invasion. The Northern newspapers of the day convinced the Yankee world that the South had "fired on the flag!" The Yankee Empire had manufactured an incident that allowed them to stampede the citizens of the United States into a war against their peaceful Southern neighbor. This was recognized by Northern Democrats at the time.

Senator James A. Bayard was a pro-peace Democrat from the state of Delaware. While visiting the South at the time of the first shots being fired at Fort Sumter he warned that Lincoln and the Republicans were manufacturing an excuse to invade the Confederate States.

> The course of the admin at Washington has, I doubt not, been intended to provoke a conflict with two ideas—one that their forces [the United States military] would be easy victors and that the attack on Sumter being commenced by the Govt here [the Confederate States] would concentrate the sentiment in the Northern States in support of war.... This pretext of enforcing the laws and protecting [United States] Govt property as a cover for invasion the people will sooner or later see through...[272]

Lincoln had sent Lt. Gustavus Fox on a secret mission to conspire with the Yankee commander (Major Anderson) who had illegally occupied Fort Sumter in violation of the armistice agreement then in place. The mission to land troops and supplies eventually failed because the Confederate government became aware of Lincoln's secret invasion plan when the invasion fleet was outside of Charleston, Harbor. But Lincoln, in a letter to Lt. Gustavus Fox, May 1, 1861, admitted:

---

[272] McClanahan, Brion, "'The Avenger without Mercy': Delaware under the Federal Heel," *Northern Opposition to Mr. Lincoln's War*, 124.

You and I both anticipated that the cause of the country would be advanced by making the attempt to provision Fort Sumter, *even if it should fail*; and it is no small consolation now to feel that *our anticipation is justified by the results.*[273] [Emphasis added]

After its successes against the Confederacy, the same technique of manufacturing an event for military intervention was used to create an *excuse* to send the *USS Boston* and Yankee Empire troops into the peaceful Kingdom of Hawaii; remove the legitimate Hawaiian government and install a puppet government—not unlike the ones the Yankee Empire had installed in the former Confederate States. In Cuba, they used Yellow Journalism and the excuse that the Spanish sunk the *USS Maine*. Instead of allowing the Yankee Empire to stampede it into war with emotional cries of "Remember the *Maine*," Americans should have asked, "What incentive would the faraway, weak nation of Spain have to secretly attack a modern battleship belonging to a giant industrial power of the United States?" As in Lincoln's war—the question was never allowed to be publicly asked or discussed. It was not in the Yankee Empire's interest to allow the gullible public to know who had the most to lose and who had the most to gain from an aggressive war. Where then lies the incentive for releasing the "dogs of war?" Was Spain the culprit, or was an "aggressive abroad" Yankee Empire the culprit?

The Yankee Empire invaded the Philippines as a part of their war with Spain but refused to allow the people of the Philippines or Cuba to form a government based upon their free and unfettered consent—instead, they installed a puppet government in each of its newly acquired territories. In

---

[273] White, Jonathan D., "Introduction," *Northern Opposition to Mr. Lincoln's War*, 2; citing *Collected Works of Abraham Lincoln*, Volume 4, 351.

all cases, public and private properties of the invaded country were ruthlessly destroyed by the invading Yankee troops. After the conquest, the invaded countries' resources were used as a means to enrich the Yankee Empire's commercial and financial elite. As a result, the people of these captive nations suffered impoverishment. This impoverishment, imposed by the victorious Yankee Empire, was not unlike the impoverishment imposed upon the defeated and occupied people of the Confederate States of America.

Retaliation Against Civilians

During the invasion of the Confederate States of America, the Philippines, and Cuba, the military forces of the Yankee Empire used retaliation against noncombatant civilians in an effort to prevent attacks against the occupying military and to convince the local population not to support their fellow countrymen who were fighting against the Yankee invaders. This effort was often referred to as "pacification." In such circumstances, thousands of innocents—men, women, children, and infants—were killed, starved, or died from disease. Today these harsh inhuman effects are buffered by ignoring the human beings who are killed and referring to such causalities as "collateral damage."

Installing Puppet Governments

After the active military and reconstruction phases were completed in the conquered Southern territories, the Yankee Empire then installed puppet state governments to rule the defeated Confederacy. These puppet governments were not created with the free and unfettered consent of the people but were governments founded upon Yankee compulsion—nothing less than bayonet constitutions forming illegitimate governments. These puppet governments gave the appearance of self-government, but as noted, they violated the principle of "consent of the governed." Because these governments violate the principle of "consent of the governed," they were and still are *illegitimate* governments. The

Yankee Empire uses the veiled threat of military force to maintain these illegitimate governments. But more important than the veiled threat of military force is the overwhelming outpouring of the Yankee Empire's propaganda from its cronies in education, media, and political institutions. No opportunity is allowed for a fair hearing from the opposing side—it is a form of "soft censorship." The conquered people are kept pacified by the opium of pro-Yankee, anti-South propaganda. Its propaganda cronies were and still are handsomely rewarded for their work, while any counter voice is silenced by being ostracized, and his career / employment is limited or destroyed.

In foreign nations, the Yankee Empire made sure the foreign puppet politicians and those allied to the puppet politicians prospered, but the common people struggled with poverty, starvation, and disease. The Yankee Empire's commercial and financial allies were given a virtual free hand to exploit the occupied nation's resources, even if it destroyed the environment.[274] The "free hand" given to the empire's commercial and financial allies resulted in Yankee profits, but, as in the case of all empires, it resulted in impoverishment for the people, black, brown, or white[275] of the occupied "captive" nation. This was a new form of imperialism, referred to as economic imperialism or dollar diplomacy. It is a form of imperialism that depends upon puppet governments installed by the Yankee Empire. Internationally these puppet governments are controlled by pro-American foreign dictators who are euphemistically referred to as

---

[274] For an explanation of the environmental impact of Passive Reconstruction in the South see Kennedy & Kennedy, *Punished With Poverty*, 185-186.

[275] White Southerners are the only "white" people to suffer long-term Yankee domination and impoverishment.

"our kind of guy."[276] The Yankee Empire has installed and removed such puppet leaders all over the world. Current Southern politicians can also be classified as the Yankee Empire's "our kind of guys."

Divide and Rule

The technique of "divide and rule" used so successfully by former empires was also a key element in the success of the Yankee Empire's efforts to control the occupied people of the Confederacy. The Yankee Empire learned how to use the "divide and rule" technique in the South and then applied it to Cuba, the Philippines, and Central America. After the Yankee Empire perfected the "divide and rule" skills during its efforts to reconstruct the conquered territories of the South,[277] it then was ready to apply it to other nations. In other nations, it would divide the population along economic lines—the haves versus the have-nots. Agents of the Yankee Empire would make lucrative business deals with businesses in large cities which helped to convince them to reject the local freedom fighters. It established a system in which the relatively rich and politically connected local inhabitants were split away from the rest of their native society. Just as in the United States today, there is a schism between the rich and politically connected elite (on Wall Street, K Street, Silicon Valley, and national / local donor-class) and the average working men and women (residing in what the elites call "fly-over country" or "Podunk, U.S.A."). This effort was so successful in Central America that a local journalist declared that any hope for improving the economic status of the average people was "terminated by the US-trained armies

---

[276] Chomsky, *Rouge States*, xvii, 3, 29, & 31.
[277] Kennedy & Kennedy, *Punished With Poverty*, 13, 51, 66, 123, 135, 189, 194.

that caused the disappearance of the most vocal proponents of sharing the land."[278] As for "divide and rule," all empires have used this technique, but none have used it more efficiently than the Yankee Empire.

Cultural Genocide

If an empire is to incorporate a conquered territory into its domain successfully, the inhabitants of the conquered territory must not be allowed to remember their history—rising generations must not be allowed a historical connection to their land, their people, or the days of freedom before the arrival of the invader. New generations must not be allowed to remember days of freedom and prosperity when the now conquered, occupied, and exploited people were the masters in their own homes. The empire understands that the native culture must be destroyed or at least marginalized to the point that only the most ardent nationalists would still yearn to throw off the invader's yoke and return to freedom and the hope of prosperity. Therefore, the occupied people's culture must be destroyed. This campaign to destroy local or national identity is referred to as "cultural genocide."

The classic example of this is the Yankee Empire's efforts to destroy the culture, especially the language, of the Native Americans of the western plains.[279] In 1887, the Yankee Empire's Congress passed The

---

[278] As cited by Chomsky, *Rogue States*, 139.

[279] "Cleveland signs the Dawes Severalty Act," Hostory.com, www.history.com/this-day-in-history/cleveland-signs-the-dawes-severalty-act (Accessed 08/15/2017); Picotte, Tristan, "The True Impact of the Dawes Act of 1887," Partnership with Native Americans, blog.nativepartnership.org/the-true-impact-of-the-dawes-act-of-1887 (Accessed 08/15/2017); "Dawes General Allotment Act," Encyclopedia Britannica, www.britannica.com/topic/Dawes-General-Allotment-Act (Accessed 08/15/2017).

Dawes Act. It was named for its author Senator Henry Dawes, Republican from the New England state of Massachusetts. It was a typical Yankee plan to "reeducate" lesser people such as Native Americans and turn them into second-class Yankees. The Act's intention was to require Native Americans, now completely under the empire's control, to become farmers. Native American children were required to be educated in a strictly New England fashion where they would be punished for speaking their Native language or wearing Native apparel. The Yankee Empire would "give" each family land for farming. Note: The Yankee Empire was "giving" Native Americans land—land the empire had stolen from these very same Native Americans! But industrious, thrifty Yankees managed to keep the best lands and "give" the Native American families land of poor quality barely fit for farming. This is the history of all empires when dealing with defeated peoples. The current reality of high crime, as well as drug and alcohol abuse, on the Yankee Empire's "Indian Reservations" is a direct result of cultural distortion arising from the Yankee Empire's destruction of the Native American's natural lifestyle and the imposing of an alien lifestyle on America's native people.

Cultural genocide is (and must be) an ongoing element of an empire's efforts to suppress the captive nation's memory of freedom. In the immediate post-war South, the Yankee authorities prohibited the wearing of gray coats associated with uniforms of the Confederate army; they even posted guards at cemeteries to prevent widows from placing flowers on the graves of Confederate soldiers, and display of Confederate flags was looked upon as an act of treason to the Yankee Empire. In order to maintain control and prevent the possible outbreak of resistance or revolt, the empire must maintain its campaign of cultural genocide. A monument to a former freedom fighter, such as General Robert E. Lee, C.S.A., just might inspire locals not only to respect the past but to remember the cause of freedom—such memories would be a potential threat to the Yankee Empire. If the Southern people begin to recognize and understand that their Confederate ancestors were fighting for freedom—it would be a disaster for the Yankee Empire's ruling elite. Thus, today (2017), the politically correct effort, supported by elected

Southern officials, to remove all things associated with the Confederacy.[280]

Extermination and Repopulation

Another aspect of Southern reconstruction that can be seen in the history of other conquered territories is the attempt of the Yankee Empire to exterminate as many of the local inhabitants as possible and then to repopulate the conquered territory with its own "loyal" citizens. This was and still is being done in the South.[281] The use of "repopulation" and the exclusion of native Hawaiians from voting enabled the Yankee Empire to completely control the Kingdom of Hawaii,[282] thereby, denying the native inhabitants the right of a government based upon their free and unfettered "consent of the governed." Note the similarity to what the Yankee Empire did to the South during the South's reconstruction—disenfranchisement of the native population and repopulation of the conquered territory with "loyal" citizens. This technique is used only when the Yankee Empire intends to formally bring the conquered

---

[280] For an example of pacified Southern officials demanding the removal of "All things Confederate." See Bellamy, Cliff, "All traces of Confederacy must go, NC law enforcement group says," *The Herald Sun* (Durham, NC), www.heraldsun.com/news/local/counties/durham-county/article171725987.html (Accessed 09/11/2017).

[281] Kennedy & Kennedy, *Punished With Poverty*, 69, 77, 157-159, 168.

[282] Depopulation of a country does not always require the complete extermination of the native population. The native population can be dispossessed of their country, as was the case of the Kingdom of Hawaii, by simply flooding the targeted nation with the empire's loyal subjects. This has been accomplished in modern times in the Southern States of Maryland and Virginia where thousands of liberal voting federal government employees now make up the majority vote in many of these previously conservative Southern States' counties.

territory into the Yankee Empire as a state (actually as a province because the Yankee Empire no longer allows sovereign states to exist). In other territories, such as Cuba and the Philippines, the Yankee Empire established its puppet government and maintained the right to intervene any time the puppet government dared to resist the Yankee Empire's commands.

The Dangers of Empire

A valuable lesson that history teaches is that all empires are expansive and must always be seeking new people and territories to conquer and exploit. In modern times, empires try to hide their exploitation of weaker peoples by claiming the empire's intervention is for the weaker nation's good, or it is the weaker nation's fault that the intervention is necessary.[283] Or in the case of the Yankee Empire, it denies that it is an empire at all! It claims it is merely helping the downtrodden and policing the world to keep the world safe from the latest villain de jour.[284] But the "downtrodden" often have differing views—they understand that empires have no spiritual connection to the land:

> Your government calls these people Communists, terrorists, and narcotics traffickers, but the truth is they're just people with families who live on lands your company is destroying."[285]

---

[283] Johnson, *The Sorrows of* Empire, 255; Kinzer, *Overthrow*, 4-5.

[284] Examples of villains for which the Yankee Empire has fought to keep the world "safe" would include: evil Southern slave holders, enemies of democracy, communists, drug cartels, rogue dictators with weapons of mass destruction, and terrorists.

[285] Perkins quoting citizen of country under control of EHM, 133.

Empires are dangerous to humans because they concentrate power in the hands of a select few (the ruling elite and their crony allies) who benefit from the use or misuse of that power. The empire's ruling elite are "preoccupied with governance of empire"[286] and are not concerned with the daily travails of those who are not a part of their privileged global club. The empires' elite are never at risk when their power creates massive poverty and inhuman collateral damage. Those with power will eventually achieve their murderous ends. "It simply waits for an excuse, an event of some sort, an assassination, a massacre ... to justify the beginning of murder *en masse*."[287] The elite who control the empire's power view themselves as having exceptional ability to diagnose and treat other people's problems—always in a manner that is the most economically beneficial to the ruling elite and their commercial / financial allies. Those who dare resist the empire's intellectually superior rulers are viewed as being outside of the superior's moral universe—inherently evil people who must be controlled, reeducated, or destroyed (exterminated) to assure continued progress and commercial gains.

Post-war (after the Confederate military surrender in 1865), the United States federal government under Republican control began formalizing through legislation, constitutional amendments, and Federal Supreme Court rulings, the federal government's centralized and supreme power in Washington, D.C. The result was a rejection and destruction of America's original constitutionally limited Republic of Republics. The original constitutionally limited United States of America

---

[286] Bacevich, *The Limits of Power*, 3.
[287] Rummel, *Death By Government*, 22.

morphed into an empire—the Yankee Empire—the South and the world have paid a high price ever since.[288]

---

[288] The difference between the legitimate U.S.A. and the current one is similar to the difference between Rome of the Republic and Imperial Rome of the Caesars. Rome of the Caesars still had the same name, same symbols, same capital, and the Senate. All the trappings of the old Republic were still visible for public consumption, but a major change had occurred in the manner in which power was exercised. The Republic was dead, and an Empire now controlled the power of Rome. Similar to the way in which Jesus described the religious establishment of his day—they were like sepulchers [tombs] painted white, beautiful on the outside but on the inside full of dead men's bones. (Matthew 23: 27, *Holy Bible*). Today the U.S.A. has the symbols but not the reality of the original Republic.

United States troops inspecting the eradication of a Moros village during the post-Spanish-American War occupation of the Philippines. According to a story carried in the New York Times March 11, 1906 over 900 men, women and children were killed. The Yankee Empire labels such human causalities as collateral damage. As Stalin said: "A single death is a tragedy, a million deaths is a statistic." Glory, Glory Hallelujah, the Yankee Empire goes marching on. [289]

---

[289] "Women and Children Killed in Moro Battle," *New York Times,* March 11, 1906. www.query.nytimes.com/mem/archive-free/pdf?res=9A0DEED7103EE733A25752C1A9659C946797D6CF (Accessed 03/13/2018).

Chapter 5: Republics Avoid Foreign Interventions

AMERICA'S FOUNDING FATHERS DID NOT intend to establish an empire when, in 1776, they seceded from their "indivisible" union with Great Britain.[290] They did, in fact, establish the American Republic composed of sovereign states leagued together as the united States of America (note plural "States" and lowercase "united" as in the original document).[291] There were a few High Federalists, under the leadership of Alexander Hamilton, who wanted to establish a system of government similar to the one in Great Britain with a senate elected for life; an executive with almost limitless power; and a central government that could nullify state legislation. This proposal was submitted at the beginning of the Constitutional Convention in 1787 before all the state delegates had arrived. The mere plan for a supreme, sovereign, central government that would replace the Sovereign States almost caused a disbanding of the Convention. The Convention soundly rejected such

---

[290] The British, just like all empires, considered their empire to be "indivisible" and would fight a war (1776-1783) to keep it together. They even offered freedom to American slaves if they joined the fight to keep the "indivisible" British Empire together. Lincoln followed the British example and today pacified Southerners swear allegiance to Lincoln's "indivisible" Yankee Empire.

[291] "The unanimous Declaration of the thirteen united States of America," www.archives.gov/founding-docs/declaration-transcript (Accessed 06/29/2017).

ideas[292] and set about drafting a constitution that maintained the states as sovereign entities and strictly limited the powers of the federal government.

Under the original constitution, the federal government was *allowed* to exercise certain specific and enumerated powers, but the federal government never possessed original sovereign authority—sovereign authority remained with the states because the states were the sovereign entities responsible for authorizing the creation of their agent, the federal government. This federal government would be known to the world as the United States of America and, from an international perspective, would exercise international sovereign authority on behalf of the sovereign states composing the United States. The thirteen sovereign states that created the United States of America under the Constitution of 1787 did not, by so doing, dissolve themselves as sovereign entities—these thirteen sovereign states did not commit suicide when they individually ratified the Constitution of 1787! As sovereign American states, they maintained their "sovereignty, freedom, and independence" as proclaimed in Article II of the Articles of Confederation which preceded the Constitution. Nowhere in the Constitution as ratified did these sovereign states agree to surrender, renounce, or irrevocably delegate to the federal government their "sovereignty, freedom, and independence."

During the debates in the various states over the possible ratification of the proposed constitution, many notable Southerners warned their countrymen about the dangers associated with joining a union with people in the North (New England and New York, especially Wall Street)

---

[292] Kennedy, *Nullification: Why & How*. See chapter 13, "The Federal Government Rejected by the Founding Fathers," 75-92. [Free download available at: www.kennedytwins.com/Nullification_Book_2012.pdf]

who had radically different economic and social interests than the people of the South. These Southerners saw a fearful future in which the Northern majority would use their majority position in the United States' Congress to support the North's commercial / financial interests at the expense of the minority in the South.[293] The political struggle between the North and the South from the ratification[294] of the Constitution (1787-1790) until 1861 consisted in the struggle between the High Federalists, holding what is known as a loose-construction view of the Constitution, and Moderate Federalists and Anti-Federalists, collectively known as strict constructionists. Strict constructionists upheld the principle of state sovereignty or states' rights, whereas High Federalists wanted to remove power (sovereignty) from the states and centralize it in the federal government. The High Federalists were followers of Alexander Hamilton (of New York) who wanted to interpret the Constitution in a manner that would greatly expand the power of the federal government, while the strict constructionists were followers of Thomas Jefferson (of Virginia) who advocated a strictly limited interpretation of the Constitution.[295] Slavery became an issue only because of its potential impact on the North's voting power in Congress. It had nothing to do with the North's falsely asserted love for their black brothers and sisters held in the

---

[293] Kennedy & Kennedy, *Punished With Poverty*, 33-39.

[294] The Constitution, and therefore the establishment of the federal government, was accomplished by the individual acts of each sovereign state. The term so often misrepresented of "We the people of the United States" did not mean the American people acting in unison. It meant "We the people of each sovereign state acting for the people of that specific state and only that specific sovereign state." It did not mean "We the people of the United States" in the aggregate—acting as one people of a new nation. Such would have been the act of creating an empire not a "compound republic," "an association of republics," a "Republic of Republics," or a Republic of Sovereign States.

[295] Kennedy & Kennedy, *Was Jefferson Davis Right?*, 217-239.

bondage of chattel slavery. Northern politicians[296] and crony capitalists knew that if a new "slave" state were admitted to the Union, it would be pro-Southern, and therefore the new state would give additional votes in Congress to those favoring the Jeffersonian view of strict construction of the Constitution. The High Federalists, from the beginning of the United States, had a slight majority in Congress and were determined to do whatever it took to maintain their grip on federal power. Remember, the Yankees' only guiding principle is profit—regardless of how crooked the pathway may be to the fulfillment of their hearts' desire.

From 1790 to 1860, Southern political power stood in the way of Yankee (Republican by 1861) political and economic ambitions. Knowing that they could not make political converts in the South, Republicans decided to destroy (exterminate) the South politically. Republicans became "anti-slavery" because it gave them a potent weapon to use in their war against the South's political power.[297]

---

[296] The belief in liberal vs strict interpretation of the Constitution crossed the geographical divide between the North and South. There were High Federalists or Whigs in the South as well as strict constructionists in the North. But a loud and vocal minority in the North (a majority in New England) advocated High Federalist views whereas the majority in the South held to strict construction of the Constitution. The vocal minority in the North, who wanted to expand their political and economic power, saw the limitations of the Constitution as a barrier that needed to be breached, whereas the majority in the South, who sought protection from an aggressive and vocal North, viewed the barriers to federal power in the Constitution as an indispensable protection and safeguard. The Constitution was a gentleman's agreement between Sovereign States and would last only as long as gentlemen were in control.

[297] DeRosa, Marshall, "President Franklin Pierce and the War for Southern Independence," *Northern Opposition to Mr. Lincoln's War*, 21. Also recall that slavery was not a logical reason to deny Independence to the Thirteen American Colonies, even though every Colony had laws allowing for slavery, and the New England Colonies were actively engaged in the nefarious international slave trade. The thirteen stripes on the U.S. flag represent thirteen former slave-holding colonies and, with independence,

The South realized that a consolidated or centralized federal government would result in a supreme federal government that would seize the right to be the sole judge of the extent—if any—of its powers. This form of government, a government that is the sole determinate of its powers, was recognized by Southerners as the very essence of tyranny. It makes very little difference if the one making the decision as to the extent of government power is an absolute monarch, dictator, or the ruling elite of a consolidated federal government—tyranny is the result. The Yankee Empire would never have developed if it had not developed a centralized, supreme federal government. An empire must have centralized control of the government. In the arena of foreign relations, a republic tends to mind its own business while empires look for excuses to exercise (project) their power over weaker nations. The empire's projection of power allows it to exploit weaker nations. In contrast to the current Yankee Empire, America's original constitutionally limited Republic of Republics sought to avoid international meddling.

In his Farewell Address to the nation, America's first president, George Washington (of Virginia), took the occasion "to warn against the mischiefs of foreign intrigue."[298] While he understood the desire of the commercial section of the country to engage in foreign trade, he warned that international trade should be accomplished with:

> Harmony, liberal intercourse with all nations, are recommended by policy, humanity, and interest. But even our commercial

---

thirteen slave-holding states. Slavery was not the C.S.A.'s sin—the C.S.A.'s sin was their attempt to remove Southern wealth from Lincoln's newly emerging Yankee Empire.

[298] "Washington's Farewell Address 1796," The Avalon Project, avalon.law.yale.edu/18th_century/washing.asp (Accessed 06/27/2017).

> policy should hold an equal and impartial hand; neither seeking nor granting exclusive favors or preferences [299]

It was an early warning against what would become known as crony capitalism in modern times. George Washington saw the danger to the new Republic in allowing America's foreign commerce to draw the Republic into foreign entanglements.

> The great rule of conduct for us in regard to foreign nations is in extending our commercial relations, to have with them as little political connection as possible.[300]

These are not the kind of instructions that an empire would follow. It is the guiding principle for a republic whose commerce would bring it into contact with foreign nations with different cultures, historical experiences, and governments. President Washington admonished Americans to "Observe good faith and justice towards all nations; cultivate peace and harmony with all. Religion and morality enjoin this conduct."[301] In addition, he warned about the danger of national debt, which was viewed as a tax upon unborn generations. One warning that is especially important if a republic is to avoid the slide into an empire is the danger of a large, standing military:

avoid the necessity of those overgrown military establishments which, under any form of government, are inauspicious to liberty, and which are to be regarded as particularly hostile to republican liberty.[302]

---

[299] *Ibid.*

[300] *Ibid.*

[301] *Ibid.*

[302] *Ibid.*

This warning would be echoed by President Eisenhower in his 1961 Farewell Address when he warned the nation about the emerging military-industrial complex.[303]

Even President and High Federalist John Quincy Adams, was concerned about the possibility of the new nation becoming involved in foreign intrigues. He saw such intrigues as a danger to the Republic and warned Americans:

> Wherever the standard of freedom and Independence has been or shall be unfurled, there will her [the United States] heart, her benedictions and her prayers be. <u>But she goes not abroad, in search of monsters to destroy.</u> She is the well-wisher to the freedom and independence of all. She is the champion and vindicator only of her own...her policy would insensibly change from *liberty* to *force*.... She might become the dictatress of the world. She would be no longer the ruler of her own spirit.[304] [italics in original—underlining added]

As evidenced by these words of a President from New England, it is clear that the founders of the United States did NOT intend to create a vast worldwide commercial, financial, and military empire.

A review of Thomas Jefferson's views would give modern day Yankee and pacified Southern "conservatives" a reason to pause and ask, "Is this the same nation that we live in today?" And of course, the answer would be, "No, this current nation (better described as the Yankee Empire) is not

---

[303] "Military-Industrial Complex Speech, Dwight D. Eisenhower, 1961," The Avalon Project, avalon.law.yale.edu/20th_century/eisenhower001.asp (Accessed 06/29/2017).

[304] Adams, John Quincy, "Warning Against the Search for 'Monsters to Destroy,' 1821," Mount Holyoke, www.mtholyoke.edu/acad/intrel/jqadams.htm (Accessed 06/27/2017).

the United States of Jefferson's days." Review Jefferson's views on foreign relations:

- "concerning themselves or other nations, we wish not to intermeddle in word or deed." Thomas Jefferson to T. Pinckney, 1792
- "We surely cannot deny to any nation that right whereon our own government is founded, that every one may govern itself according to whatever form it pleases and change these forms at its own will, and that it may transact its business with foreign nations through whatever organ it thinks proper, whether king, convention, assembly, committee, president, or anything else it may choose. The will of the nation is the only thing essential to be regarded." Thomas Jefferson to G. Morris, 1792
- "Our desire is to pursue ourselves the path of peace as the only one leading surely to prosperity." Thomas Jefferson to G. Hammond, 1793
- "I am for free commerce with all nations, political connection with none, and little or no diplomatic establishment. And I am not for linking ourselves by new treaties with the quarrels of Europe, entering that field of slaughter to preserve their balance, or joining in the confederacy of Kings to war against the principles of liberty." Thomas Jefferson to E. Gerry, 1799 [Emphasis added]
- "Commerce with all nations, alliance with none, should be our motto." Thomas Jefferson to T. Lomax, 1799
- "The presumption of dictating to an independent nation the form of its government is so arrogant, so atrocious, that indignation as well as moral sentiment enlists all our partialities and prayers in favor of one [independent nations] and our equal execrations against the other [dictating to other nations]." Thomas Jefferson to J. Monroe, 1823
- "Although we have no right to intermeddle with the form of government of other nations, yet it is lawful to wish to see no emperors nor kings in our hemisphere." Thomas Jefferson to J. Monroe, 1823.

- "Our first and fundamental maxim should be never to entangle ourselves in the broils of Europe." Thomas Jefferson to J. Monroe 1823.[305]

From Thomas Jefferson's statements listed, it is easy to see that a radical change in the character, beliefs, and morality of those who controlled the federal government (more appropriately the Yankee Empire) occurred from the 1820s to 1861. Those advocating a commercial / financial empire seized power, and thereby the political origin of an empire occurred. The birth of the Yankee Empire occurred in 1865 with its successful invasion, conquest, and occupation of a formerly free and prosperous nation, the Confederate States of America. The newly created Yankee Empire continued to grow until today; it employs worldwide economic hit men (EHM), Jackals, and when necessary, the U.S. military. The startling and embarrassing question for pacified Southerners is, "Would Thomas Jefferson pledge allegiance to this new *one nation, indivisible*?" Lincoln, the Republican Party, and their crony capitalist allies used vicious military force to convert a former republic into an aggressive empire. Lincoln and the Republican Party created an empire that is, as General Robert E. Lee, CSA, predicted, "aggressive abroad and despotic at home." All done, according to Lincoln's apologists, out of necessity in order to "save the Union."

A noted liberal Yankee historian and Lincoln apologist approvingly declared that Lincoln, in his Gettysburg Address, "performed one of the most daring acts of open-air sleight-of-hand ever witnessed by the

---

[305] Coates, Eyler, "Foreign Relations & Jeffersonian Principles," eyler.freeservers.com/JeffPers/jefpco30.htm (Accessed 06/29/2017).

unsuspecting."[306] In his Gettysburg Address, Lincoln abandoned the tradition of referring to the United States as a "union" and used the word "nation" five times.[307] Lincoln's mere unfounded words replaced the Constitution and, using military compulsion, replaced America's Republic of Sovereign States with a unitary nation / state. Harvard Professor George Ticknor (1791-1871) writing after the War declared that "It does not seem to me as if I were living in the country in which I was born."[308] Southern scholar, Marshall DeRosa, noted that because Lincoln was willing to "dispense with the rule of law in order to achieve political objectives favorable to the dominant political class" he became America's first Caesar—a promoter of empire.[309]

Modern Yankee historians, who are actually well-rewarded propagandists for the Yankee Empire, try to hide Lincoln's dictatorial actions by claiming that his "own loyal and unselfish nature" tended to "check the excessive use of absolute power" and after all, Lincoln was "a benevolent dictator."[310] This is said without a hint of embarrassment when faced with the fact that Lincoln and his fellow Republican co-conspirators were responsible for the arrest of between 10,000 to 38,000 U.S. citizens without benefit of civilian judicial proceedings.[311] It should

---

[306] Wills, Gary, *Lincoln at Gettysburg: The Words that Remade America* (New York: Simon & Schuster, 1992), 38.

[307] Hummel, *Emancipating Slaves, Enslaving Free Men*, 329.

[308] Ticknor as cited in Hummel, *Emancipating Slaves, Enslaving Free Men*, 333.

[309] DeRosa, Marshall, "President Franklin Pierce and the War for Southern Independence," *Northern Opposition to Mr. Lincoln's War*, 12.

[310] White, D. Jonathan, "Copperheads: History and Historiography," *Northern Opposition to Mr. Lincoln's War*, 89.

[311] *Ibid.*, 90.

be pointed out here that these citizens were citizens of *Northern States*—they were not Southerners. In other words, Lincoln and his Republican cronies waged war upon their own people while waging war upon the people of the Confederate States of America. One of the first domestic acts of Lincoln's new Empire was to enact unconstitutional policies whose purposes were to chill free speech and other constitutional rights.

One does not have to arrest every Democrat to send a clear message to voters that opposition will not be tolerated. One does not have to arrest the entire Federal judiciary to let judges know that deciding a case against the administration may result in house arrest or worse.[312]

Lincoln's exercise of unconstitutional powers set a precedent that other U.S. Presidents used to excuse their use of unconstitutional powers. The excuse of "necessity" would become a common justification for the use of force, or the restriction or invasion of personal liberties in the Yankee Empire. During the Bush Administration, it was often used to justify spying on or detaining citizens—they reasoned that "Lincoln had done it, so it must be okay."[313]

Military necessity in Lincoln's Federal Empire meant that a state of war or "national emergency" operates as an amendment to the Constitution overriding all other amendments or Constitutional restraints on use of government force. Lincoln was to the United States' original Republic what Caesar was to the original Roman Republic. After Caesar, Rome was never again a Republic—after Lincoln, the United States is no longer a republic. Under both Caesar and Lincoln, republics were destroyed and replaced by a cruel, dictatorial empire. In both

---

[312] *Ibid.*
[313] *Ibid.*

former Republics, the trappings of the old Republic remained for public consumption (flags, senate, titles of offices, holidays, *etc.*), but the restraint on governmental force no longer remained—in each case a republic was replaced with an empire that maintained the exclusive right to be the judge of the extent of its powers.

Democratic Lawyer John C. Bullitt (circa 1860) from Philadelphia, Pennsylvania, understood the dangers of allowing a president to use "necessity" as an excuse for violating the Constitution. "The act of today becomes the precedent for tomorrow."[314] Half a century later, President Woodrow Wilson used the precedent established by Lincoln to arrest citizens who opposed the U.S. participation in World War I, approximately two decades later, President Franklin D. Roosevelt used Lincoln's precedent to round-up and incarcerate American citizens of Japanese lineage during World War II, and President Bush (the younger) used Lincoln's precedent to justify spying on Americans and other unconstitutional actions. "Necessity" as an excuse for tyrannical acts is as old as government itself. John Milton, the 17th century English writer, described it like this: "So spake the fiend, and with *necessity*, the tyrant's plea, excused his devilish deeds."[315] [Emphasis added]

A constitution that secures and protects citizens in their rights only in time of peace is a fraud. It would amount to putting liberty in danger anytime a power-hungry president or ruling elite desired to announce *or create* some new public disaster, crisis, or distress requiring immediate

---

[314] As cited by Trask, Arthur, "Philadelphia against the War," *Northern Opposition to Mr. Lincoln's War*, 256.

[315] Milton, John, *Paradise Lost*, Book IV; in *John Milton Complete Poems and Major Prose*, Merritt Y. Hughes, editor (Indianapolis & New York: The Odyssey Press, 1957), 287.

and vigorous government intervention. As recent United States history has taught—power hungry politicians "never let a crisis go to waste."[316] And just like Lincoln at Fort Sumter—if a convenient "crisis" is not available, then the Yankee Empire will manufacture one—just like Yankee Greenbacks (fiat paper currency first issued by the Lincoln Administration to finance Lincoln's invasion of the Confederacy); it will be created out of thin air and passed off on an unsuspecting world as real.

---

[316] Rahm Emanuel, chief of staff for President Barack Obama, www.youtube.com/watch?v=_mzcbXi1Tkk (Accessed 11/20/2016).

Yankee troops beheaded Jack Hinson's two teenage sons falsely claiming the boys, who had been out hunting, were guerrilla troops intending to ambush the U.S. Army. Their severed heads were brought back and posted in front of their home in full view of their mother and father to serve as a warning to all who dared to resist Yankee domination. Until then, Jack had been a pro-Union Southerner—he took his revenge! [317]

---

[317] Kennedy, *Uncle Seth Fought the Yankees*, 373-376.

CHAPTER 6: AN EVIL EMPIRE'S FIRST INVASION

THE YANKEE EMPIRE HAS done a masterful job developing excuses for invading a country that contains resources or a strategic global position coveted by the Empire. The effort to deceive the Southern Peace Commissioners who were sent to Washington in March 1861 by the Confederate government to negotiate in good faith was the Yankee Empire's first foray into such international intrigue. Lincoln kept the Confederate Peace Commissioners at arm's length, communicating with them only through a third party, Associate Justice John Archibald Campbell of the United States Supreme Court, and delaying them with repeated false assurances that the United States did not intend to use force against Fort Sumter in South Carolina nor Fort Pickens in Florida. All the while, Lincoln was sending secret communications to the U.S. Navy to make clandestine preparations for a forced landing in the South and communicating with the Yankee Commander who had occupied Fort Sumter in violation of the truce or armistice then in place. With an invasion fleet offshore and an unfriendly Yankee force occupying Fort Sumter, the Confederacy had no choice but to reduce the Fort before it was reinforced and threatened the civilian population in the city of Charleston.[318] It is worthy to note that international law, recognized at the time, declares that it is not the one who fires the first shot who is responsible for initiating hostilities. Instead, it is the one who makes

---

[318] For timeline and discussion of Lincoln's secret war plans against the Confederate States of America, see Kennedy, *Uncle Seth Fought the Yankees*, 341-351.

firing (in self-defense) the first shot necessary who is responsible for initiating hostilities. The aggressor nation (the United States of America), by making certain threatening moves against a peaceful nation (the Confederate States of America), intentionally places the peaceful nation in the position of striking first before the more powerful aggressor could land his invasion forces.[319]

The propaganda effect on a gullible Northern public was Lincoln's primary reason for attacking Fort Sumter. He told Lieutenant Fox (one of the many Yankee secret war conspirators) that even though their attempt to reinforce Fort Sumter had failed, it nonetheless did achieve its purpose.[320] The emerging "Yellow Journalists" of the North began beating the "war drums" and "rattling war sabers" by telling their Northern readers that evil, slaveholding Southerners had attacked the U.S. flag and honor demanded a vigorous war of invasion and retribution. Yankee "Yellow Journalists," in league with radical abolitionists, crony capitalists, and Republicans demanded blood revenge for such an alleged "unprovoked" attack upon the country's honor. Lincoln and his Republican co-conspirators used trickery, treachery, and deception to convince the average person in Yankee America that the "evil" South deserved to be invaded and punished. In the not too distant future the Yankee Empire would apply this well-learned lesson to other nations

---

[319] The United States fired the first shots of the Pacific War which began the U.S. involvement in World War II! Hours before the Japanese attacked Pearl Harbor, the U.S. navy dropped depth charges on a Japanese mini-sub attempting to enter the harbor. Such "first shots" are viewed not as an act of aggression but as acts of self-defense. Thus, the firing on Fort Sumter, with a Yankee invasion fleet offshore and a hostile foreign (Yankee) force occupying the fort, was a similar act of self-defense.

[320] White, "Introduction," *Northern Opposition to Mr. Lincoln's War*, 2; citing *Collected Works of Abraham Lincoln*, Volume 4, 351.

anytime the Yankee Empire discovered a foreign nation that had resources or a strategic global position coveted by the Yankee Empire. Empires maintain control of their "loyal" population by deceiving their citizens about the reason or justification for each new war, invasion, or other use of imperial power against a new international "enemy."

Admiral Raphael Semmes of the *CSS Alabama* noted that during the War for Southern Independence, Yankee newspaper reporters sought after "sensational" stories, and if they could not find them, then false stories—19th century version of fake news—would be created by Yankee reporters. He feared that if the South lost its struggle for independence, "Such is the stuff out of which a good deal of the Yankee histories of the late war will be made."[321] Thus, even before the term "Yellow Journalism" had been coined, the Yankee Empire's journalists were busily engaged in their efforts to dehumanize those who stood in the way of the Yankee Empire's expansion. The cry "Remember the Maine" was used by the Empire's Yellow Journalists to convince the American public to engage in an aggressive military expansion in the Caribbean and the Philippines. The trick worked well against the Confederacy and has been used time and time again to "convince" a gullible American public to support the Yankee Empire's worldwide military interventions and numerous no-win wars.

North and South—Not just Different but Antagonistic

Southerners had been warned from the beginning of the United States about the dangers of joining a league or union with Northerners. The cultural, religious, social, and economic differences were so extreme that

---

[321] Semmes, *Memoirs of Service Afloat*, 235-236; 401.

early on it was apparent that the two would not be able to live together in peace under the same government. Confederate States President Jefferson Davis, noted the vast difference between Southerners and Northerners. He described Benjamin Franklin—American Founding Father from Pennsylvania—as typical of the Yankee spirit:

> Franklin's soul was a true type or incarnation of the New England character—hard, calculating, angular, unable to conceive any higher object than the accumulation of money. He was the most material of great intellects. None of the lighter graces or higher aspirations found favor in his sight.... The hard, grasping, money-grubbing, pitiless and domineering spirit of the New England puritan found in Franklin a true exponent.[322]

New Englanders were descended from the ancient English enemy of the Celtic peoples of Scotland, Ireland, Wales, and the Northern English border shires. While the English immigrants and descendants populated New England, the South was populated primarily by Celtic immigrants.[323] These Southern immigrants were often referred to as Scotch-Irish. They brought with them their historical hatred of all things English. Actually, the Celtic or Scotch-Irish mindset was one that was opposed to any outside authority. Their spirit of rugged individualism was a major concern for the central Spanish and English authorities in Colonial

---

[322] Davis, as cited in McWhiney, Grady, *Cracker Culture-Celtic Ways in the Old South* (Tuscaloosa, AL: University of Alabama Press, 1988), 139.

[323] Celtic immigrants made up a substantial part of the Southern population, but Southerners are a blend of Scot-Irish and Welsh (Celtic), as well as African, Native American, English, German, Hispanic, French and others, all of whom have contributed their unique culture and blood to the making of a unique people known as "Southerners." See-Clyde Wilson, "Is the South Celtic?," The Abbeville Blog, www.abbevilleinstitute.org/blog/is-the-south-celtic (Accessed 11/13/2017).

America.[324] By the beginning of the War for Southern Independence (1861), they and their descendants outnumbered the combined total of all other white settlers in the South. Their culture became the dominant culture of the South—a culture[325] that was radically different from the money-worshiping culture of New England. The conflict between North and South was a conflict of cultures; a conflict of differing values; a conflict that was shaped by the ancient roots of these English-speaking people. It was not a conflict of brother against brother but a conflict of culture against culture. And it should be noted that at this early period of American Colonial history, slavery was actively practiced in both sections—North and South. Slavery did not cause the conflict between these two-differing people, but by 1861, it had become a convenient Yankee excuse for aggressive war.

Ralph Waldo Emerson was an outspoken champion of New England and a vicious critic of the South. His idolatry of England is evidenced by his declaration "England is the best of actual nations." He concluded that Yankees or New Englanders and English looked alike and dined alike, and that the Yankee stock was the continuation of England in the New World.[326] In contrast, he summed up the Yankee view of the people

---

[324] Ste. Claire, Dana, *Cracker-The Cracker Culture in Florida History* (University of Florida Press: 1998), 43.

[325] It is of interest that the Celtic people who settled the South had a culture based on blood relations in a clan or tribe, family, weapons, and manly pursuits such as hunting, warfare, and the general pursuit of a leisurely lifestyle. This Celtic culture is very similar to the culture of the Africans who were brought to America by New Englanders engaged in the nefarious slave trade. Though different in many ways, black and white Southerners still merged together to form a unique society despite the burdens of slavery.

[326] McWhiney, *Cracker Culture*, 30.

populating the South by declaring that the Celts in Ireland were "an inferior or misplaced race."[327]

While New Englanders found England to be an ideal nation, Southerners saw less to admire in England. Jefferson Davis, writing in 1845, called England "the robber nation of the earth, whose history is a long succession of wrongs and oppressions, whose tracks are marked by the crushed rights of individuals—to England I cannot go for lessons of morality and justice."[328]

Premodern Celts and pre-war Southerners valued leisure far higher than work, but the opposite was true for the New Englander. It was often said that a Northerner would not eat anything he could sell whereas the Southerner would not sell anything he could eat! Hard work and productive activity were the essence of the Yankee's social condition—the constant striving after material gain for no other purpose than its acquisition. Life for the Yankee was indeed hard in their cold climate where livestock had to be fed and sheltered during harsh winters. By contrast, Southerners raised their livestock on the open range, and the South's temperate climate did not require Southerners to tend their cattle and hogs during the relatively mild winters. When an industrious Yankee would chastise a "lazy" Southerner for not being actively involved in productive work, the Southerner would reply, "Why work when you do not need to work?" Life was to be enjoyed, and work was to be taken up only when necessary. Indeed, most people, both black and white, did not seem to work too hard in the South. One study noted:

---

[327] *Ibid.*, 28.

[328] *Ibid.*, 35.

> Nobody seems to have worked very hard in the Old South ... even if one ... assumes that only slaves worked in the Old South, and that no white person ever lifted a finger, then each black field hand would have had to labor about 147 ten-hour days a year.[329]

This would be equal to a work year of 1470 hours. The standard work year for a full-time employee in the U.S. today is 2080 hours. Samples of the actual work done by Southern plain folk (non-plantation whites) indicate that four randomly selected families labored a total of perhaps 423 hours per year.[330] This leisurely work ethic provided one of the highest standards of living in the world at that time.[331] Prior to the War for Southern Independence, Southerners (black and white) consumed almost five times the amount of protein recommended for adults by the federal government in 1978. After Yankee invasion, conquest, and occupation, the Southern people suffered massive malnutrition resulting in a South-only disease, Pellagra—a disease caused from deficient intake of protein.[332] Pellagra, which lasted in the South until the late 1940s, was a "gift" to the conquered Southern people from the Yankee Empire! Starvation and malnutrition tend to follow empires, but the ruling elite and their cronies never suffer want; they are "too big to fail!"

The radical difference between the people of the North and the South was noted by pre-War foreign travelers. Foreigners noticed that Northerners were more concerned with materialistic pursuits, whereas Southerners were more inclined toward leisure and things of spiritual

---

[329] *Ibid.*, 47.

[330] *Ibid.*, 47.

[331] Kennedy & Kennedy, *Punished With Poverty*, 15-31.

[332] *Ibid.*, 111-112.

values—not all such values are necessarily religious but include pleasurable activities such as socializing, charitable endeavors, music, horse racing, as well as a high sense of personal honor. One foreign visitor was quoted as saying:

> The southerner very often prosecutes his amusements as actively as the northerner engaged in sterner occupations...The people of the Northern States, as a whole, probably enjoy life less than any other civilized people.[333]

These observations by foreigners did not cease after the States created the federal government by ratifying the Constitution of 1787. The unsure union between the North and the South did not mitigate these differences, it actually accentuated these differences and eventually turned them into points of political conflict. A European visitor in 1855 left this testimony:

> Proceeding towards the South, I find the manners soften as well as the voice, more frankness and cheerfulness: the rather stiff formality of the Northern States is replaced by ease, and at the same time the young people are merry without being boisterous, and no one objects to those games and amusements which the spirit of the puritanical times has handed down as crimes to ... their New England descendants.[334]

The conflict between the United States and the Confederate States was not a conflict of brother against brother, or a conflict of anti-slavery versus pro-slavery, it was a conflict of culture against culture. The United States was and is today a culture based on dollar-worshiping materialism, the roots of which are English. Even contemporary (2008) New England "intellectuals" have admitted that American character is typified by a

---

[333] As cited in McWhiney, *Cracker Culture*, 105.

[334] *Ibid.*, 109.

"restless searching for a buck" and a willingness to eliminate anyone standing in the way of profit.[335] The Confederate States' culture was leisure-oriented—a culture that did not object to money but money was not the most important aspect of pre-war Southern society.[336] As one Southern historian noted, "Relatively few of the plain folk, however, seem to have had a desire to become wealthy."[337] The roots of Southern culture are decidedly anti-English—taking their lineage from the Celtic peoples of Scotland, Ireland, Wales, and the northern border shires of England.

Conditions among the inhabitants of the English uplands, Wales, Scotland, and Ireland had long been adverse to the perpetuation of their traditional ways. In the American South migrants from those areas could preserve those ways and flourish. Indeed, in a manner of speaking, their entire history had prepared them to be Southerners.[338]

It is important to point out that even though Celtic immigrants had a major influence on Southern culture—Southerners are a unique people composed of a blend of many different people and cultures. The people

---

[335] See Bacevich, *The Limits of Power*, 17.

[336] This contrast between the money-grubbing Yankee and the spiritual Southerner remains today and can be seen in the radical difference between the charitable giving of the two sections. For example, the affluent Yankee state of Massachusetts is among the lowest in per capita charitable giving, whereas the poorest state in the current United States, the Southern State of Mississippi, has the highest per capita charitable giving. Kennedy & Kennedy, *Punished With Poverty* (Maps in center section).

[337] Owsley, Frank L., *Plain Folk of the Old South* (1949, Baton Rouge, LA: LSU Press, 1982), 134.

[338] McDonald, Forrest, in "Prologue," McWhiney, *Cracker Culture*, xliii.

of the South are a blend of Celtic, English, French, German, Spanish, Hispanic, Native American, and African people.[339]

Yankee post-war propaganda has imposed upon the world the false history that the so-called "Civil War" was fought over slavery. But the truth of history stands in radical contradiction to prevailing Yankee myths. However, as a conquered people and a captive nation, the South has had limited means to counter generations of slanderous anti-South Yankee propaganda. Yet, the truth is difficult to destroy even with the aid of a massive Yankee propaganda machine that includes America's news media, Hollywood, the educational, financial, and political establishments. Despite their best efforts to *exterminate* the traditional South—the truth remains and demands to have its story told. Truth, though crushed to the earth—just like our Southern nation—shall rise again!

Early Warnings of the Danger of Maintaining a Close Union with Yankeedom

Patrick Henry, from Virginia, was very direct when he warned Virginia and the South about the dangers of forming a union with "those people"[340] of the North. Patrick Henry had worked with Northerners during the War for American Independence (1775-1781). He quickly realized that Northerners were different from Southerners and warned that the Northern states were then a slight majority and Northerners would eventually use their majority status to oppress the Southern

---

[339] Kennedy, *Uncle Seth Fought the Yankees*, 14-15.

[340] "Those people" is the gentlemanly term General Robert E. Lee often used when referring to Yankee invaders.

minority. He warned that the proposed Constitution of 1787 would create a federal government that would become a dreadful danger to the South.

> The [proposed] government subjects everything to the Northern majority.... How can the Southern members prevent the adoption of the most oppressive mode of taxation in the Southern states, as there is a majority in favor of the Northern States? Sir, this is a picture so horrid, so wretched, so dreadful, that I need no longer dwell upon it.[341]

Patrick Henry was not alone in his fear of an aggressive Northern majority. Another Virginian, George Mason, added his voice to those who were warning the South.

> The eight Northern States have an interest different from the five Southern States.... The Southern States had therefore grounds for their suspicions.[342]

General Charles Cotesworth Pinckney, South Carolina, clearly saw what would become of the South if it were to go into union with the North. He declared that under the proposed federal government,

> the regulation of trade is to be given to the General Government [federal government created under the Constitution], they [the Southern States] will be nothing more than overseers for the Northern States"[343]

Were these early predictions of the impoverishment and oppression of the Southern minority by the Northern (Yankee) majority justified? Were

---

[341] Patrick Henry, as cited in Kennedy & Kennedy, *Punished With Poverty*, 125-126.

[342] George Mason, *Ibid.*, 126.

[343] Pickney, *Ibid.*, 126.

these warnings merely hysterical rantings of "ignorant and radical Southerners?"

In 1828, a mere forty years after the establishment of the federal government, Senator Thomas H. Benton of Missouri gave an impassioned speech in the United States Senate denouncing the economic exploitation of the South by the North. He noted that 75% of the revenues collected by the federal government came from the South. Most of this Southern wealth was spent on "internal improvements" benefiting Northern commerce and industry. Senator Benton declared "Wealth has fled from the South and settled in regions north of the Potomac."[344] It is worth noting—although Yankee history will never do so—that Senator Benton was opposed to the expansion of slavery and was considered to be anti-slavery.

North-South Trade Imbalance

By the mid-1830s, cotton shipments accounted for more than half the value of all exports from the United States.[345] This takes into account only cotton! To gain a complete picture of the South's active international trade, other Southern products must be added to cotton exports. Other agricultural products were produced in the South such as tobacco, sugar, and indigo. In addition, cattle and hogs supplied to the domestic and international markets must be added. According to the 1860 census, the

---

[344] Senator Thomas H. Benton, *Ibid.*, 38.

[345] Ransom, Roger L., "The Economics of the Civil War," Economic History Association, eh.net/encyclopedia/the-economics-of-the-civil-war (Accessed 07/06/2017).

value of cattle and hogs was nearly equal to the value of all crops produced that year.[346]

> Neither slavery nor the plantation system was as widespread or as distinctively southern as the raising of livestock, especially hogs and cattle, on the open range.[347]

This demonstrates the dramatic positive impact the plain folk of the old South, with their vast herds of hogs and cattle, had on the Southern economy. These were non-plantation whites who made up the largest portion of the South's white population. They also represent the often cited "80%" of the Confederate army who did not own slaves. These plain folks in the Confederate Army were not fighting so that a few rich plantation owners could keep their slaves—they were fighting for their Freedom!

Northern Opposition to Lincoln's Illegal War

The Yankee Empire's propagandists [348] have convinced the world that the people of the North were united in their support of Lincoln and his invasion of the democratically elected, peaceful, sovereign nation, the Confederate States of America. The truth is that slightly over sixty percent

---

[346] McWhiney, *Cracker Culture*, 52; also see, Ste. Claire, *Cracker-The Cracker Culture in Florida History*, 10; & Owsley, *Plain Folk of the Old South*, 32.

[347] McWhiney, *Cracker Culture*, 52.

[348] Propagandists masquerade as intellectuals, scholars, fair and balanced news media, and Hollywood producers all doing the Yankee Empire's bidding. They are rewarded for serving the Empire, while anyone who offers counterviews is socially ostracized and shunned and their professional careers are severely limited or destroyed. It is nothing less than "polite" or "soft" censorship—in the Yankee Empire the politically correct mob performs the dirty work of censorship, leaving the ruling elite's hands "clean."

of the American people had voted for someone other than Lincoln in the 1860 presidential election. Lincoln, with less than 40% of the vote, was a "minority" (numerical minority) president. His primary support came from political radicals of New England, crony capitalists, and Northerners who had been brainwashed by generations of slanderous, anti-South propaganda and influenced by the ravings of the North's Yellow Journalists. The radicalism of New England had planted the seeds of disunion and hatred. By 1861, the seeds of anti-South hatred and disunion had germinated and would soon bring forth its bloody and tyrannical fruit.

It was not only Southerners who had a harsh opinion about New England Yankees. The Canton, Ohio, *Stark County Democrat* declared, "the crazy descendants of Plymouth Rock" possessed hearts "as bloodless as the Rock."[349] New England's greed, as evidenced by its constant demands for protective tariffs, had driven a wedge of bitterness and distrust between the commercial North and the agricultural South. But Southerners were not the only ones to suffer from New England's greed. Midwestern Democrats, representing non-slave states, criticized these tariffs, because it transferred money from Midwestern farmers while enriching "manufacturing monopolists."[350] Notice how these Northern agriculturalists complained about the same issues as did Southern agriculturalists—tariffs transferring wealth from the productive sector (agriculture) to the parasitic commercial centers in New England and Wall Street.

---

[349] As cited by White, "Copperheads," *Northern Opposition to Mr. Lincoln's War*, 91-92; Plymouth Rock, Massachusetts is where the Pilgrims landed in 1620.

[350] *Ibid.*, 92.

Early in American history, the people of New York developed a strong dislike for the New England Yankees who were moving into New York.[351] New Yorkers had little use for the New England Yankees describing them as "money-worshipers" whose central purpose in life was striving after the "almighty dollar." New Yorkers described New Englanders as having "no manners and chased dollars too avidly and successfully. [Yankees] were tireless in extolling the superior virtues of New England and its institutions."[352] Mary Lydig Daly of New York, writing in her diary in 1864, lamented:

> We are at present ruled by New England, which was never a gentle or tolerant mistress, and my Dutch and German obstinate blood begins to feel heated to see how arrogantly she [New England] dictates and would force her ideas down our throats, even with the bayonet.[353]

Many Northerners never fully supported Lincoln's unconstitutional war. Even the infamous Yankee General William T. Sherman was forced to admit before Congress that the Yankee army of some three million men was forced to use half that number fighting in or otherwise securing "loyal" states.[354] Despite generations of slanderous anti-South propaganda, many people in the North understood what Lincoln, the Republicans, and their crony capitalists were doing to America's Republic. In an editorial, an Indiana newspaper, the *New Albany Ledger*

---

[351] Wilson, *The Yankee Problem*, 18-26.

[352] As quoted by Valentine, R.T., "Yankees and Yorkers," *Northern Opposition to Mr. Lincoln's War*, 163.

[353] Daly, *Ibid.*, 193.

[354] Valentine, "Yankees and Yorkers," *Northern Opposition to Mr. Lincoln's War*, 196.

declared, "It will be a sorry day for the people of Indiana, when they sacrifice the friendship of their Southern neighbors for that of the cold and calculating Yankees and grasping Wall Street jobbers."[355] Many Peace-Democrats realized that Lincoln and his cronies were replacing the Southern agricultural aristocracy with a profit-driven Northern financial/commercial aristocracy.

The resistance to Lincoln's unconstitutional war against the Confederacy was active not only in the Midwestern states but also in Eastern states such as Pennsylvania. Prior to the War, in 1859, between 20,000 and 30,000 people attended a mass meeting in Philadelphia, Pennsylvania, in support of states' rights and the Jeffersonian view of the Constitution. None of the speakers were in favor of slavery, but all wanted to maintain a Union in which the South would be treated fairly.[356] A prominent Philadelphia, Pennsylvania, Democrat recognized that:

> The same spirit of persecution, which in the history of New England manifested itself from its earliest colonial period, and fastened, from time to time, upon various objects, has for the last twenty-five years been concentrated on the South.... The North cruelly and long goaded them [the South] to it [secession].[357]

Peace Democrats would often point out that "the great Lincoln army of the North" was part of the "fanatical and mercenary communities and bankrupt railroad corporations." They understood that crony capitalists of the railroad industry wanted a "Northwestern route [for the proposed

---

[355] As cited in Chodes, John, "Oliver P. Morton, Indiana's War Governor," *Northern Opposition to Mr. Lincoln's War*, 198.

[356] Trask, Arthur, "Philadelphia against the War," *Northern Opposition to Mr. Lincoln's War*, 231-2.

[357] *Ibid.*, 234.

trans-continental railroad], the adoption of which is to galvanize the insolvent corporation which center at Chicago, and to turn the commerce of the West exclusively into the lap of [New York City]."[358] It became apparent to those of the North who loved the original Republic that Lincoln and his Republican cronies were conducting a revolution designed to destroy the Republic. William B. Reed, a prominent citizen of Philadelphia, Pennsylvania, warned that if the United States were successful in its war against the South, it would result in "some new form of consolidated government, alien to our habits and education."[359] Many in the North recognized the fact that Lincoln and his cronies were actively engaged in an illegal (unconstitutional) destruction of America's original Republic of Republics. They realized that while Lincoln was claiming to be in a war to preserve the Union, what he was actually doing was using dictatorial methods to destroy America's constitutional Republic and thereby create an empire!

Lincoln the Tyrant

Lincoln is a god to those who worship in the Temple of the Yankee Empire. Without Lincoln, the Yankee Empire would not exist. Without the Yankee Empire, Hawaii would still be ruled by its native inhabitants; American troops would not have killed thousands of Cuban and Filipino freedom fighters; Yankee gunboat diplomacy would not have dominated Central and South America; and, the world would never have been blessed with economic hit men working with the CIA to undermine

---

[358] *Ibid.*, 240.

[359] Reed, as cited in *Ibid.*, 262.

foreign nations. Also, the people of the South would not have been punished with poverty. It is ironic that in America Abraham Lincoln is worshiped by both liberals and conservatives. Those on the left ignore Lincoln's racist views and his attachment to crony capitalism, while those on the right ignore Lincoln's unconstitutional exercise of dictatorial powers and his destruction of America's original Constitutionally limited Republic of Sovereign States. In the Temple of the Yankee Empire, Yankee conservatives, pacified Southerners, and liberals join hands while obediently supplicating themselves before the idol of their god—Abraham Lincoln.

Lincoln, during his presidency, would not tolerate dissenting opinions. Even a former President came under attack when he refused to endorse Lincoln's war. Former President Franklin Pierce, from the Yankee state of New Hampshire, was a firm defender of limited federalism and real states' rights. While President, he sent a veto message to Congress in which he noted: "It is, in my judgment, to be taken for granted, as a fundamental proposition not requiring elucidation that the Federal government is the creature of the individual states...."[360] In addition, Pierce was a friend of Jefferson Davis. In 1853, President Pierce appointed Davis as his Secretary of War. The friendship between a former United States President and the Confederate States President posed an embarrassing problem for Lincoln. But Lincoln knew how to silence Americans, even a former President.

Lincoln and his Republican co-conspirators were never reluctant to use deceit, falsehoods, or slander if it would help them to promote their cause—the cause of expanding the Hamiltonian dream of a Northern

---

[360] DeRosa, "President Franklin Pierce and the War for Southern Independence," *Northern Opposition to Mr. Lincoln's War*, 23.

commercial empire. In December of 1861, Lincoln's Secretary of State, William Seward, manufactured a claim of treason against former President Franklin Pierce.[361] Pierce, then living at home in New Hampshire, was a personal friend of Confederate President Jefferson Davis and an outspoken opponent of Lincoln's war. No proof of the allegation of treason was ever found, but the smear on Pierce's character remained. It served to "chill" free speech—today we would call this "soft censorship." This is but one of many examples of how Lincoln and his cronies would manufacture incidents or fake news to destroy their enemies and engage in "soft" censorship—a violation of the American principle of free speech. Lincoln and his cronies were well aware of how to produce and use "fake news" to their full advantage.

The ease with which Yankee mishandling of the truth and how easy this distorted "truth" can become common history is demonstrated by the way in which they labeled Lincoln's opponents as "Copperheads." A copperhead is a venomous North American snake found primarily in the American South. The April 8, 1861, edition of the Philadelphia *Inquirer* reported that two venomous snakes were found in mail bags from Florida. The original news article made no connection between the snakes and Florida's recent secession. The following day, another Yankee newspaper picked up the story adding a few "facts." On April 10, the New York *Times* repeated the story adding the assumption that the snakes were included in the mailbags as an act of "unmanly warfare." The story was eventually picked up by the New Hampshire *Sentinel*. In the New Hampshire story, it was stated that the snakes had been mailed from secessionists in Florida directly to President Lincoln in an attempt to assassinate him.[362] In

---

[361] *Ibid.*, 10.

[362] White, "Copperheads," *Northern Opposition to Mr. Lincoln's War*, 76-77.

reality, the snakes were sent to the Smithsonian as zoological specimens, but the hysterical Yankee public, a public that was being whipped into a saber-rattling frenzy by Northern Yellow Journalists, assumed the worst. It was easy for Northerners to believe the worst about Southerners, because for generations, Yankee propagandists had inaccurately informed the public about the intrinsically evil, sinful, and hate-filled folks down South.

Lincoln's willingness to use terror against civilian populations is evidenced by the fact that he authorized United States military authorities to bombard the city of Baltimore, Maryland,[363] if necessary, to prevent the Maryland legislature from seceding or if Maryland attempted to delay the movement of Yankee troops through the state. Lincoln's Secretary of War, Simon Cameron, ordered the U.S. military to arrest as many of the duly elected legislators in Maryland as necessary to prevent a successful vote for secession.[364] It was reported that Lincoln was prepared to arrest Chief Justice Taney of the United States Supreme Court due to his anti-Lincoln decisions. Ward Lamon was a close, personal friend of President Abraham Lincoln and the U.S. Marshal in Washington, D.C. He stated that Lincoln had issued a warrant for the arrest of Chief Justice Taney because of Taney's unfavorable rulings against Lincoln's unconstitutional assumption of powers. In addition, Lincoln's Secretary of State William Seward ordered the house arrest of a Federal Judge in Washington, D.C. and ordered the withholding of the Judge's pay.[365] The dictatorial exercise of power by Lincoln and his cronies was not limited to a few high-

---

[363] *Ibid.*, 78.

[364] *Ibid.*, 83.

[365] *Ibid.*, 79.

ranking government officials. The United States War Department on August 8, 1862, issued an order authorizing all United States Marshals and Chiefs of Police of any city or town "to arrest and imprison any person or persons who may be engaged by act, speech, or writing ... in any way giving aid and comfort to the enemy or any other disloyal practices against the United States."[366] Even though no Confederate armies were invading the United States, Lincoln nonetheless turned the United States into a quasi-military dictatorship in which no United States citizen could be secure in his constitutional rights. Lincoln was keenly aware that you don't need to arrest too many judges or private citizens or close too many newspapers before they all get the message: "The United States' federal government will NOT allow dissenting opinions!"

In Delaware, as in other Northern states, the United States military was used to intimidate voters in order to lower anti-Lincoln/pro-Democrat turnout. Yankee troops arrested numerous Democrats and held them without warrants and in flagrant violation of the constitutional right of due process. A leading Republican admitted that troops were used to prevent Republicans from being "beaten badly" in elections.[367] The state of Delaware suffered in the East, while the Yankee state of Indiana suffered in the mid-West. "Indiana today is completely under military rule ... a large portion of the people are willingly bowing their necks to receive the yoke of despotism."[368] Lincoln's Republican War

---

[366] As cited in Trask, "Philadelphia against the War," *Northern Opposition to Mr. Lincoln's War*, 260.

[367] As cited in McClanahan, "The Avenger without Mercy," *Northern Opposition to Mr. Lincoln's War*, 140-1.

[368] As cited in Chodes, "Oliver P. Morton," *Northern Opposition to Mr. Lincoln's War*, 211.

Governors also assumed and used tyrannical powers in their efforts to keep their states "loyal" to Lincoln. Governor Oliver P. Morton, of Indiana, declared, "I am the state" and disbanded courts and the state legislature. He also relied on United States military to intimidate via arrests and threats to arrest those who opposed Morton's rule and to close newspapers that were not "loyal" to his or Lincoln's regime.[369] In addition to the overt use of the United States military to prevent anti-Republican (anti-Lincoln) turnout during elections, the Republicans also used mobs to intimidate, silence, and censor opponents to Lincoln's invasion of the Confederacy. Lincoln's strategy to defeat free speech is not that dissimilar from the way modern day politically correct mobs prevent open and free discussion in the Yankee Empire.[370]

Lincoln's unconstitutional suspension of the writ of *habeas corpus* caused an early clash between U.S. Supreme Court Chief Justice Taney and Lincoln. Taney issued a decision that stated a constitutional fact that had never been in question. Acting as a dictator, Lincoln suspended this essential constitutional guarantee of personal liberty. The Chief Justice did not approve! He knew that only Congress has the legal (Constitutional) authority to suspend the ancient common law writ of *habeas corpus*. English common law tradition saw this "right of Englishmen" as being so critical that it could be suspended only in case of rebellion or invasion and then only by Parliament. Even the English King was not authorized to violate this basic common law right! America's

---

[369] *Ibid.*, 196.

[370] For example, see "Who Truly Imperils Our Free Society?" buchanan.org/blog/truly-imperils-free-society-127663 (Accessed 09/20/2017); and, "Antifa Activists Say Violence is Necessary" thehill.com/policy/national-security/350524-antifa-activists-say-violence-is-necessary (Accessed 09/14/2017).

Founding Fathers followed this English common law tradition by allowing for the suspension of the writ of *habeas corpus* only during rebellion or invasion[371] and then only by an act of Congress. The suspension is authorized in Article One of the Constitution which outlines the powers delegated to Congress and is NOT mentioned in Article Two which outlines the powers delegated to the president. Pre-Lincoln authorities that agree with the Chief Justice's view would include such notables as the first attorney general of the United States, Edmund Randolph, early authors of texts on the Constitution, such as, St. George Tucker, William Rawle, and Joseph Story, and the second Chief Justice of the United States Supreme Court John Marshall.

In addition to Lincoln's war against Northern citizens' civil liberties, he also initiated policies that attacked the economic welfare of the average citizen in the North. An economic depression occurred in the Midwest in 1861, as a result of the initiation of Lincoln's invasion of the Confederacy. Out of 112 banks in Illinois, only seven survived.[372] But far worse was the manner in which Lincoln chose to finance his aggressive war against the Confederacy. It was a technique that all tyrants eventually find necessary to finance their military adventures—debasing the currency. The Lincoln Administration's Legal Tender Act of 1862 flooded the country with irredeemable paper money (Greenbacks) that drove sound money out of circulation. As with all government-created inflation or debasement of the currency, those who have close connections to the ruling elite, such as

---

[371] No state that had elected to remain in the Union was in a state of rebellion nor were any of these states being invaded or in danger of being invaded. If one of these had been the case, it would have been the duty of Congress to debate and decide whether to suspend this common law right so necessary for individual liberty.

[372] White, "Copperheads," *Northern Opposition to Mr. Lincoln's War*, 82.

bankers and financiers, have first use of the new money and therefore get the full value as stated on the face of the newly printed currency. Think of counterfeit money—the counterfeiter gets the full benefit. But by the time debased government fiat currency circulates to the common man, the newly printed money (money created out of thin air) has lost much of its stated value. As with all such banking/financing schemes, it provides a windfall for the government and the elites connected with the central bank (Federal Reserve today), but we the people end up paying the cost in higher prices and eventually via "bailouts" paid by taxpayers.

Actually, the devalued government money has lost much of its stated *purchasing power* and now requires more money to purchase the same quantity of goods or services. Politicians and central bankers prefer for people to think that prices are somehow mystically going up (referring to increasing prices of goods and services as "inflation") and thereby shift the blame to the marketplace. If people understood that politicians' policies were causing the decline in the purchasing power of their money, then the peoples' anger would be directed toward politicians. Therefore, inflation is always described as increasing *price* rather than *decreasing purchasing power* of government money.[373] The people must pay the price because big banks, the Federal Reserve, and politicians are too big to fail—while we the people are too small to count.

The Yankee Empire's War of Extermination

The Republican Party was established as an instrument to further the agenda of the Yankee's financial / commercial interests. Abolitionist Wendell Phillips noted that the Republican Party was a "sectional party ...

---

[373] Kennedy, *Reclaiming Liberty*, 127-145.

pledged against the South."374 Their primary goal was to destroy (exterminate) the South's political power in Congress. Southern author Andrew Nelson Lytle writing in the early 1930s noted:

> If the South could be broken politically, it could be forced into a position of economic serfdom, depending on those who would control the strongly centralized government.375

Republicans supported radical abolitionists, because it provided them with a weapon (slavery) to use against their archenemy—the South. The Republican Party's primary issue was not slavery—though it provided the pro-high tariff Republicans with a useful tool—their primary aim was to destroy the political power of the South and then to erect even larger protective tariffs. The Republican Party's antagonism toward the South was evident in its 1856 Platform that called for a transcontinental railroad by the "most central and practical route."376 This would, and eventually did, exclude the South from any economic benefit from this major "national" internal improvement. To add "insult to injury" this railroad "internal improvement" would be paid for primarily by money directly and indirectly extracted from the people of the South. Southerners, on the other hand, wanted a more southerly route for the proposed transcontinental railroad.377

---

374 Phillips as cited by, Lytle, Andrew Nelson, *Bedford Forrest and His Critter Company* (1931, Nashville, TN: J.S. Sanders Co., 1992), 31.

375 Lytle, *Ibid.*, 30.

376 DeRosa, "President Franklin Pierce and the War for Southern Independence," *Northern Opposition to Mr. Lincoln's War*, 17.

377 Cooper, *Jefferson Davis—American*, 257.

By 1860, Southerners realized that they were no longer an equal partner in the federal government. New England ideas and their money-worshiping commercialism had seized control of the United States' political thinking and its political machinery. The Universal American idea to which all good Americans must now submit was advocated by Reverend Samuel Harris of Maine in 1861 when he declared that an American "who is not in sympathy with the American idea ... is an alien unworthy to bear the name of American citizen."[378] Thus Southerners who rejected such Yankee logic were "aliens" who needed to be exterminated or expelled from Yankee America. The word "extermination" was not just an offhand declaration. The Yankee's unmitigated hatred of the South is demonstrated by the outspoken demands to remove Southerners and repopulate the South with new people who would be more amenable to following the new "American idea."

The desire to depopulate or exterminate the people of the South was openly expressed by United States political leaders[379] and vocal supporters of the newly created Yankee Empire. A Tennessee Unionist, who also happened to be proslavery, announced his anti-Southern attitude when he declared,

> If I had the power... [I would] exterminate every rebel from the face of God's green earth—every man, woman, and child south of the Mason-Dixon line ... crowd the rebels into the Gulf of Mexico, and drown the entire race, as the devil did the hogs in the Sea of Galilee.

---

[378] Harris, as cited in DeRosa, "President Franklin Pierce and the War for Southern Independence," *Northern Opposition to Mr. Lincoln's War*, 43-44.

[379] Kennedy & Kennedy, *Punished With Poverty*, 69-87.

His extreme pronouncement was met with enthusiastic applause.[380]

His opinion did not change with the ending of the War. In 1866, at a meeting in Philadelphia, he declared, "As for the Rebel population, let them be exterminated."[381] Dr. Edward Everett Hale of Boston in 1862 declared, "We are to introduce into the South and Southwest new men, new life, and a higher civilization."[382] The religion of New England found in the idea and mission of extermination and repopulation of the South a new religious zeal—an anti-South zeal unmatched by anything since the infamous New England witch-trials in 1692-1693. In 1865, Dr. Bacon called for volunteers to use "bayonets fixed," and beginning in the upper South, "drive every man" not loyal to the federal government "into the Gulf of Mexico." (Great Applause from the crowd).[383] Reverend Justin D. Fulton, Baptist minister of Boston, recommended that all Confederate leaders should be hanged and their property confiscated by the federal government. As for the general population of the South, he thought that they "might" one day be forgiven but only after they had been completely "re-educated."[384] The theme of "re-educating" ignorant Southerners was often heard—a more accurate term would be "forcefully brainwashing new generations of Southerners." The April 15, 1865, issue of the Boston *Universalist* declared "we must educate the people we have conquered."[385] Note the word "conquered." The Reverend G.S. Weaver

---

[380] Stromberg, "Blood on the Pulpit," *Northern Opposition to Mr. Lincoln's War*, 51.

[381] *Ibid.*, 51-52.

[382] *Ibid.*, 53-54.

[383] *Ibid.*, 64.

[384] *Ibid.*, 65.

[385] *Ibid.*

from Lawrence, Massachusetts, urged the nation to "Give them [Southerners] a strong master until they learn obedience."[386] The question remains to be answered as to whether modern-day Southerners have "learned obedience." Judging from the actions of pacified Southerners, it would appear that too many Southerners have indeed learned to be obedient to their masters and accept their assigned position as second-class Yankees in this "one nation indivisible."

The South Suffered First but the World Would Follow

The emergence of Lincoln's newly created Yankee Empire would bring death, starvation, and continuing poverty to black and white people of the formerly free and prosperous Confederate States of America. The Yankee Empire's first foray into imperialistic military aggression would not end with the defeat, occupation, and exploitation of the South. A 20th century Southern historian, Francis B. Simkins, pointed out that "Northern capitalism was eagerly imperialistic" and that Yankees "tore down in order that they might rebuild. To tear down the civilization that lay to their south was but a chapter in their history."[387] Empires have a relentless appetite for more lands and people to exploit. And as in the case of the Yankee Empire's invasion of the peaceful, democratically elected sovereign nation, the Confederate States of America, the Yankee Empire can always manufacture an excuse for the exercise of its military power in foreign nations. As one contemporary, pro-Southern scholar noted in 2014, Lincoln and the Republican Party's war upon the South had become:

---

[386] *Ibid.*, 65.

[387] Francis Butler Simkins, as cited in *Punished with Poverty*, 21.

> [A] permanent template for subsequent American crusades.... From the Free-Soil argument of the 1850s, through two World Wars, Cold War, and down to Iraq and beyond, American leaders insist that their last [most recent] enemy is both inherently expansionist and committed to some form of slavery. It is therefore the duty of the new enemy to surrender "unconditionally" and undergo reconstruction and re-education for the good of all mankind *and the end is not yet in sight*.[388] [Emphasis added]

Such observations are not new. In 1930, Southern scholar Andrew Nelson Lytle described the condition of the South in Lincoln's new Union—that is the Yankee Empire:

> Since 1865 an agrarian Union has been changed into an *industrial empire* bent on *conquest* of the earth's goods and ports to sell them in. This means *warfare*, a struggle over markets, leading, in the end, to actual military conflict between nations.[389] [Emphasis added]

Now recall General Robert E. Lee's warning written to Lord Acton in 1866. General Lee predicted that if the federal government centralized its power by becoming the sole judge as to the extent of its powers, then the United States would become "aggressive abroad and despotic at home."[390] Writing in 1868, Admiral Raphael Semmes, CSN, former Captain of the *CSS Alabama,* predicted that "The form of government having been changed by the revolution, there are still other acts of the

---

[388] Stromberg, "Blood on the Pulpit," *Northern Opposition to Mr. Lincoln's War*, 74.

[389] Lytle, Andrew Nelson, "The Hind Tit" in *I'll Take My Stand*, 202.

[390] Kennedy & Kennedy, *The South Was Right!*, 41.

drama to be performed."[391] Admiral Semmes understood, as did most Southerners of his day, that if the Yankee Empire was successful in its war against the Confederacy, then the old Republic would be molded by evil hands into a consolidated nation / state that would refuse to recognize any constitutional limits upon its powers. He warned that if the Yankee nation won "Constitutional liberty will disappear."[392] Non-pacified Southerners understand these inconvenient truths that pacified Southerners ignore—empires are always "aggressive abroad and despotic at home," and we, the citizens of a defeated and occupied nation, are currently the *subjects* of the Yankee Empire and citizens of an intentionally impoverished captive nation.

---

[391] Semmes, *Memoirs of Service Afloat*, 833.

[392] *Ibid.*, 285.

The Yankee Empire claims it fought the so-called "Civil War" to end slavery. But as the photographs from the Library of Congress taken *circa* 1940 demonstrate, the real purpose was to exterminate the South's position of economic and political power in the United States. These impoverished Southerners and their descendants have more in common with each other than they do with the ruling elite of both national political parties, the crony capitalist elites on Wall Street, or the "deep state" donor class on K street in Washington, D.C. The War exchanged 4.5 million chattel slaves for 8.5 million sharecropping slaves. Sharecropping was a new and even more evil form of slavery that lasted for almost a century after the defeat of the South in the War for Southern Independence.[393] The motto of the Yankee Empire should be: *Vae Victis*—Woe to the Vanquished. (Courtesy LOC)

---

[393] Kennedy & Kennedy, *Punished With Poverty*, 105-119, 173-195.

Chapter 7: Southern Efforts to End Slavery

There was little difference between the North and the South in the volume and vigor of ANTISLAVERY expression.
—Francis Butler Simkins [394]

NOWHERE IN THE WORLD can there be found a more successful propaganda campaign than the evil, slanderous, "false-news," Yankee account of slavery in the United States. Fifty years before the defeat of the Confederate States of America by the Yankee Empire, an ongoing Yankee propaganda campaign was already actively portraying the South as the land of evil slaveholders while praising Yankees as noble humanitarian champions of freedom. Yet, as historian Francis B. Simkins points out, early in its history, the South was just as eager and more earnest in its efforts to find a way to end slavery than the North. The statement by Simkins quoted above was made in reference to the abolition movement in America circa 1830. As Simkins points out, the goodwill and mutual effort to end slavery by the two sections was given a fatal blow by the emerging Radical Abolition movement in the North.[395]

Most Americans and surely most foreigners have heard only one side of the story about slavery in America—the side told and enforced by the victor of the War for Southern Independence, that is, the Yankee Empire's

---

[394] Simkins, *A History of the South*, 96.

[395] *Ibid.*, 103-105.

side. As such, they find it hard to believe that it was the South which led the way for the elimination of the African slave trade and promoted the idea of limiting the movement of slaves into the Northwest Territories of the United States. When told that slavery existed for 72 years LONGER in the Yankee State of Massachusetts than in the Southern State of Mississippi, most people reject the information as a falsehood. Yes, the New England state of Massachusetts has a longer history of chattel slavery (in addition to its commerce in the nefarious international African slave trade) than almost half of the Southern States that comprise the Confederate States of America. Yet, the world is assured by the Yankee Empire's propagandists that Northerners were the ones who strove to free slaves and that Southerners promoted slavery. As has already been pointed out, it is to the benefit of the Yankee Empire to promote this vile slander upon the South in order to hide its naked aggression against a peaceful and once prosperous people of the Confederate States of America. It should also be remembered that the invasion, conquest, reconstruction, and occupation of the Confederacy became the template or pattern for worldwide imperial Yankee aggression. As stated previously, this trend of aggressive Yankee imperialism was predicted by the South's most noted military leader, General Robert E. Lee, shortly after the defeat of the Confederacy. It was Lee who, in a letter to Lord Acton, predicted that the "new" America would become a nation that was "aggressive abroad and despotic at home."[396]

A short review of the history of the South's efforts to end slavery in the early history of the United States will prove that the South was indeed a

---

[396] Lee's letter to John Emerich Edward Dalberg-Acton (1834-1902), British author, historian, and political philosopher. Online Library of Liberty, oll.libertyfund.org/titles/acton-selections-from-the-correspondence-of-the-first-lord-acton-vol-i#lf1480_head_058 (Accessed 11/28/2017).

leader, if not the leader, in the abolition of slavery in America. To reduce confusion about terms, it should be noted that there is a very significant and distinct difference between an abolitionist and a *radical* abolitionist. An abolitionist was one who desired to see an end to slavery by peaceful and equitable means. Men such as George Washington, American's first president under the Constitution of 1787, and Thomas Jefferson, America's third president, were both slaveholders and abolitionists. As shall subsequently be pointed out, many of the first abolitionists were also slaveholders. Radical abolitionists were a different nature of men than abolitionists. Radical abolitionists held the view that slavery was so abhorrent and evil that anyone associated with the institution was to be treated as subhuman.[397] After dehumanizing all Southerners by making them appear to be subhuman due to their association with slavery, the North could then justify any violent and aggressive act against Southerners as being necessary to "break the bounds of slavery." According to radical abolition propaganda, the massacre of all white men, women, and children in the South was justifiable if the end result was the abolition of slavery. While abolitionists were men of the North and the South, slaveholders and non-slaveholders, *radical* abolitionists were mostly Yankees with their origins in New England. These radical abolitionists soon attached the stigma of the vile slaveholder not only to

---

[397] Ewing, E.W.R., *Northern Rebellion and Southern Secession* (Richmond, VA: J.L. Hill Co., 1904), 257-258.

the minority of Southerners who owned slaves[398] but to EVERY Southerner.

Haitian Slave Revolt killing both slave owners and non-slave owners. Northern radical abolitionists promoted the same type of slave rebellion down South | Courtesy of LOC

This meant that the large non-slaveholding South found itself in danger of a Haitian style slave insurrection in which white men, women, and children of non-slaveholders would suffer the same fate as slaveholding families.

---

[398] Various historians have given the number of slaveholders in the South as low as 5% (McWhiney) to as high as 28% (Simkins). Most use the approximation of 20% slaveholders leaving 80% of Southerners as non-slaveholders.

The fear of a Haitian-style massacre of whites by blacks was evident even in Northern states where there were relatively few black residents. In 1831, there arose such a fear of an imminent massacre of whites in Detroit, Michigan, that troops had to be dispatched to quell white fears.[399] If such fear could be aroused in the North with only a few thousand black residents, it should be obvious that a much greater fear would arise in the South with millions of black residents plus the constant agitation by anti-South Radical Abolitionists promoting slave uprisings.

From the early 1830s, radical abolitionists demanded immediate emancipation (something no Northern State had done) without compensation to slaveholders (again, something no Northern State had done). At the time of the War for American Independence, 1776, there were thirteen American States. These thirteen States consisted of four from the deep South (Georgia, South Carolina, North Carolina, and Virginia) two from the upper South (Maryland and Delaware) or a total of six Southern States. The remaining seven were Northern States (mid-Atlantic: Pennsylvania, New Jersey, New York, three states; New England States: Connecticut, Rhode Island, New Hampshire, and Massachusetts, four states) or seven Northern States. In *all* thirteen States, North and South, slavery was a legal institution. In those States where there were fewer slaves per capita, that is, in the North, African slave trading was a large and important feature of their economy. But in the South where there were more slaves per capita, the African slave trade barely existed. No American State was free of the issue of slavery. The fact that the thirteen stripes on the United States flag represent the original thirteen "slaveholding" States of America is skillfully hidden from the general public by Yankee propagandists in the media, education, and Hollywood.

---

[399] Ewing, *Northern Rebellion and Southern Secession*, 275.

The Radical Abolition movement, based primarily in New England, conducted a campaign of slander against the South by claiming that the South alone was responsible for American slavery. This same "fake news" narrative about slavery was used during the War, Reconstruction, and up unto this very day to slander the defenseless people of a defeated and occupied nation, The Confederate States of America.

The obvious question to ask is, "Does Southern history offer an argument about the issue of slavery that is contrary to that promoted by the conquering Yankee?" The answer is, "Yes of course it does!" The history of the South speaks boldly to this issue. Yet, as a captive nation, the South has had very limited means to reply to this intentional slander.[400] As already mentioned, slavery existed in every American state in 1776. The history of the South's efforts to curb and eliminate slavery goes back to the time when America was a colony of Great Britain. In the early 1700s, the elected government of Virginia passed laws to curb the influx of slaves into Virginia. This law was vetoed by the English Parliament over the objections of Southerners. On October 5, 1778, (note this was two years after Virginia had seceded from its indivisible union with Great Britain) Virginia's governor Patrick Henry, a slaveholder, signed into law an act outlawing the additional importation of slaves into the state. Notice that this was two years after Virginia had seceded from its indivisible union with Great Britain and was free to act without British permission on the subject of the African slave trade. Virginia was joined by other Southern States as they began to shut down the African slave

---

[400] Again, it must be pointed out that this ongoing campaign of anti-South slander must be maintained IF the Yankee Empire is to maintain its façade of legitimacy! Worldwide recognition of the truth would destroy the Yankee Empire's false narrative that it must have to justify its very existence.

trade into their states. Even in the face of these facts, Yankee propaganda proclaims that Southerners were and are evil defenders of slavery.

Virginia did not stand alone in its early effort to end the African slave trade. In 1760, South Carolina attempted to restrict the flow of slaves into the colony only to be rebuffed by the King's government in London. In 1798, the State of Georgia passed a constitutional amendment prohibiting further importation of slaves into the State. This was done ten years before the federal Congress legislated against the nefarious trade. Over the objection of many Southerners (*and with the enthusiastic endorsement of many New England States*), the African slave trade was given Constitutional protection for twenty years.[401] When in 1808 it became legal for Congress to outlaw the African slave trade, 98% of all delegates in Congress voted in favor of the bill to prohibit the African slave trade. Delegates from four states voted to keep the nefarious trade alive. Those delegates voting to keep the African slave trade open were evenly divided, two from the South and two from the North. By 1807, the African slave trade had been permanently prohibited in all Southern States except South Carolina. This was done before the Federal Congress had acted to eliminate the nefarious trade.[402] Where then is the vaunted Southern "slaveocracy" defending and promoting slavery? It did not exist during this time nor did it ever exist as such. Radical Abolitionists incorrectly stated the issue by falsely claiming that there existed a Southern "slaveocracy" conspiring to spread slavery as a labor system throughout the nation. This was never true. What Southerners desired more than

---

[401] For more information on this subject see, Kennedy, Walter D., *Myths of American Slavery* (Gretna, LA: Pelican Publishing Co., 2003), 21-30; also see Kennedy & Kennedy, *The South Was Right!*, 72-74.

[402] Simkins, *A History of the South*, 117.

anything else was to be allowed to act upon the slavery issue just like the people of the New England states, New York, New Jersey, and Pennsylvania had done. In each of these states, a system of gradual emancipation was adopted which allowed the owner of the slave to recover some of his investment in his slave property and adjust his society in such a way as to prevent social and economic collapse. The Yankee Empire did not allow this alternative for the people of the South.

The desire to end slavery was so strong in the South, that by 1827, the bulk of all American abolition societies were in the South. But even more shocking is the fact that the founding members of some of the early and most prominent abolition societies were slaveholders.[403] The passing of the Northwest Ordinance in 1787, limiting the movement of slave property into that vast territory, offers a perfect example that the South was not seeking dominance for the slave culture. The Northwest Territory was taken from Great Britain during the War for American Independence by the military forces of Virginia. From this territory, six new states would be established extending from Ohio to Wisconsin. In 1787, Virginia ceded this vast territory to the United States with the provision that no slave property would be allowed in the ceded territory. The vote in the United States Congress to accept this grant of territory was unanimous, with all Southern delegates voting to accept the grant of territory with the elimination of slavery. Again, we ask the question, "Where is the alleged Southern 'slaveocracy' forcing slavery on America?" In 1820, Governor Thomas Randolph of Virginia declared slavery as "the deplorable error of our ancestors" that had been fixed upon the South by "copying a civil institution from savage Africa."[404] Notice here that the governor of the

---

[403] Kennedy, *Myths of American Slavery*, 28.

[404] Thomas M. Randolph, as cited in, Simkins, *A History of the South*, 98.

Southern State of Virginia understood that slavery was not just a "white" or European thing but something that had its beginning in Africa with Africans enslaving Africans. Eight years after Virginia's governor condemned slavery, Mississippi's legislature condemned slavery as a "national evil" in which there was much "regret" but one that could not easily be eliminated.[405] In 1828, Governor Gerard Brandon, of Mississippi, declared that slavery was "an evil at best."[406] A mere 29 years before Virginia seceded from the Union with the North, her legislature was considering adopting a system of gradual emancipation to eliminate slavery.

It should be obvious that the issue of slavery is not something that belongs only to the South, but it was an American institution. Prior to the War, there were many different views on the subject of slavery. What was needed was cool, *civil*, and respectful discussions on how to eliminate slavery in a manner that would benefit all parties concerned, which of course included the enslaved people. From the beginning of the United States until around 1830, cool heads did prevail and progress was made toward the elimination of slavery in the United States. For example, the number of manumissions (the freeing of slaves by the slaveholder at his own expense) of slaves was steadily increasing; organized efforts to promote the freeing and returning of freed slaves to their ancestral homeland was gaining acceptance; legislation to suppress the African slave trade was passed through Congress with the support of an overwhelming number of Congressmen from both the North and the

---

[405] Gerard C. Brandon cited in Bettersworth, John K., *Mississippi: A History* (Austin, TX: The Steck Co., 1959), 194.

[406] *Ibid.*

South. From this, it is evident that there was no inherent resistance from the South to the elimination of slavery in America.

By the second decade of the 1800s, it seemed that the issue of slavery was well on the way to being successfully addressed. This was true until arrogant, meddling Yankees, in the form of Radical Abolitionists, destroyed the *mutual* efforts of Americans to eliminate slavery.[407] Where once Southerners spoke of slavery as a necessary *evil* of which they were eager to assist in its demise, after 1830, a bunker mentality took hold in the South. With an ever-increasing attack upon all things Southern by Yankee Radical Abolitionists, Southerners began to "circle the wagons" to protect themselves from those seeking not just the elimination of slavery but the bloody and violent elimination of Southerners both slaveholders and non-slaveholders alike.[408] Although Radical Abolitionists were loud, crude, and insulting, they were not strong enough to cause a major problem by themselves, but they had powerful Northern allies.

From the earliest days of the Republic under the United States Constitution, powerful business and banking elements of the North viewed the South as an obstacle to their profit-making desires. From early in the history of the Republic, the North's economy was more dependent upon commerce, banking, and industry than the South's economy. The South's economy was based more upon agriculture. Two major forms of

---

[407] A classic example of Northerners and Southerners working together for the elimination of slavery is demonstrated in the life of William Rawle of Philadelphia, Pennsylvania (Pennsylvania is a Northern State). Mr. Rawle, an abolitionist, worked very closely with Southerners in their efforts to end slavery so much so that he served for many years as President of the Maryland Society for the Elimination of Slavery. Maryland was a very Southern state at that time, yet the people of these two states worked together for their common cause—Rawle was NOT a Radical Abolitionist.

[408] Bettersworth, *Mississippi: A History*, 196.

agriculture were practiced in the South: plantation agriculture where cotton, tobacco, sugar, and rice were grown, and private homesteads where more often a system of open range grazing of hogs, cattle, sheep, and small-scale grain production was practiced. While many Northerners in derision would refer to the non-plantation class as "poor white trash," this was a gross misrepresentation of these people. Yes, these people were white, but they were seldom poor or trash.[409] Each year the small farms and open range stock production of the South equaled the dollar value of plantation produced goods. Just ten years before the secession of the Southern States from the United States, two-thirds of the nation's exports came from the fields, farms, and forests of the South.[410] Greedy Northern business interests viewed the South as a rich marketplace for their goods and services. The one thing the dollar-worshiping Yankee did not desire was for this Southern market to slip into the hands (pockets) of European merchants. Since Southerners exported their produce to European markets, Southern commerce tended to flow to European markets rather than to Yankee markets. In order to keep the Southern buyers at home buying Northern goods, Northern politicians supported a high protective tariff on imported goods thereby making Yankee goods more price competitive—in 20th century Italy, this crony capitalist business and government relationship would become known as Fascism.

Being forced into higher-priced Northern markets was only one complaint the South had against the North. The higher tariff was imposed on all ports in the United States, but as much as three-fourths of the

---

[409] For a more complete analysis of both Southern wealth and the life of the small farmers of the old South, see, Kennedy & Kennedy, *Punished with Poverty,* Chapter 3, "Prosperity Beyond Belief."

[410] Simkins, *A History of the South*, 130.

federal revenue was collected in Southern ports. The South was a minority section of the United States (by population and therefore representation in Congress), but Southerners were paying most of the cost of running the federal government. To add insult to injury, the bulk of the money collected in Southern ports was spent to improve Northern infrastructure.[411] As long as the North could maintain control of the federal government, it could pass laws that were profitable to its business interests, but the South stood in its way.

The Northern desire to reduce the power of the South in the United States Congress was the driving force which produced an alliance between Northern business and Northern Radical Abolitionists. Each viewed the South as an obstruction in its path of remaking America in the Yankee image and in making more and more profits. The Republican Party was founded in the mid-1850s. It was America's first political party that had as its goal the forming of a business-government alliance to promote profits and to create an activist federal government dedicated to perennial social reform. It should be no surprise that this revolutionary big government party was very attractive to American and newly arriving European Marxists and socialists. [412]

---

[411] Kennedy & Kennedy, *Punished with Poverty*, 39.

[412] For more information on this subject see Benson & Kennedy *Lincoln's Marxist*.

Slave auction in New Amsterdam (now New York) in 1655, painted by Howard Pyle, 1917 | Courtesy WikiMedia Commons

While the history of the South's efforts to end slavery and the slave trade is seldom recognized it is equally true that the arrogance of the Imperial Yankee will not admit to its sins of slavery, slave trading, and overt racism. The arrogance of the imperial Yankee prevents him from ever admitting his culpability in the sins of slavery and racism. From the Yankee's point of view, those things belong to the South, or so the self-righteous Yankee will assure the world, and the slandered South, being a captive nation, has no adequate means of responding in its own defense. Nevertheless, slavery existed in various areas of the North from 1626 until the ratification of the Thirteenth Amendment on December 6, 1865.

The Dutch founders of New Amsterdam imported African slaves into the colony in 1626. When the English took control of New Amsterdam, they renamed it New York. Chattel slavery existed in New York from 1626 until circa 1830—one hundred and thirty-nine years longer than slavery existed in the Southern State of Mississippi. Even with the end of chattel slavery, New York maintained a brisk commerce in the illegal African slave trade, supplying the slave markets of South American and the Caribbean nations until circa 1870. The *Nightingale,* one of the last slave ships captured just before the War for Southern Independence, was built in Massachusetts, her captain was from New York and she sailed under the protection of the U.S. flag. When captured, she had over 900 slaves on board with a death rate of four to six slaves per day. According to Black historian, W.E.B. Dubois, even during the War for Southern Independence, Central American colonies and nations were still actively involved in the African slave trade.[413]

The history of legislation legalizing slavery in the English colonies of America can be traced back to 1642 when the colony of Massachusetts became the first American colony to pass a law that allowed slavery in

---

[413] Dubois, W. E. B., *The Suppression of the African Slave Trade 1638-1870* (1896, New York: Russell and Russell, 1965), 162-3, 298.

their colony.[414] Prior to that Massachusetts became involved in the African slave trade when her ship, the *Desire*, brought slaves to Massachusetts in 1637. The African slave trade became a lucrative business for not only Massachusetts but also most of the New England Colonies. After chattel slavery was ended in the State, Massachusetts established a system of laws which discouraged the movement of African-Americans into their state. One such measure was the election of a local "Negro Whipper." It was the function of this agent of the New England state of Massachusetts to give notice to any "black, mulatto, or Indian" who came into the State of Massachusetts and remained two months to leave the state or be publicly whipped.[415] It should come as no surprise to anyone that the African-American population in Massachusetts steadily decreased over the following years—so much for the so-called humanitarian Yankee. But their well-kept "secret" system of flogging Africans worked wonders in removing black people from their "fair" state.

Northerners demonstrated their dislike for the African-American from the time Massachusetts elected its first official charged with whipping (flogging) African-Americans who dared to remain in their State until well after the War for Southern Independence. Many Northern States passed "exclusion" laws which prevented free people of color from moving into a Northern State. Throughout the North, free African-Americans were relegated to the status of second-class citizens, denied the right to vote and to serve on juries, or in many places, they were not allowed to give

---

[414] The first slaves sold in the English North American colonies were at Jamestown, Virginia, in 1620. Massachusetts was the first English colony to *pass a law* recognizing the right of ownership of a slave.

[415] Moore, George H., *Notes on the History of Slavery in Massachusetts* (New York: D. Appleton & Company, 1866), 228-229.

testimony in court against a white citizen.[416] Even in the far West of the United States, the California Supreme Court upheld a State law that prevented "blacks, mulattoes, and Indians from testifying as witnesses" against any white person. The court also expanded this California law to prohibit the testimony of Chinese against white people.[417] In 1858, the State of Oregon was admitted into the Union as a "free" state. It was admitted to the Union as a free state—if by free state one means free from slavery *and* from African-Americans. The first State Constitution of Oregon prohibited the movement of African-Americans into the state and established punishment for anyone bringing African-Americans into the State of Oregon. Notice that both of these states (California and Oregon) were part of the Yankee-dominated states that are constantly touted as "free" states—free to white people but not free to blacks, mulattoes, Indians, and Chinese.[418] The Radical Abolitionist, William Lloyd Garrison, lamented the fate of free people of color in the North explaining that "The free colored people were looked upon as an inferior caste to whom their liberty was a curse, and their lot worse than that of the slaves."[419] Even during the War for Southern Independence, the people of Illinois (Lincoln's home state) passed a constitutional amendment to their state constitution prohibiting freed slaves from moving into the Northern State of Illinois.[420] In the 1850s, Illinois law provided that any

---

[416] Kennedy, *Rekilling Lincoln*, 62-64 and Kennedy, *Myths of American Slavery*, 40-60.

[417] Limerick, Patricia Nelson, *The Legacy of Conquest: The Unbroken Past of The American West* (New York: W. W. Norton & Company, 1987), 261.

[418] Kennedy, *Rekilling Lincoln*, 66.

[419] William Lloyd Garrison, as cited in, Munford, Beverly B., *Virginia's Attitude Toward Slavery and Secession* (Richmond, VA: L.H. Jenkins, Inc., 1915), 163.

[420] Kennedy & Kennedy, *The South Was Right!*, 55.

free black who refused to leave, "shall at public auction proceed to sell said negro or mulatto to any person..."[421] This law was passed in Lincoln's home state of Illinois in the 1850s. It amounted to nothing less than a Yankee state slave auction! This is just one more example of Yankee hypocrisy.

Numerous non-Southern historians have documented the second-class status of the African-American in the North, but this information seems to get lost in the North's frenzied attacks upon the evils down South. Race has been used by the politicians of the North before the War for Southern Independence to induce Northerners to elect politicians who would go to Congress and stand up to the evil "slaveocracy" of the South. After the defeat of the Confederate States of America and during the active phase of Reconstruction (military occupation and rule), race was used to divide black and white Southerners into warring camps thus providing the Republican Party with its majority in the Yankee Empire's Congress. This "divide and rule" strategy gave the Republicans the vast majority of elected offices in the defeated and militarily occupied South. This provided the Republicans in Congress the votes needed to plunder the South further. What was good for the Republican Party was disastrous for the people of the South. It created a social environment of violence and poverty for both black and white Southerners. The actions of the Republican Party were so wicked and despicable that Hiram Revels, the first African-American elected to the United States Senate, resigned from the Republican Party. In his letter to Republican President Grant, Revels states:

> The Bitterness and hate created by the late civil strife ... would have long since been obliterated in this state, were it not for some

---

[421] Ewing, *Northern Rebellion and Southern Secession*, 268.

unprincipled men who would keep alive the bitterness of the past, and inculcate a hatred between the races, in order that they may aggrandize themselves by office, and its emoluments, to control my people, the effect of which is to degrade them.[422]

Notice that here we see the words of the first African-American United States Senator, holding the seat once held by Jefferson Davis (first President of the Confederate States of America and former U.S. Senator from Mississippi), and yet he is condemning the Republicans who at that time were using racial division to promote their crony-capitalist allies at the expense of all Southerners—both black and white. This is just one more piece of evidence that the Yankee Empire was not then, nor is it now, the champion of African-Americans as its propagandists are so eager to proclaim.

Since the early days of the Pilgrim Fathers of New England, the Yankee has eagerly proclaimed to the world that they were the inhabitants of a heavenly "City on a Hill."[423] The world is put on notice that this Yankee "city" is so perfect that its glory draws men from every nation to its portals to be taught the truth of an enlighten Yankee world. This Yankee self-conceit and arrogance continues today. The late Charles Krauthammer, of the Northeast corridor [424] "intellectual school," declared in an article written in 1989 titled "Universal Dominion" that America was destined to bring universal peace and harmony to the world. Another Northeast corridor ideologue, William Kristol, declared in 1996 that America was

---

[422] Hiram Revels, cited in www.hornfans.com/threads/letter-from-first-black-us-senator-to-grant-1875.22347 (Accessed 09/04/2017).

[423] Bacevich, *Limits of Power*, 20; also see Bradford, *Against the Barbarians*, 18-19.

[424] Northeast corridor—from Washington, D.C. through New York and into New England.

destined to establish a "benevolent global hegemony" that would exercise "authority over all others in its domain."[425]

Rather than the vaunted heavenly "City on a Hill," the imperial Yankee resides in a bleak fortress on the edge of a swamp from which he will sally forth to do battle with anyone who stands in the way of Yankee profits and/or his most recently adopted sociological fad. Those who become ensnared by the embrace of the Yankee do so not by consent but by coercion—often the coercion of bloody Yankee bayonets. The Confederate States of America was simply the first victim of Imperial Yankee aggression. Having caused over one million deaths in the war and postwar "peace" in the South, the calloused, Imperial Conscience of the Yankee had no problem in putting to death any number of American Indians, Native Hawaiians, Cubans, Filipinos, Latin Americans, or any other group Yankees surveyed with envious eyes from their so-called "City on a Hill." While displaying a counterfeit claim of humanitarianism, the ever profit-minded Yankee sought more ways to bring under his control those nations and people who would fill his blood-lined coffers with more ill-gotten wealth. The imperial Yankee would always expand his empire while proclaiming his humanitarian and peaceful "good intentions" toward the downtrodden upon whom he had so callously trod.

Since its victory over the Confederate States of America and especially after the turn of the present century, the Yankee Empire continues using its control of "information" to promote and enforce the concept of Yankee purity and Southern guilt. For example; if one views the "documentary" film at the Vicksburg National (federal, i.e., Yankee) Battlefield in Vicksburg, Mississippi, one is led to believe that black Southerners fully

---

[425] Hazony, "Is 'Classical Liberalism' Conservative?," www.wsj.com/articles/is-classical-liberalism-conservative-1507931462 (Accessed 10/31/2017).

supported the North's invasion of the South. Never is the story told of the thousands of black Confederate troops on the battlefield and black laborers on the home front who fought and struggled alongside their white Southern friends defending the South. The "documentary" even extols how Yankee occupation of the City of Vicksburg became the model for Southern Reconstruction after the defeat of the South. The viewer is gleefully informed about how "Civil Rights" were being extended to African-Americans in this Southern city. What is not told is that these same Northerners who were imposing these measures upon the South had prohibited the movement of African-Americans into Northern States, denied African-Americans the right to vote in Northern States, and did not allow African-Americans to testify against white citizens in most Northern States. These propaganda films <u>never</u> inform the viewer that, while claiming to "free the slaves," the Yankee Empire actually enslaved free men, black as well as white, into the slavery of rank poverty under the system of debt peonage known as sharecropping. Such mass poverty and malnutrition bordering on starvation were unknown in the South before the Yankee invasion, conquest and occupation. As already pointed out, the victorious Yankee Empire used and is still using racial division in the South to keep the formerly free and prosperous people of the Confederate States of America divided, fighting each other, and passively remaining under the Yankee Empire's control. The Yankee Empire must relentlessly pursue its propaganda efforts to slander the South by claiming evil Southerners were fighting to keep blacks in the chains of slavery while the virtuous North fought a cruel war to free their black brothers from slavery. But as Governor Joel Parker of the Yankee state of New Jersey stated during the War (1863) "Slavery is no more the cause of this war than gold is the cause of robbery."[426]

---

[426] Governor Parker cited in Wilson, *The Yankee Problem*, 78.

200

CHAPTER 8: CONSTITUTIONAL REPUBLIC OR COMMERCIAL EMPIRE

SOUTHERNERS LOOKED TO the government under the Second Continental Congress (1775-83) as a means of organizing a joint effort in defeating the British and securing their independence. The first "federal" government of the United States was created by America's thirteen Sovereign States joining (acceding to) the Union under the Articles of Confederation in 1783. Several years later, the same Sovereign States seceded from that Union as they acceded to the new Union under the Constitution proposed in 1787. In all three systems of government (Continental Congress, Articles of Confederation, and the Constitution), the people of the states [427] looked to the government thus created as a means to formalize a joint effort to protect the States from foreign enemies. In addition to protecting the borders, this new federal government, or Union, would allow for free trade among the sovereign states. Patrick Henry of Virginia clearly stated the prevailing Southern view of the American government when he declared, "The first thing I have at heart is American *liberty*; the second thing is American *union*."[428] In 1814, John Randolph of Roanoke, Virginia, declared that he always

---

[427] The federal government created by the original constitution as ratified by the Sovereign States (1787-1789) died with the assumption of power by Lincoln and his Republican cronies in 1861—the Republic was replaced with a supreme federal government that would henceforth be the sole judge as to the extent of its powers.

[428] *Patrick Henry: Life, Correspondence and Speeches*, W.W. Henry, ed. (Harrisonburg, VA: Sprinkle Publishing, 1993), Vol. III, 449.

thought that the union "was a means of securing the safety, liberty, and welfare of the confederacy [the union of states under the original Constitution] and not in itself an end to which these should be sacrificed."[429] He agreed with Patrick Henry that liberty trumps government. Southerners followed the political idea as announced in the Joint Declaration of Independence (1776) that plainly declared that when any government becomes destructive of liberty "...it is the Right of the People to alter or abolish it, and to institute new Government...." This concept, the right to abolish an oppressive government and establish a new government, was held by the generation of Southerners who seceded from the Yankee-controlled union in 1861.[430]

In 1861, James P. Holcombe, professor of law at the University of Virginia, described the feelings of most Southerners when he declared, "Whenever this Union and your liberties cannot exist together, throw the Union to the winds, and clasp the liberty of your country to your hearts."[431] Professor Holcombe was advocating the same ideas as expressed not only in the Declaration of Independence but also the opinions expressed by James Madison and Thomas Jefferson in the Virginia and Kentucky Resolves of 1798. In these Resolves, both founding fathers and future U.S. presidents plainly declared that the federal government was not the sole judge of its own powers—their use of the

---

[429] Randolph as cited in White, "Introduction," *Northern Opposition to Mr. Lincoln's War*, 5.

[430] Actually, South Carolina seceded from the union on December 20, 1860 and the other Southern States followed in 1861.

[431] Holcombe, as cited in White, Jonathan D., "Introduction," *Northern Opposition to Mr. Lincoln's War*, 5.

term "federal government" includes the Federal Supreme Court.[432] Prior to the Lincoln revolution, the ultimate constitutional judge, as to what was or was not constitutionally correct, belonged to the people of the sovereign state(s). Should a conflict arise between the federal government and a sovereign state, the state possessed the sovereign authority to take whatever steps it determined to be best to arrest the federal government's encroachment upon the sovereign states' rights or the rights of the people of that specific state. The fact that the political philosophy espoused in the Kentucky and Virginia Resolves of 1798 was the primary view of a substantial part of the country is demonstrated by the 1852 Democratic Party Platform. The 1852 Democratic Party Platform declared, "That the democratic party will faithfully abide by and uphold the principles laid down in the Kentucky and Virginia resolutions of 1798."[433] Unlike the Republican Party, the Democratic Party was not a regional party, it was a major political player in all states both North and South. In May of 1860, Senator Jefferson Davis of Mississippi introduced a resolution in the United States Senate declaring that "in the adoption of the Federal Constitution, the states adopting the same acted severally as

---

[432] It is assumed today that the Federal Supreme Court has the "final word" on issues between the states and the federal government. This is true TODAY because the United States is no longer a Republic of Sovereign States but is governed by an ILLEGITIMATE government created by Lincoln and his co-conspirators—the legitimate Republic founded by the consent of sovereign states was replaced by an ILLEGITIMATE empire created by the compulsion of bloody bayonets. And never let it be forgotten that it is Southern blood on those bloody, Yankee bayonets!

[433] As cited by DeRosa, "President Franklin Pierce and the War for Southern Independence," *Northern Opposition to Mr. Lincoln's War*, 18; In 1821 the Ohio Legislature endorsed the "Doctrine of 1798," Kilpatrick, James Jackson, *The Sovereign States*, (Chicago: Henry Regnery Co., 1957), 154.

free and independent sovereignties."434 [Emphasis added]. Senator Davis' resolution was debated and voted on in the United States' Congress less than a year before the beginning of the secession of Southern States. Senator Davis' resolution passed by a vote of 36 in favor and only 19 in opposition! But this democratic debate and vote occurred before the criminal Lincoln took command of the federal government and turned it from a Republic into an aggressive and evil empire. The view of the intrinsic authority of the sovereign state was so strongly held in the United States—before the Lincoln revolution—that it had adherents in the federal judiciary well into the modern era, although they were by that time a definite minority. For example, in a 1936 case, *Carter v. Carter Coal Company*, Federal Supreme Court Justice Sutherland declared, "The States were before the Constitution; and, consequently, their [the states] legislative powers antedated the Constitution."435 Similar "shadows" of 1798-thinking also can be seen in many of the dissenting opinions issued by Justice Clarence Thomas436 of the current (2017) Federal Supreme Court.

The Southern minority (a minority in the U.S. Congress) saw the Constitution as a means to protect the reserved rights of the people of

---

434 Davis as cited by Masters, *Lincoln the Man*, 419.

435 As cited in DeRosa, Marshall, "President Franklin Pierce and the War for Southern Independence," *Northern Opposition to Mr. Lincoln's War*, 37.

436 Justice Clarence Thomas is the only African American currently on the U.S. Supreme Court. He was born in Georgia and therefore is the only Southerner on the Supreme Court. For a review of the impact his "originalist" views have had, see Lovelace, Ryan, "Former Trump candidate for Supreme Court praises Clarence Thomas' disagreements with Antonin Scalia," *Washington Examiner*, www.washingtonexaminer.com/former-trump-candidate-for-supreme-court-praises-clarence-thomas-disagreements-with-antonin-scalia/article/2630541 (Accessed 10/25/2017).

each sovereign state. The New England majority (the Northern majority in the U.S. Congress) saw the Constitution as a barrier used by rich Southerners to prevent them (the North) from creating a vast, glorious, commercial empire. From the very beginning of these United States, the South was by far the wealthiest part of the new country. The dollar worshippers of New England cast their covetous eyes southward and saw vast riches just waiting to be exploited. The two peoples, Northern and Southern, were different in culture, in social morals, in economic activity, and political outlook regarding the role of the federal government. As Southern historian Simkins noted, "Had their Southern rival not possessed slavery, some other Southern sin could have been shrewdly conjured up for moralizing purposes."[437]

Alexander Hamilton's High Federalist Curse on Liberty

Alexander Hamilton was one of the leading High Federalists who argued from the very beginning of the United States in favor of a strong central government. His original plan called for a federal government with an executive with almost kingly powers, Senators elected for life exercising power similar to the House of Lords, and a Congress that could override (veto or nullify) state legislation. The essence of his vision of a supreme federal government was presented to the early arrivals at the Constitutional Convention,[438] but Hamilton's vision of a supreme federal government was so extreme that it almost caused the dissolution of the

---

[437] Kennedy & Kennedy, *Punished With Poverty*, 132, footnote 311.

[438] The Constitutional Convention which drafted the original Constitution was a meeting of delegates selected by each sovereign state and met in Philadelphia, Pennsylvania, from May 25 to September 17, 1787.

Constitutional Convention.439 Cooler heads took control, and they eventually crafted the original Constitution that was then submitted to the sovereign states for their individual ratification or rejection. From the beginning, High Federalists such as Alexander Hamilton and John Jay, both from New York, were determined to convert the sovereign states into a centralized, energetic, federal government that would establish a commercial and financial empire controlled by the North. It is interesting to note that both of these High Federalists had offices on Wall Street in New York City. Hamilton would become President George Washington's Secretary of the Treasury, and John Jay would become the first Chief Justice of the Federal Supreme Court. High Federalist Chief Justice John Jay saw the federal court as an instrument in Federalists' hands that could be exploited to gain federal supremacy over the states and force the states to submit to the federal government.440

Hamilton of New York, just like most of the Founding Fathers North and South, was a slave owner.441 In New York City in the late 1790s up to 25% of New Yorkers owned slaves! Slavery did not end in New York until the 1850s.442 The great debate between High Federalists (primarily

---

439 Kennedy, *Nullification: Why and How*, 79-83.

440 *The Oxford Companion to The Supreme Court of the United States*, Kermit L. Hall, ed. (New York: Oxford University Press, 1992), 447.

441 Hamilton's ownership of slaves has been a subject of much discussion, but one thing is for sure, he never objected to the making of profits as it related to the subject of slavery.

442 DiLorenzo, Thomas J., *Hamilton's Curse-How Jefferson's Archenemy Betrayed the American Revolution and What it Means for Americans Today* (New York: Crown Forum, 2008), 10.

Yankees) and Jeffersonian Republicans [443] (a majority in the South and many Northern states) was not a debate over slavery but a debate as to whether the United States would become a commercial empire centered on New England and New York, especially Wall Street, or remain a Republic of Sovereign States. Hamilton's vision of the United States was that it should follow the British model. He hoped to establish a system of government that would vigorously promote "national greatness and imperial glory."[444] He saw the use of tariffs as a means of collecting money from the haves (the South) and using it to develop the North's commerce. The first tariff after the ratification of the Constitution was Hamilton's work.[445] Hamilton's vision of a supreme federal government that would promote commercial / financial imperialism was radically different from the vision of the vast majority of Southerners. The agricultural South viewed commerce as a private affair and saw any government interference with free trade as an attempt of a ruling elite to promote "their" allies at the expense of those "others" who did not control the federal government. Southerners followed the Jeffersonian vision of a limited federal government that would be kept in control ultimately by the exercise of states' rights. Southerners took great comfort (in reality—too much comfort) in the Constitutional guarantees announced in the Ninth and Tenth Amendments. Jefferson understood that most foreigners did not understand the role of the Sovereign States in the American federal system. Today, pacified Southerners should be added

---

[443] Jeffersonian Republicans of the early 1800s were the very opposite of the Lincoln Republicans of the 1860s. Other than the name "Republican," there is no similarity between the two.

[444] DiLorenzo, *Hamilton's Curse*, 12.

[445] Masters, *Lincoln the Man*, 445.

to "foreigners" who do not understand the proper role of *real* states' rights. In an 1824 letter Jefferson wrote:

> With respect to our State and federal governments, I do not think their relations [are] correctly understood by foreigners. They generally suppose the former [State] is subordinate to the latter [federal government]. But this is not the case. They are coordinate departments of one...integral whole. To the State governments are reserved all legislation and administration, in affairs which concern their own citizens only, and to the federal government is given whatever concerns foreigners, or the citizens of other States.[446]

Note that Jefferson described the relation of the Sovereign State to the federal government as "coordinate departments." James Madison, in *Federalist* Number 51 and 62, described the relationship as being a "compound republic." The creators of the federal government (the Sovereign States) delegated specific and limited sovereign powers to their creature, the federal government, while retaining unto themselves all ultimate sovereign authority. Also note that citizenship, prior to the illegal enactment of the Fourteenth Amendment, meant citizenship to a specific state, not to the nation.

Federal protectionism, favoritism, and financial support[447] for Northern commerce and industry (today we would call it corporate welfare) was one of Hamilton's primary means for creating a vast commercial empire. A federally controlled central banking system was

---

[446] Jefferson, as cited in DiLorenzo, *Hamilton's Curse*, 15-6.

[447] Hamilton advocated hyper-protective tariffs and federal dollars given to selected industry or, as he referred to it, "pecuniary bounties & premiums." DiLorenzo, *Hamilton's Curse*, 111.

his chosen method for creating an American financial empire—both banking and commerce would be centered in New York and New England. Hamilton's plan was the first step toward crony capitalism in America. Hamilton wanted to use the power of the federal government to create "a monopoly of the domestic market."[448]

An early but short run of Federalist Party Presidents was ended with the election of a strong States' Rights president, Thomas Jefferson. The Federalist Party was thoroughly defeated and subsequently disbanded. This was merely a temporary setback for those advocating an American crony capitalist commercial empire. A new political party, the Whig Party, was formed and began a campaign promoting central banking and use of federal monies for internal improvements and subsidies for commerce, industry, and finance. The new party called their plan to use federal power and money to support commerce, and finance "The American System." Henry Clay of Kentucky was its major advocate and spokesman. Edgar Lee Masters (1868-1950), attorney, poet, novelist and biographer born in Kansas but lived in Illinois, described Clay thusly:

> Clay was the champion of that political system which doles favors to the strong in order to win and keep their adherence to the government. His system offered shelter to devious schemes and corrupt enterprises ... [Clay followed] Alexander Hamilton with his corrupt funding schemes, his superstitions concerning the advantage of a public debt, and a people taxed to make profits for enterprises that cannot stand alone ... its principles were plunder and nothing else.... Whigs adopted the tricks of the pickpocket who dresses himself like a farmer in order to move

---

[448] DiLorenzo, *Hamilton's Curse*, 110.

through a rural crowd unidentified while he gathers purses and watches.[449]

Clay was an unsuccessful presidential candidate in three elections. It should be noted that even with three efforts to gain the presidency, those advocating crony capitalism were defeated by those advocating the principles of the Kentucky and Virginia Resolves of 1798. After Clay's death, the Whig Party dissolved and most of its members joined the newly created sectional party (Northern states), the Republican Party.

Lincoln, elected by only 39% of popular vote, and his Republican allies installed a system of dictatorial rule in which Constitutional fine points such as "due process," "*writ of habeas corpus*" and "trial by jury" were dispensed with and replaced by Lincoln's strong-man arbitrary rule. William Henry Seward of New York and United States Secretary of State under Lincoln typifies the arbitrary nature of "civil rights" under Lincoln's regime. Seward told Lord Lyons, "I can touch a bell on my right hand and order the arrest of a citizen of Ohio. I can touch the bell again and order the arrest of a citizen of New York. Can Queen Victoria do as much?"[450] Seward was bragging about having the power to send people to jail without a warrant or due process. This alone is enough to brand the Lincoln regime as a tyranny. But note that Seward was talking about United States citizens in states that were not in "rebellion" but were for the most part supporting or at least passively accepting the edicts from Lincoln's federal government! Lincoln and company cannot even use the excuse that they were actively putting down a rebellion in Northern states! While conducting an illegal, imperialistic invasion of a peaceful,

---

[449] Masters, *Lincoln the Man*, 26-27.
[450] Seward, cited *Ibid.*, 411.

democratically elected nation—the Confederate States of America—Lincoln and his co-conspirators were also conducting an unconstitutional invasion of civil liberties within the United States. Lincoln, the Republican Party and their crony capitalist allies were responsible for the death of the original American Republic and for setting the United States on the "path toward empire."[451] The unlimited power of the federal government was celebrated by the ruling elite and their cronies during the War. Yankee General William Sherman's brother, Senator John Sherman, declared that with a federally controlled central banking system in place, it would help to create "a powerful national government and an *internationally dominant* American nation,"[452] [Emphasis added]. Republican George Julian celebrated the fact that "the days of Conservatism, of State Sovereignty, are over, and the reign of [Republican] Radicalism has been fairly ushered in.... From the crucible of War and the sacrifice of blood, would come the most perfect civilization that the world has ever seen."[453] The arrogant Yankee's lust for empire could not be satisfied with merely one victory in 1865 against the Confederate States of America—it continues today!

By the end of the War for Southern Independence, it was clear—even before Reconstruction—that the United States was no longer a Republic but was now an empire that exercised the right to be the sole judge as to the extent of its powers. United States President, Woodrow Wilson, while a professor at Princeton University, wrote "The War Between the States established ... this principle, that the Federal government is, through its

---

[451] *Ibid.*, 498.

[452] Sherman, cited in DiLorenzo, *Hamilton's Curse*, 129.

[453] Julian, as cited in Chodes, "Oliver P. Mortn," *Northern Opposition to Mr. Lincoln's War*, 199.

courts, the final judge of its own powers."454 In other words, the Republic was destroyed by massed, bloody bayonets, and an empire now stands where once the Jeffersonian Republic of Sovereign States stood. And never let it be forgotten that the blood on those bloody Yankee bayonets is Southern blood.

When confronted with international rage, Yankee and pacified Southerners wonder, "Why do they hate us?" They act confused as to why so many people around the world do not trust the Yankee Empire. They wonder why so many people around the world seem to agree with Lenin who declared that, "A handful (less than one-tenth of the inhabitants of the globe) ... plunder the whole world simply by clipping coupons."455 This is the image the majority of the world has when they think about the vast, self-serving interest of Wall Street, the Federal Reserve, International Monetary Fund, or the World Bank. This is one of the primary reasons so many of the world's impoverished people willingly support communist (anti-capitalist) insurgents. Yankee-Americans and pacified Southerners do not understand this simple fact. But Lenin's analysis was not entirely accurate. What Lenin labeled as "capitalism" was actually "crony capitalism." Free market capitalism in America has been perverted by the Yankee Empire. Free market capitalism begins to die the moment government begins to show favors to one economic actor over another. Crony capitalism is the match applied to the gunpowder of the free market. A great explosion of energy initially occurs, but the very substance of that energy—the gunpowder representing the free market— is eventually completely consumed. Crony capitalism has become the

---

454 Wilson, cited by DiLorenzo, *Hamilton's Curse*, 84.

455 Lenin, V. I., *Imperialism; The Highest Stage of Capitalism* (1917, New York: International Publishers, 1939), 13.

accepted American (Yankee Empire) version of national socialism or economic fascism—also described as corporatism, corporatocracy, corporate welfare, a partnership between business and government, or favored businesses "too big to fail." What we see today is the end result of Lincoln's destruction of a Republic and the emergence of first a North American, then a Western Hemisphere, and eventually a worldwide commercial, financial, and military empire—the Yankee Empire. An empire that never would have emerged had the Confederate States of American won its freedom and independence in 1861-1865. For those Americans who were raised as the generation of Cold War, anti-communist warriors, it may be embarrassing to read the words of a Communist dictator who—though he did not make a distinction between capitalism and crony capitalism—he nonetheless stated a truth when he said, "We ask, is there under capitalism any means of removing the disparity [between the haves and have-nots] … other than war?"[456] Note the similarity to Andrew Nelson Lytle's analysis (Lytle was a Southern author writing in the 1930s):

> Since 1865 an agrarian Union has been changed into an industrial empire bent on conquest of the earth's goods and ports to sell them in. This means warfare, a struggle over markets, leading, in the end, to actual military conflict between nations.[457]

---

[456] *Ibid.*, 98.

[457] Nelson, "The Hind Tit," *I'll Take My Stand*, 202.

Empires Impose Death, Destruction, and Misery

Empires by their very nature are aggressive. They use military power to impose the empire's will on foreign people and nations. Many innocent people die as a result of the empire imposing its will on foreign nations. The invaded nation's military will resist, and many of these soldiers will be killed or wounded; many of the empire's soldiers will also be killed or wounded, but most of the death and destruction will fall on the non-combatants—civilians, men, women, children, and infants. Today, Americans euphemistically refer to these innocent civilian causalities as "collateral damage." Many civilians will be killed or murdered by direct military actions. Many more will die of disease, malnutrition, and starvation produced by the destruction of invaded nation's civil society. It is a story as old as man himself. It has been played out in all ages in every civilization. Yankee conservatives and pacified Southerners cannot bring themselves to accept the fact that "their" nation is an evil empire that has inflicted its share of death and destruction on innocent civilians—not only in the South during the War for Southern Independence but on innocent men, women and children in this current generation.

When dealing with foreign nations, empires do not seek international justice, peace or fair play. Empires seek commercial, financial, and military advantage for the empire's ruling elite. The Yankee Empire tells its soldiers that they are fighting to "preserve the Union," (1861) when in reality, the empire is fighting to preserve its ability to extort revenue from the Southern people; the Yankee Empire tells its soldiers it is fighting to avenge the "sinking of the *Maine*," (1898) when actually, it is fighting to extend its commercial and military power in the Caribbean, Central America, South America, the Philippines, and eventually China. In Vietnam (1960s) the Yankee Empire told its soldiers it was fighting to preserve democracy, but was that true? How many people died in that no-win war—a war in which the original American Republic would never have become involved but one in which the Yankee Empire saw no reason to avoid?

The Vietnam War demonstrates the Yankee Empire's ability to engage in self-deluding, arrogant thinking to rationalize sending young men to die in a war that had already seen the destruction of the French empire by the determined efforts of the Vietnamese people. But even worse was the fact that the Yankee Empire was instrumental in setting the stage for the American portion of the Vietnam War—a war, with all its death and destruction that could have been avoided. The blame for the horrors of a useless war belongs not to the soldiers who honorably obeyed their country's call to duty but to the Yankee Empire's ruling elite. As was true in the war initiated by Lincoln and his co-conspirators in 1861, the Vietnam War was "A rich man's war but a poor man's fight."

In the mid-1940s, Ho Chi Minh began working with the United States Office of Strategic Services (OSS was a precursor to the CIA) in military actions against the Japanese in Vietnam and South China. In 1945, he delivered an interesting speech in Hanoi, Vietnam. In his speech, Ho Chi Minh quoted the American Declaration of Independence.[458] He was hoping that the United States would support Vietnam's claim to independence. It was said that Ho Chi Minh had a "lifelong admiration for Americans."[459] He attempted to gain support from the United States by sending letters to President Truman and General George Marshall but to no avail.[460] During World War II, the Vichy French allowed the Japanese to occupy Vietnam. At the end of World War II, the Vietnamese people wanted to establish a government of their own choosing—but the Yankee Empire had other ideas. The Yankee Empire supported the French imperial claim to Vietnam, and with American support, the French became embroiled in a vicious guerrilla war in Vietnam. By 1954,

---

[458] "Ho Chi Minh, President of North Vietnam," *Encyclopedia Britannica*, www.britannica.com/biography/Ho-Chi-Minh (Accessed 11/03/2017).

[459] Kinzer, *Overthrow*, 150.

[460] *Ibid.*

the French were defeated and ready to leave Vietnam. A peace agreement was signed in Geneva that would have ended the conflict. The Yankee Empire's representative at the peace conference was Secretary of State John Foster Dulles.[461] The peace agreement called for a halt to the fighting; a *temporary*, two-year division of Vietnam; followed by a nationwide vote in 1956 in which the North and South would be united. There was no doubt as to who would win the vote. Even President Eisenhower thought that Ho Chi Minh would win the vote of "possibly eighty percent of the population."[462] In other words, the democratic will of the people of Vietnam was in favor of unification under the leadership of Ho Chi Minh. The Yankee Empire found this to be unacceptable. The excuse offered was that Ho Chi Minh was a communist. But so was Josip Tito of Yugoslavia, and the Yankee Empire had friendly relations with him. Furthermore, in 1972, "conservative" President Nixon would become best "buds" with Mao Zedong in Communist China. But for reasons we mere mortals may never know, the Yankee Empire, which by this time had installed its puppet government in South Vietnam, decided not to allow the scheduled 1956 vote. This was a violation of an international agreement (the 1954 Geneva Peace Accords) of which the Yankee Empire had been a quasi-party. But remember, the Yankee Empire has a history of breaking and violating firm agreements, such as the Constitution, if it will advance its commercial, political or military power.

---

[461] John Foster Dulles was born in Washington, D.C. to a politically prominent (Yankee) family. He attended Princeton University and practiced law in New York. "John Foster Dulles Biography," Biography.com, www.biography.com/people/john-foster-dulles-9280687 (Accessed 10/21/2017).

[462] Kinzer, *Overthrow*, 153.

The American phase of the Vietnam War could have been avoided, but empires seldom choose to do those things that would be best for the average person in the empire and are especially calloused when dealing with the people of other nations. What was the result? Vietnam was eventually united! But what was the human cost? American deaths during the Vietnam War were 58,220.[463] In 1956, when President Eisenhower (Republican) was in office, the ruling elite of the Yankee Empire thought the risk of war in Vietnam was worth taking. Empires never consider the human cost of their adventures—"Rich man's war, poor man's fight."

The prior data covers only the Yankee Empire's human cost of waging a no-win, politically inspired war. The people of Vietnam also paid an enormous price. It has been estimated that approximately three million Vietnamese died between 1954 and 1987.[464] These deaths plus the American deaths represent deaths that would not have occurred had the Yankee Empire honored the Geneva agreement of 1954. How much "collateral damage" (innocent civilians killed) has occurred since Lincoln unleashed his "vigorous war policy"[465] against the civilian population of the Confederate States of America?

After more than a century and a half as a captive nation, perhaps it is time for the Southern people to recognize that Southerners are no longer citizens of America's original Republic of Sovereign States but are in fact subjects of the Yankee Empire, and as such, the South is a captive nation.

---

[463] "Vietnam War U.S. Military Fatal Casualty Statistics," National Archives, www.archives.gov/research/military/vietnam-war/casualty-statistics.html (Accessed 10/21/2017).

[464] Rummel, *Death By Government*, 280.

[465] Kennedy & Kennedy, *Punished With Poverty*, 59, 70, 73-74,76-77.

As long as pacified Southerners remain a docile part of the Yankee Empire, the empire will continue to use Southern resources and Southern blood to expand and maintain its commercial, financial, and military empire. Perhaps it is time to take the steps necessary to reclaim the South's rightful inheritance of liberty, freedom, and peaceful prosperity.

Chapter 9: U.S. Army Invades the Confederate States of America

AT THE BEGINNING OF THE WAR for Southern Independence,[466] the radical leaders of the Republican Party in the United States Congress made it very clear what they intended to do to the South once the forces of Yankee invasion had won final victory. "Our generals have a sword in one hand and shackles in the other," proclaimed Pennsylvania's Republican Congressman Thaddeus Stevens.[467] The Yankee's bloody sword would be used to conquer a free people, force them to submit to Yankee rule, and, as pacified subjects of the Yankee Empire, meekly wear Yankee shackles! Once the South was conquered, Congressman Stevens proposed to deal with the South "by the laws of war and conquest."[468] He was determined to "punish" the South and to use force to make sure land belonging to Southerners was "confiscated."[469] The post-war scalawag governor of Tennessee, a former Methodist minister, publicly advocated the "extermination of all Confederates and their families."[470] By 1861, generations of virulent, slanderous, anti-South propaganda had produced

---

[466] Southern Historian Dr. Clyde Wilson of South Carolina has noted that while from the Southern point of view it was a *War for Southern Independence*, from the Yankee's point of view it was a *War to Prevent Southern Independence*!

[467] Stevens, as cited in Bowers, *The Tragic Era*, 72.

[468] Stevens, as cited *Ibid.*, 73.

[469] *Ibid.*

[470] As cited in, Mitcham, *Bust Hell Wide Open*, 300.

a Northern zeitgeist[471] set upon the total destruction and *extermination* of the "evil" South. Generations of anti-South propaganda created this evil, anti-South, Northern "spirit of the age" that would be the primary and overriding "frame of reference"[472] when Yankees considered questions relating to the South. It was a zeitgeist of unmitigated hatred, bigotry, and prejudice against the people of the Yankee Empire's newly conquered territory—the formerly free and prosperous people of the Confederate States of America. This evil Yankee zeitgeist continues today in the form of ever-increasing waves of politically correct, anti-South, cultural genocide!

The evil intent of the Yankee Empire to punish and exterminate the Southern people is documented in numerous accounts of terror, rape, murder, and pillaging that the Empire's soldiers inflicted upon the South's civilian population (both black and white).[473] It can also be seen in the "official" explicit or implicit authorization given by the Yankee Empire's political and military leadership to the invading Yankee armies—instructions to exterminate all who dare to resist the Yankee Empire.

During the First World War, many Southerners who had lived through the Yankee invasion of their Southern homeland were dismayed by the degree of Yankee hypocrisy when dealing with the claims of German attacks against innocent Belgium civilians. At the outbreak of World War I, Yankee Yellow Journalists were busy writing horror stories about the claims of brutality by the Germans in violation of the sacred laws of

---

[471] Zeitgeist: Spirit of the age or time that controls the thinking of a society.

[472] Frame of reference: A set of assumptions, basic ideas, or standards that regulates and sanctions an individual's behavior or how the individual perceives a given situation.

[473] Kennedy & Kennedy, *Punished With Poverty*, 69-87.

civilized warfare. Yet, during the War for Southern Independence, Yellow Journalists from these same papers had been open champions of far worse crimes against innocent Southern civilians.[474]

Yankee Yellow Journalism played a major role in creating and maintaining this anti-South zeitgeist. Yankee Yellow Journalism before and during the War for Southern Independence helped to "dehumanize" the people of the South and thereby justify the cruel and immoral acts committed by the United States military against innocent Southern civilians. It is a well-known fact that before you can exterminate a people, you must first "dehumanize" them. Northern Yellow Journalists, writers, and rabble-rousers performed this function for the Yankee government prior to and during the so-called "Civil War." After the War was over and continuing through today, the Yankee Empire's propagandists—masquerading as journalists, educators, and Hollywood elites—continue the effort to "dehumanize" the Southern people, our Cause, and anyone who dares to defend the right of the South to be an independent nation.

Yankee arrogance regarding their assumed ability to quickly destroy the "evil" Southern nation was displayed in the New York *Tribune* which promised the world, "The nations of Europe may rest assured that Jeff Davis & Co. will be swinging from the battlements at Washington, at least, by the 4th of July [1861]. We spit upon a later and longer deferred justice."[475] Not to be outdone, the New York *Times* predicted that it would take only 30 days to destroy the Confederacy. Next, it demonstrated the North's virulent hatred of the South by declaring: "We only have to send

---

[474] See "Yankee Hypocrisy—Germans in Belgium vs. Yankees in Georgia" in Kennedy, *Uncle Seth Fought the Yankees*, 335-340.

[475] As cited in Pollard, E. A., *Southern History of the War* (1866, New York: The Fairfax Press, 1977), Vol. I, 76.

a column of 25,000 men across the Potomac to Richmond and burn out the rats there."[476] Notice how the people of the South are referred to as "rats." This is just one of many examples of Southerners being dehumanized by the Yankee press. Yankee propagandists were setting the stage for the extermination of the South. But before the emerging Yankee Empire could justify exterminating the people of the South, it first had to dehumanize the people it had targeted for extermination. Once the aggressor nation (the United States in this example) successfully brands the people of the targeted nation (the people of the Confederate States) as "evil," "sinners," and "cruel and subhuman," it becomes illogical NOT to rid the world of such vile human vermin. The Philadelphia *Press* demonstrated its contempt for the people of the South by declaring: "The rebels [are] a mere band of ragamuffins, will fly, like chaff before the wind on our approach."[477] Such was the arrogance of the Yankee press that the Chicago *Tribune* was convinced that the Southern people would fold once the might of the North invaded the South. The *Tribune* asked that Illinois be given the sole honor of whipping these ignorant Southerners into line. "Illinois can whip the South by herself. We insist on the matter being turned over to us."[478] It did not take long for evil Yankee words to turn into evil Yankee deeds.

In May of 1861, the Yankee Empire sent 8,000 invaders across the Potomac River and occupied Alexandria, Virginia. The town was undefended. The prior week, a local pro-Union man had been accosted by a group of angry Southerners. The pro-Union man was rescued by Mr. Jackson, the proprietor of the Marshall House, a local hotel. Mr. Jackson

---

[476] *Ibid.*, 77.

[477] *Ibid.*

[478] *Ibid.*

was a strong supporter of Southern independence, yet, seeing the injustice playing out before him, he was motivated to stop the harassment by coming to the Union man's rescue. All the while, Mr. Jackson proudly flew a Southern flag on the top of his hotel. He and his family lived in a private residence in the hotel. In the middle of the night, as the Yankees were occupying the town, a Yankee, Colonel Ellsworth, decided he would take the flag as a "prize of war." Mr. Jackson was awakened by the sounds of Colonel Ellsworth and three other Yankees coming down the hotel stairs carrying Mr. Jackson's Confederate flag. The Yankee Colonel informed Mr. Jackson that the flag was a prize of war. Mr. Jackson informed the Yankee Colonel that he would not live to enjoy his prize and discharged both barrels of his shotgun into the Yankee's chest. Mr. Jackson was killed by the other three Yankees. Yellow Journalists in the North branded Mr. Jackson as an "assassin," but in truth, he was a martyr for the Cause of Freedom. Mr. Jackson became the first civilian casualty of the War for Southern Independence. He died defending his home, his family, and his country's flag.[479] He would not be the last.

The list of Yankee atrocities is virtually limitless, but they cannot be found in standard Yankee history textbooks. The well-rewarded sycophants of the Yankee Empire, masquerading as scholars, intellectuals, journalists, or mainline media personalities, are careful to cover up or ignore such evidence. The average Southerner, much less the average Northerner or foreigner, will never be exposed to the vast array of Yankee atrocities—atrocities cataloged in books that are seldom, if ever, allowed national exposure. Yankee atrocities such as what happened in Kentucky where Yankees shot a small child as she was playing in her front yard. They shot her because her father would not pledge allegiance to the

---

[479] *Ibid.*, 81.

United States flag.[480] In Virginia, Yankees captured a fourteen-year-old boy who was serving with Confederate Major John Singleton Mosby's cavalry. They tried him as a spy and wanted to hang him, but he was spared hanging by one vote. The Yankee judge then sentenced the fourteen-year-old boy to life in prison. The boy was told that he could avoid the sentence if he claimed that he had been drafted into Confederate service, but the boy refused—he wanted the world to know that he had volunteered to defend his home, his people, and his country.[481] In Stevenson, Alabama, Yankee Captain Gates burned the home occupied by a woman and her children. He set the house ablaze while the woman and her children were still in the house. They escaped with nothing but the clothing they were wearing. The house burning was in retaliation for Confederate soldiers firing on a Yankee supply ship in a nearby river.[482] Soldiers under the command of Yankee General Payne murdered Confederate prisoners-of-war as well as numerous civilians in Tennessee.[483] In Shepherdstown, Virginia, Yankee General Hunter ordered the burning of civilian homes. In one of the homes he ordered to be burned lived the descendant of a 1776 Revolutionary War hero who had built the home, and General Hunter's own niece was residing in the house! Homes of innocent women and children were burned all across the South—so much so that many Southern towns and cities were referred to as "Chimneyville," because all that was left standing were chimneys where once fine homes had stood.[484] Yankee atrocities included the

---

[480] Kennedy, *Uncle Seth Fought the Yankees*, 21-25.

[481] *Ibid.*, 62-65.

[482] *Ibid.*, 90-93.

[483] *Ibid.*, 114-116.

[484] *Ibid.*, 288-291.

beheading of two young Southerners falsely accused of being guerrilla fighters. After killing these innocent boys, Yankee soldiers severed their heads and took them to the boys' home where they mounted the severed heads on the fence leading to the front door of the boys' home. It was done to serve as a warning to all Southerners who dared to resist the imperial embrace of the Yankee Empire. Their father, Jack Hinson, had been a pro-Union Southerner and had even assisted Yankee General Grant as the invaders moved into Jack's area of Tennessee. But after the demonstration of Yankee honor, he became dedicated to taking revenge upon all Yankees. Jack Hinson conducted a private war of revenge as a Confederate sharpshooter. He personally killed more than one hundred Yankee soldiers—his primary targets were officers and non-commissioned officers.[485]

During and subsequent to the War, the Yankee Empire used and continues to use fake news to hide its crimes against its peaceful neighbor—the Confederate States of America. To cover its crimes against humanity, the Yankee Empire utilized the work of its Yellow Journalists to redirect attention away from actual Yankee crimes and have the world focus on "fake news" about fictitious Southern crimes. Leading up to the War, Lincoln and his cronies used "fake news" to arouse Northern sentiment against the South and redirect attention away from Lincoln's secret war conspiracy. Today the Yankee Empire sings the same song—same song, different verse!

Despite generations of slanderous anti-South propaganda in 1860, the average Northerner still believed that a sovereign state had the right to secede from the Union. This presented Lincoln and his cronies with a

---

[485] Kennedy, *Uncle Seth Fought the Yankees*, 373-376; also see McKenney, Tom C., *Jack Hinson's One-Man War* (Gretna, LA: Pelican Publishing Co., 2009).

major obstacle to their desire for an invasion of the Confederate States of America. For example, the New York *Tribune*, a pro-Lincoln/Republican newspaper, declared in 1860:

> We hold, with Jefferson, to the inalienable right of communities to alter or abolish forms of governments that have become oppressive or injurious; if the cotton States shall decide that they can do better out of the Union than in it, we insist on letting them go in peace... We hope to never live in a republic whereof one section is pinned to the residue by bayonets.[486]

The New York *Herald* added its voice to this general feeling:

> Each State is organized as a complete government ... possessing the right to break the tie of the confederation as a nation might break a treaty and to repel coercion as a nation might repel invasion. Coercion, if it were possible, is out of the question.[487]

These two examples demonstrate the difficulty faced by the warmongering Lincoln and his cronies. To initiate an invasion of the Confederate States, Lincoln and his cronies had to devise a way to mobilize Northern public opinion in favor of war. Lincoln was elected with only 39% of Americans voting for him—he realized that the average person in the North did not want war. But, matters became critical for the North's crony capitalists once the Confederacy established their relatively low tariff rates. Yankee financial and commercial empires depended upon a high protective tariff collected in Southern ports! This was admitted by leading New Englanders in the late 1820s. Senator Daniel Webster from Massachusetts received a letter from his political

---

[486] Kennedy, *Uncle Seth Fought the Yankees*, 342.

[487] *Ibid.*

and economic advisor, Abbott Lawrence,[488] who wrote boastfully that the tariff: "If adopted as amended will keep the South and West in debt to New England the next hundred years."[489] If the South seceded, then the North would not be able to use the federal government to protect Northern markets from foreign competition and continue their exploitation of the Southern people via confiscatory protective tariffs! Something had to be done to convince the Northern general public to support military aggression against the democratically elected, peaceful, sovereign nation—the Confederate States of America. If nothing else, Lincoln was a master of seducing the public with half-truths, deceit, and hidden agendas. Lincoln's maneuvering to initiate a war with the Confederate States was a deceitful work of Machiavellian political cunning.[490]

President James Buchanan was in office when Lincoln was elected President in November 1860. Buchanan remained in office until March 1861. During that time and before Lincoln was sworn in as United States President, six Southern States had seceded from the United States and formed the Provisional Government of the Confederate States of America. President Buchanan acknowledged that the Constitution does not delegate power to the federal government to invade a Sovereign State in

---

[488] Abbott Lawrence was a major New England industrialist and developer of textiles mills that depended upon slave grown cotton. "Abbott Lawrence, American Merchant," *Encyclopedia Britannica*, www.britannica.com/biography/Abbott-Lawrence (Accessed 02/03/2018).

[489] Gov. Sam Houston Jones, "The Plundered South," The Abbeville Blog, www.abbevilleinstitute.org/blog/the-plundered-south (Accessed 01/31/2018). Reprint of a speech given by Louisiana Governor Sam Houston Jones in 1943.

[490] For a more complete detail and timeline of Lincoln's deceitful maneuvers to initiate a war, see Kennedy, *Uncle Seth Fought the Yankees*, 341-351.

order to keep it in the Union. In his December 1860 State of the Union address he noted:

> Suppose such a war should result in the conquest of a State; how are we to govern it afterwards? Shall we hold it as a province and govern it by despotic power? War would not only present the most effectual means of destroying it but would vanish all hope of its peaceable reconstruction.[491]

As it became clear that the South would establish low tariffs, crony capitalists in the North began to demand action by the federal government to force the seceded states back under the control (i.e., tariff collecting authority) of the federal government. President Buchanan rejected the idea of federal coercion even though he was under great pressure including threats of physical harm. His decision not to threaten the South with military invasion was based upon a sound interpretation of the Constitution.[492]

Propagandists for the Yankee Empire continue to promote falsehoods about the War—done to create a "smokescreen" between Yankee lies and the public understanding. This "smokescreen" of slanderous lies allows

---

[491] From President's Buchanan's State of the Union Address, 03 December 1860, teachingamericanhistory.org/library/document/1860-state-of-the-union-address (Accessed 12/12/2017). President Buchanan was following the thoughts of Hamilton as expressed in the *Federalist Papers* Number 28, "It may safely be received as an axiom in our political system, that the State governments will, in all possible contingencies, afford complete security against invasions of the public liberty by the national authority."

[492] The original Constitution established the limits of federal powers. Such powers were called "enumerated" powers. If a power was not "enumerated" or listed in the Constitution's plain language, then the federal government had NO constitutional authority to exercise such powers. The authority for the federal government to engage in an invasion of a Sovereign State is NOT listed except upon the application of that State's governing body.

the Yankee Empire to hide the truth about its aggressive war against the people of the Confederate States of America. There are four primary lies that demonstrate how effective Yankee propaganda was and still is! Those lies are (1) the South started the war by firing the *first* shot at Fort Sumter, (2) the evil South intentionally caused the death of Yankee prisoners-of-war at the Southern POW camp at Andersonville, Georgia, (3) Confederate General Nathan Bedford Forrest deliberately engaged in a massacre of black Union troops at Fort Pillow, and, (4) the war was fought over slavery.

Fort Sumter

The *New York Herald* openly declared in its April 5, 1861, edition, some seven days BEFORE the April 12, 1861, firing on Fort Sumter, that Lincoln's administration was attempting to maneuver the Confederate States into a position in which it would have to "fire the first shot" in order to defend the South from invasion:

> We have no doubt Mr. Lincoln wants the [Confederate] Cabinet in Montgomery [Montgomery, Alabama—the provisional capitol of the Confederate States] to take the initiative by capturing ... forts in its waters, for it would give him the opportunity of throwing the responsibility of commencing hostilities.[493]

In the following issue, April 7th, the same paper declared:

> Unless Mr. Lincoln's administration makes the first demonstration and attack, President Davis says there will be no bloodshed. With Mr. Lincoln's administration, therefore, rests

---

[493] Stokes, "Fort Sumter and the Siege of Charleston," *To Live or Die in Dixie*, 165-166.

the responsibility of precipitating a collision, and the fearful events of protracted war.[494]

The "secret" plot to invade the South had moved from mere rumor to open discussion in Northern newspapers. For example, the New Jersey *American Standard* in its April 12th edition proclaimed that Lincoln and company were attempting to conceal their true intention by pretending to be seeking a peaceful solution while actually preparing for an aggressive war of invasion:

> The measure is a disingenuous feint ... a mere decoy to draw the first fire from the people of the South, which act by the pre-determination of the government [U.S. federal government] is to be the pretext for letting the horrors of war. It dare not itself fire the first shot or draw the first blood and is now seeking by a mean artifice to transfer the odium of doing so to the Southern Confederacy.[495]

By the time the previous words were published in New York and New Jersey, Lincoln and his cronies had already equipped and dispatched a Yankee invasion armada to Charleston, South Carolina. On April 8, 1861, Governor Pickens of South Carolina received a message from Lincoln that an armed naval flotilla would reinforce Fort Sumter by force if necessary. Fortunately for the South, a gale prevented the Yankee invasion fleet from attempting to enter Charleston Harbor. It was clear, to those who wanted to know the truth, what Lincoln and his cronies had done. After word reached the North about the South's retaking its fort in Charleston Harbor, several papers acknowledged as much:

---

[494] *Ibid.*, 166.
[495] *Ibid.*, 167.

- April 13, *The Providence Daily Post* [Rhode Island]; "We think the reader will perceive why Mr. Lincoln saw an opportunity to inaugurate civil war without appearing in the character of an aggressor.[496]
- April 16, the *Buffalo Daily Courier* [New York]; "The affair at Fort Sumter, it seems to us, has been planned as a means by which the war feeling at the North should be intensified, and the [Lincoln] administration thus receive popular support for its [war] policy...War is inaugurated, and the design of the [Lincoln] administration is accomplished.[497]

The truth is that it was Lincoln and his cronies who initiated the War. Unfortunately, the victor writes the history and uses his political and military power to enforce his version of the victor's war of aggression. The victor writes the history while the people of the captive nation must suffer insults and slander in meek, docile silence in order to maintain their status as pacified subjects of the Empire. One can only wonder when the people of the South will ask at last: "What price for my soul?"

Andersonville - Major Wirz

In any Yankee portrayal of the so-called "Civil War," one can count on an emotionally driven account of the alleged distress, starvation, torture, and death suffered by Yankee prisoners-of-war at the hands of evil, criminal, and sadistic Southerners. Period photographs of starving Yankee prisoners will naturally draw the desired emotional response from the audience/readers. Of course, because the South is a captive nation, it

---

[496] *Ibid.*

[497] *Ibid.*

has no means to respond effectively to such slanderous "continue-to-hate-the-South" Yankee propaganda. Yet facts, though suffocated by overwhelming and endless tidal waves of slanderous anti-South propaganda, tell a radically different story! The death rate in Northern POW camps was 12%, while the death rate in Southern camps was 15%. Yankee propagandists (also known as historians) claim that this 3% difference indicates that the South was *intentionally* starving and otherwise mistreating Northern prisoners. But during World War II, the death rate in German POW camps was 9%. What does this 3% difference between the German World War II death rate of 9% and the U.S. "Civil War" POW 12% death rate indicate? It takes more than merely looking at a set of numbers to obtain the whole picture of what was happening to prisoners both North and South during the War for Southern Independence. But the numbers of deaths in Northern vs. Southern POW camps will make evident the startling contrast between Yankee lies and Southern truth. But of course, a captive nation is never allowed to tell the truth about the invasion, conquest, and occupation of its formerly free country!

The one fact that is never told by Yankee propagandists is that the Yankee Empire's Anaconda Plan[498] was established to starve the South's civilian population into submission. In conjunction with the Anaconda Plan, invading Yankee armies were ordered to destroy Southern food production equipment and draft animals necessary to raise food crops. This caused major malnutrition and starvation among the Southern

---

[498] Yankee General Winfield Scott's Anaconda Plan was enacted to strangle the South *via* a total blockade of all Southern ports. The blockade included food and medical supplies. The blockade, plus the North's intentional effort to destroy all food production capabilities in the South, caused mass starvation among the South's civilian population as well as a severe shortage of food for Confederate soldiers and prisoners.

civilian population.[499]   Day to day life, including commerce and agricultural activities, continued in the North uninterrupted by the War. The North had plenty of food and other resources that could have been provided to Confederate POWs. But the Yankee Empire refused to supply adequate food, clothing, medicine, or housing for Southern prisoners in Northern POW camps. It should also be recalled that Southern prisoners, coming from the warm South, were not acclimated to the extremely harsh Northern winters and did not have adequate clothing to protect their bodies from the harsh Northern winter. This, plus the Yankee Empire's desire to exterminate as many Southerners as possible,[500] explains the high death rate in Northern POW camps—most of these deaths were preventable! The number of Southerners who died in Yankee POW camps was 26,436 while the number of Yankees who died in Southern POW camps was 22,576—thus, 3,860 more Southerners died in Yankee POW camps than did Yankee prisoners who died in Southern POW camps! Some Northern POW camps had low death rates, but most did not. For example:

- Elmira, New York POW camp death rate = 33%
- Alton, Illinois POW camp death rate = 21%
- Camp Butler Illinois POW camp death rate = 20%
- Camp Morton, Indiana POW camp death rate = 17%

---

[499] For discussion on the use of starvation as a Yankee technique to depopulate the South, see Kennedy & Kennedy, *Punished With Poverty*, 77.

[500] See "extermination" & "de-population" as per the index in Kennedy & Kennedy, *Punished With Poverty*.

- Fort McHenry Maryland POW camp death rate = 0.6% [501]

It should be noted that Fort McHenry POW camp was located in a Southern state that had been illegally invaded and occupied by Lincoln at the outbreak of the War. Fort McHenry is where, during the War of 1812, Francis Scott Key observed the British bombardment and composed the *Star-Spangled Banner* which was set to music and became the United States national anthem. It is also the Yankee Empire's POW camp in which Francis Scott Key's *grandson* (a civilian) was held as a political prisoner by Lincoln—such is the tragic absurdity of Lincoln's war to "save the Union."[502]

A Northerner who had been an inmate at the Southern POW camp in Andersonville noted:

> Of the thirteen prisoners that Wirz [Confederate Major Henry Wirz commander of the Andersonville POW camp] was charged with murdering on his own personal account, not the name of a victim was testified to and not a solitary one of them has been since that time! ... The dates of the alleged assaults, the facts down to the most minute particular were testified to with exactness, but in every case the most important thing—the name—was wanting.[503]

Another former POW from Andersonville, Lt. James M. Page, offered to testify on behalf of Major Wirz, but the United States military court never allowed him to testify. He was so outraged at the injustice done by

---

[501] Data collected and published as *The Confederate Handbook*, by Colonel Robert C. Woods of New Orleans, Louisiana, circa 1900.

[502] Kennedy, *Rekilling Lincoln*, 249-261.

[503] As cited in Kennedy & Kennedy, *Was Jefferson Davis Right?*, 132-133.

the United States to his former enemy, Major Wirz, that he wrote a book "in the interest of truth and fair play" defending the actions of Major Wirz at Andersonville. In his book, Page explained that the high death rate (some estimate it to be as high as 29%) at Andersonville was primarily the fault of the Yankee Empire. "...the Federal authorities failed to exercise a humane policy in the exchange of those captured in battle."[504] Lincoln and Grant both rejected the policy of prisoner exchange that had been established early in the war. There were two main reasons why the Yankee Empire did not want to engage in prisoner exchange—even when the South offered to exchange at a rate of multiple Yankee prisoners for one Southern prisoner. Lincoln and his military and political cronies opposed exchange because (1) when a Southern prisoner was exchanged, he typically rejoined his military unit, but (2) when a Northern prisoner was exchanged, he rarely rejoined his military unit, and when at home, he would tell the truth about how determined the Southern people were to be free of Yankee domination. This inconvenient truth would cause great political trouble for the Lincoln administration and the Republican Party in upcoming elections. Lincoln felt that it was better to let Northern soldiers die of Northern-induced starvation, caused by the North's Anaconda Plan, than to allow Southern prisoners of war to rejoin their units or to allow Northern POWs to go home where they would tell their Northern friends and neighbors the truth about Lincoln's war of aggression.

After the War, the Yankee Empire tried Major Wirz for war crimes. The Yankee Empire's military court's trial of Major Wirz was worse than a show trial—if the truth were ever to be known, it would damn and convict the Yankee Empire of far worse crimes than that for which it

---

[504] *Ibid.*, 134.

falsely accused, convicted, and eventually hanged (lynched) Confederate Major Wirz.[505]

The treatment of enemy POWs during an ongoing war is difficult even for modern nations blessed with enormous industrial capacity. For example, during World War II, General Eisenhower ordered that food rations for German POWs be reduced by one-half. The Geneva Convention required that POWs be given the same rations as that provided to the capturing nation's soldiers. To get around this requirement, General Eisenhower changed the designation of German soldiers from POWs to Disarmed Enemy Forces and ordered that their daily food supply be cut by one-half. Conservative estimates of between 3,000 to 10,000 German POWs died as a result of starvation and lack of adequate shelter. Some have claimed that the United States intentionally caused the deaths of far more than the admitted number, but these claims have been dismissed by the Yankee Empire's "officially accepted" historians.[506]

General Forrest Massacred Black Soldiers at Fort Pillow

General Forrest was one of the most successful Confederate officers during the War for Southern Independence. To the self-proclaimed erudite and sophisticated folks of New England, Forrest represented all that was evil in the South. Forrest gained a portion of his wealth as a local slave dealer. Notice the hypocrisy of New Englanders who had gained

---

[505] *Ibid.*, 131-135.

[506] "Rheinwiesenlager," *Wikipedia*, en.wikipedia.org/wiki/Rheinwiesenlager (Accessed 08/16/2017); also see Ambrose, Stephen E., "Ike and the Disappearing Atrocities," *New York Times*, www.nytimes.com/books/98/11/22/specials/ambrose-atrocities.html (Accessed 8/16/2017).

much of their wealth engaged in the nefarious international African slave trade and were still reaping profits in that illegal trade at the outbreak of the so-called "Civil War." Also, Yankees scorned Forrest because he was uneducated having no more than a first-grade education. Yet, this unsophisticated and uneducated backwoodsman defeated every Yankee army sent to destroy him. In addition, he took his slaves to war with him, armed them, and maintained a close personal relationship with his slaves. General Forrest was often a target of Yankee Yellow Journalists because of the embarrassment he caused as a result of his success against better-equipped and more numerous Yankee armies. All manner of crimes would be attributed to him—primarily to distract from the utter failure of much larger, better equipped, Yankee armies commanded by highly educated Yankee Generals—Yankee Generals who were always unable to defeat General Forrest. The Battle of Fort Pillow became, in past and current Yankee thinking, the centerpiece of Yankee "fake news" against General Forrest.

Fort Pillow was a Yankee fort on the Mississippi River above Memphis, Tennessee. It was commanded by a second or third-rate Yankee officer who had a complement of black and white Yankee troops under his command. Local ladies from the area around Fort Pillow pleaded with General Forrest to reduce the fort because the undisciplined and intoxicated[507] troops from the fort had engaged in all manner of harassments and crimes against innocent women and children. General Forrest, always anxious for the protection of innocent women and

---

[507] Open barrels of whisky were found inside the fort by Confederate troops during the assault. Confederate officers immediately destroyed the contents for fear of what would happen if their troops began to "enjoy" the intoxicating liquor. For an excellent defense of General Forrest at Fort Pillow, see Seabrook, Lochlainn, *A Rebel Born, A defense of Nathan Bedford Forrest* (Franklin, TN: Sea Raven Press, 2010), 367-409.

children, decided to reduce the fort. After surrounding the fort, Forrest demanded its surrender. The Yankee officer[508] in command of Fort Pillow refused to surrender—perhaps he was relying on the promise of a Yankee gunboat captain[509] to support him if Forrest attacked the fort. In the attack, approximately 40% of the Yankee troops were killed. Some have claimed that 60% of the black Union soldiers were killed—this gave rise to the Yellow Journalists' claim that General Forrest had ordered a "massacre" of black Union troops during the battle. Recall that the U.S. Sixth Cavalry in one action against the Confederates in Virginia suffered a causality rate of 61%, as previously noted.

At no time during the battle did any Yankee officer offer to surrender Fort Pillow. At no time did any Yankee lower the United States flag flying over the fort—lowering the flag is an internationally recognized signal of surrender. The lanyard holding the Yankee flag to the flagpole was cut by a Confederate officer after the fort had been evacuated by the Yankees. With the U.S. (Yankee) flag removed, a general halt to the fighting began. Yankee troops had evacuated the fort, arms in hand, and fled toward the river and the promised safety of the Yankee gunboat. In their retreat from the fort, the Yankee troops unknowingly placed themselves between Confederate troops on each side of the road leading from the fort toward the river. Most of the Yankee casualties occurred at this point. After the battle, a great number of weapons were picked up at this point and at the river bank. Troops, retreating with arms in hand, cannot be viewed as having "surrendered" but are still hostile combatants. The promise of

---

[508] Major Booth was an alias. His real name was George H. Lanning. See Mitcham, *Bust Hell Wide Open*, 178-179. Booth was dead when the demand for surrender was received. The rejection of the surrender demand was done while the fort was commanded by Major Bradford.

[509] Yankee gunboat Captain James Marshall of the U.S. gunboat *New Era*.

"support" from the Yankee gunboat was broken as soon as it appeared that Forrest would capture Fort Pillow. The Yankee gunboat steamed away from the fort and out of range of Confederate cannons and snipers. Many Yankee casualties resulted from troops drowning as they attempted to hide in the turbulent waters of the Mississippi River. The fort's Yankee commanding officer was located after the battle "chin deep" in the Mississippi River—attempting to hide from General Forrest! The real culprit—the one responsible for the numerous deaths of Yankee troops—was the captain of the Yankee gunboat. Even after the battle was over and while under a white flag signaling a truce between Confederate and Yankee forces, the Yankee gunboat captain refused to come to shore to aid the wounded. He simply steamed up river and left his wounded black and white comrades to their fate. Yellow Journalists were kept busy slandering General Forrest by accusing him of orchestrating a massacre at Fort Pillow while ignoring the total incompetence of the fort's commanding officer and the refusal of the Yankee gunboat captain to fulfill his promise to "support" the fort if Forrest attacked.

It is interesting to note that many Confederate units suffered casualty rates higher than 60% and no one would use such data as evidence of an intentional Yankee massacre of Confederate troops. Also, the treatment of Confederate deserters found inside Fort Pillow indicates that if Forrest had desired to kill all black or white troops, he certainly had the means and opportunity to do so. Of the 64 Confederate deserters found hiding in Fort Pillow, 47 were executed—a rate of 73%! [510]

As a result of the hysteria trumped up by Yankee Yellow Journalists and as a way to hide Yankee military incompetence, the Yankee Empire's Congress attempted to charge General Forrest with "war crimes." Despite

---

[510] Mitcham, *Bust Hell Wide Open*, 185.

all the "fake news" and perjury—some of which was so bad that it became humorous—the Yankee Senate Committee could not find sufficient evidence to support the allegation of "war crimes." During the testimony before a U.S. Senate Committee hearing the matter, two Union soldiers who were present during the battle testified on behalf of General Forrest! Both Union soldiers were black. Private Ellis Falls testified that Forrest had commanded his men to "stop fighting" when it seemed to be getting out of control. The second black Union soldier, Private Major [511] Williams, testified that he heard Confederate troops yell out during the battle that General Forrest did not want black troops killed, but they were to be returned to their owners.[512] With such testimony, the U.S. Senate Committee took Forrest off its list of war criminals.[513] Yet, even to this day, General Nathan Bedford Forrest is branded as a war criminal and hater of all black people.

It should be noted that for a man (General Forrest) who is charged as being an evil Southern racist who hated blacks, it is surprising that his slaves would follow him to war, serve *under arms* with him, and often serve as his bodyguard. If Forrest was the evil racist man that Yankees claimed, then why did his slaves not kill him, and become heroes in the Yankee press? His black troops were some of his most loyal troops. After months of service, General Forrest, at his own personal expense, gave all of his slaves their freedom! He told them that as free men they could remain with the army or leave—the vast majority remained with General Forrest; those who elected to leave simply went back to their Southern

---

[511] "Major" was his name, not an indication of military rank.

[512] Seabrook, *A Rebel Born*, 404-405.

[513] Reports of Committees of the Senate of the United States, p. 27, as cited by Lochlainn, *A Rebel Born*, 404.

homes! Such inconvenient facts are never allowed to be published in the Yankee Empire's officially sanctioned narrative of the so-called "Civil War." The reason is very simple—the truth would destroy the Yankee Empire's claim of moral supremacy and legitimacy.

The War was Fought Over Slavery

In 1968, the local daily paper in Vicksburg, Mississippi, carried a report about a group of Norwegian tourists who traveled to Vicksburg to visit the local "Civil War" battlefield. These foreign tourists described the war of 1861-1865 as "America's Slave War." Even in 1968, it was apparent to any Southerner who took notice that the Yankee Empire had won the propaganda war against the South. Unfortunately, too many Southerners never took notice, and thus today, we see the toadies of the Yankee Empire destroying monuments to Confederate veterans all across the South. This ongoing campaign of anti-South cultural genocide was made possible by the South's own pacified people. Pacified Southerners cannot bring themselves to admit that their Confederate ancestors were fighting for freedom and the nation fighting to prevent their freedom was the United States of America. To do so would call into question whether or not the conquered people of the South are free today! The obvious answer is that Southerners do not live under a government ordered upon their free and unfettered consent—therefore they are not free. Pacified Southerners dare not ask questions about "freedom" because the answer would be personally embarrassing. It would cause them to admit that they, as pacified Southerners, are acting as protectors and agents of the very Empire that destroyed Southern freedom and reduced every successive generation of Southerners to subjects of the Yankee Empire. Because pacified Southerners refuse to take the bold stand of declaring the War for Southern Independence as a war for Freedom—the Yankee Empire's propagandists have had a free hand in labeling the war as a war to end slavery. The Yankee Empire's propagandists are free to claim that they, the aggressors, were actually fighting for freedom! *As bad as this Yankee lie is—it is not as bad as the cowardly attitude of pacified Southerners who are afraid to boldly proclaim the truth.* Their allegiance is not to the truth about our Southern heritage but to the flag of the Yankee Empire—although, to be fair, most pacified Southerners live in a fantasy world in which they dutifully pledge allegiance, thinking all the while that they are pledging allegiance to the original American Republic of Sovereign States. In reality, the constitutionally limited republic established by America's founding fathers no longer exists! Pacified Southerners have unwittingly become "useful fools"[514] that the Yankee Empire depends upon for its continued existence. Absent the benefits bestowed upon the Yankee Empire by pacified Southerners—the Yankee Empire would lose its false claim of legitimacy and eventually expire.[515]

The self-righteous and cunning Yankee informs the world that they were fighting to free the slaves and the world has accepted the Yankee's false narrative. If freeing slaves had been their motive for war then, it should be evident in the legislation passed by the Yankee Empire's Congress in 1861 immediately after it was relieved of the presence of Southern Senators and Representatives in the U.S. Congress. Shortly after the election of Lincoln, Southern Senators and Representatives from South Carolina and States in the Gulf South [516] withdrew from the Yankee Congress. Shortly after these Southern States seceded from the Yankee Union, they met and acceded to a new union thereby forming the Confederate States of America. As Southerners left the U.S. Congress, the Yankee advocates of protective tariffs seized the opportunity and enacted

---

[514] "Useful fools" is derived from "useful idiots" attributed to Lenin describing capitalists who were willing to help the communist revolution even though it would ultimately mean the destruction of capitalism.

[515] At some point pacified Southerners become Southern collaborators who actively aid in the oppression of their own people.

[516] Gulf States: Mississippi, Alabama, Louisiana, Georgia, Texas, and Florida.

the Morrill Tariff of 1861. The Act was signed into law two days before Lincoln took office. The Provisional Congress of the Confederate States of America met in Montgomery, Alabama, on February 4, 1861. Seven Southern States were represented. So, the first act of the Yankee Empire's Congress was not to free the slaves that were still held in bondage in the Northern States but to seek additional protection for the commerce and industry of the North's crony capitalists. Slavery was not ignored by the Northern-controlled Congress. The Yankee Empire's Congress authored and submitted to the states a constitutional amendment dealing with slavery. "On March 3, 1861, Congress [U.S.] passed a proposed amendment to the Constitution making it *impossible ever to amend the Constitution* to give Congress power over slavery in the States. Lincoln approved the amendment in his first Inaugural Address."[517] The purpose of the amendment was to lure the Southern States back into the Union with the assurance that the Yankee Empire would protect the South's slave property. The Yankee Empire did not care about the condition of black slaves—they wanted the South (more specifically they wanted the South's wealth) back in *their* Union in order for them to force Southerners to continue paying tribute to the South's Northern masters in the form of high tariffs. Not a single Southern State took the "generous" offer. Why? Because Southerners were not fighting for slavery, they were fighting for their freedom!

At this point the sycophants and propagandists for the Yankee Empire will cry out, "How could the South be fighting for freedom while holding so many humans in slavery?" The question alone is usually all that is necessary to have pacified Southerners scurrying away desperately looking for politically correct cover. The simple truth is that the Southern

---

[517] Livingston, Donald, "Why the War Was Not About Slavery," *To Live or Die in Dixie*, 3.

States in 1861 were no different than the Thirteen American Colonies in 1776, all of whom had laws allowing for slavery, and the New England states were actively engaged in the nefarious African slave trade! Which Americans (Northern or Southern) were truly attempting to end slavery? Prior to 1830, the South was the leader in the American abolition movement. The Southern abolition movement was halted, not by Southerners, but by Northern extremists who were promoting a Haiti style slave revolt down South that would have included the mass murder of thousands of white Southerners—men, women, children, and infants, both slave owners and non-slave owners alike.[518] One of the many ironies of Southern history is that the effort to emancipate slaves was at first a Southern effort in which Southerners personally paid the cost of emancipation but after the radicals of New England of the John Brown school, took over the abolitionist movement in the North—the Southern effort to provide freedom to slaves in the South was put on hold. But again, as a conquered and captive nation, the South has had no way of telling its side of this story—at least in a manner that would allow the South to compete against the ongoing tidal wave of vicious anti-South narrative promoted by the Yankee Empire's propagandists.

The "secret" Yankee economic motivation[519] for war was clearly explained in the United States House of Representatives on July 10, 1861, by Ohio Democrat Congressman Clement Vallandigham:

---

[518] Kennedy & Kennedy, *Punished With Poverty*, 41-50; also see, Robertson, Henry O., "In the Habit of Acting Together," *The Emergence of the Whig Party in Louisiana, 1828-1840* (Lafayette, LA: Center for Louisiana Studies, University of Louisiana, 2007), 43-45.

[519] The issue of slavery should be looked upon as a smokescreen behind which the Yankee Empire's ruling class and its crony capitalist allies could hide while pursuing their true, greedy motives for an aggressive, imperialistic war against a peaceful neighbor.

...the Confederate Congress adopted our old tariff of 1857 ... fixing their rate of duties at five, fifteen and twenty percent lower than ours. The result was ... trade and commerce ... began to look to the South ... Threatened thus with the loss of both political power and wealth ... both New England—and Pennsylvania ... demanded, now, coercion and civil war, with all its horrors.... The subjugation of the South, and the closing up of her ports— first, by force, in war, and afterward, by tariff laws, in peace, was deliberately resolved upon by the East.[520]

It was not just Southerners or "copperhead" Northern Democratic politicians who understood that the Southern people were being exploited by Northern political policy that favored Northern crony capitalists. A month after Lincoln's election, the December 10, 1860, issue of the *Daily Chicago Times* confessed that:

> The South has furnished near three-fourths of the entire exports of the country ... we have a tariff that protects our [Northern] manufacturers from thirty to fifty percent and enables us to consume large quantities of Southern cotton, and to compete in our whole home market with the skilled labor of Europe. *This operates to compel the South to pay an indirect bounty to our skilled labor, of millions annually.*[521] [Emphasis added]

A resident of Charleston, South Carolina, of English birth, wrote back to family in England explaining how the Northern political and commercial elites were exploiting the people of the South:

> Millions upon millions have the South unjustly paid under the Northern protective tariff system. With secession, this tribute

---

[520] Vallandigham as cited by DiLorenzo, *The Real Lincoln*, 241-242.

[521] *Ibid.*, 242.

payment ceases. There is no wonder that the Northerners are union men and denounce the impropriety of secession. It occasions them pecuniary loss.[522]

As we have already pointed out, the only principle that Yankee dollar-worshipers consistently adhere to is the principle of Yankee profits—regardless of how crooked or bloody the pathway to Yankee profits might be. But if this truth is allowed to become worldwide public knowledge it would bring to an end the Yankee Empire's false claims of legitimacy.

The Yankee Empire unleashed the "dogs of war" upon a people who had formerly been their countrymen. The Yankee Empire relished in the opportunity to *exterminate* the people of the South and to implement their *final solution*[523] to the political might of the South that had for so long stood in the way of their vision of a worldwide, commercial, financial, and military empire. The dollar-worshipers of Yankeedom suffered no misgivings about initiating an aggressive war against their smaller neighbor, a democratically elected government, and a people who only asked to be left alone to live under a government ordered upon the free and unfettered consent of the Southern people. But for the Yankee Empire, it was obvious that profits trump principles, an aggressive invasion was initiated, a free people were conquered, and a captive nation today lies under the foot of the Yankee Empire.

In 1875, ten years after the surrender of the Confederate military, Massachusetts historian Charles Bancroft admitted that money, profits,

---

[522] Stokes, "Fort Sumter and the Siege of Charleston," *To Live or Die in Dixie*, 173.

[523] For an account of General Sherman using the phrase "final solution" with reference to Native Americans and by inference to Confederates, see: www.lewrockwell.com/2003/02/thomas-dilorenzo/what-lincolns-army-did-to-the-indians (Accessed 10/29/2017).

and greed were the true motives for the war against the South when he declared:

> While so gigantic a war was an immense evil; to allow the right of peaceable secession would have been ruin to the enterprise and thrift of the industrious laborer, and keen-eyed businessman of the North. It would have been the greatest calamity of the age. War was less to be feared.[524]

This is the reason that, on three separate occasions, when Lincoln was asked, "Why not let the South go?" he responded: "Let the South go? Let the South go! Where then shall we get our revenue?" Or as the *Chicago Times* warned in its December 10, 1860, issue "Let the South adopt the free-trade system [Northern] commerce must be reduced to less than half what it is now."[525] As Yankee Governor Parker of New Jersey noted in 1863 "Slavery is no more the cause of this war than gold is the cause of robbery."[526] "Follow the money" is always good advice when looking for the real reason for aggressive war.

---

[524] Bancroft, as cited in Kennedy & Kennedy, *Punished With Poverty*, 79.

[525] *Ibid.*

[526] *Op cit.*

Major Heinrich "Henry" Hartmann Wirz, C.S.A. | Courtesy LOC

Post-war, the Yankee Empire conducted war crimes trial against Major Wirz, falsely accusing him of intentionally causing the deaths of Yankee prisoners at the POW camp in Andersonville, Georgia. The trial was a "show-trial." Major Wirz's attorneys resigned from the defense due to the Yankee Court's biased treatment of their client. False testimony was purchased and used against Major Wirz. He was offered a chance to avoid the death penalty if he would falsely accuse Confederate President Jefferson Davis of being part of a conspiracy to kill Yankee POWs. Major Wirz refused and was hanged by the victorious Yankee Empire.[527] Note the gallows used to "lynch" Major Wirz and the U.S.A. Capitol Dome in the background. Major Wirz, a loyal Southerner, was born in Zurich, Switzerland. | Courtesy LOC

---

[527] Kennedy & Kennedy, *Was Jefferson Davis Right?*, 131-135.

Chapter 10: Yankee Empire Plunders a Conquered South

AT THE VERY BEGINNING OF THE WAR of Southern Independence, Yankee Congressman Thaddeus Stevens (Republican from Pennsylvania and Chairman of the powerful Ways and Means Committee) declared that Yankee Generals who were invading the Confederate States of America had "a sword in one hand and shackles in the other."[528] After their successful invasion, conquest, and occupation of the Confederacy, Representative Stevens announced the Republican plan to treat the South as a "conquered province" and to confiscate its property.[529] This was not the ranting of one lone Republican maniac. A leading Northern newspaper called for terrible retribution against Southerners: "We mean to conquer them, subjugate them.... Never would traitors be permitted to return to peaceful and contented homes; instead they must find poverty at their firesides and see privation in the anxious eyes of mothers and the rags of their children."[530]

---

[528] Bowers, *The Tragic Era*, 72.

[529] Stevens, Thaddeus, "Reconstruction," *A Just and Lasting Peace*, John D. Smith, ed. (New York: Signet Classics, 2013), 71, 77.

[530] As cited by Simkins, *A History of the South*, 219.

The Southern People—From Riches to Rags

As documented in *Punished With Poverty-the Suffering South*[531] during the early 1700s, the Southern Colonies were the wealthiest section of the American colonies. This wealth was not due to the plantation system alone but also included the wealth-generating capacity of thousands of cattle and hogs belonging to the plain folk of the old South. These vast herds required little tending while they freely roamed the South's vast open range which consisted primarily of forest that provided ample (free) food for hogs and upland savannas that provided ample (free) grazing for cattle. This Southern wealth included not only financial comfort but also allowed for a leisurely lifestyle enjoyed by antebellum Southerners. Even slaves in such a society were able to participate in the benefits afforded by living in a society that had a generally higher standard of living and participating in that leisure-oriented lifestyle.[532] This shocking fact (shocking to those who only know the South as depicted by the Yankee Empire's propagandists) is evidenced by the fact that slaves in the South had a longer life expectancy than white workers in the North or in Europe.[533] Other studies have shown that slaves in the South worked fewer hours per year than Northern white farmers. According to the 1850 census of the 569,000 farms in the South, only 30% owned one or more slaves.[534] A study of the workload of slaves in

---

[531] Kennedy & Kennedy, *Punished With Poverty*.

[532] This is not an attempt to justify human slavery but to contrast slavery as practiced in the South with slavery as practiced in the large, industrialized, absentee-landlord plantations of the Caribbean.

[533] Fogel & Engerman, *Time on the Cross*, 126.

[534] McDonald & McWhiney, "The South from Self-Sufficiency to Peonage: An Interpretation," *The American Historical Review* (Vol. 85, No. 5. Dec. 1980), 1096.

Alabama demonstrated that if one assumes that slaves did all the work necessary for Alabama's agriculture production (an absurd assumption considering the number of white farmers who owned no slaves) the total hours per year required would be 147 ten-hour days or 1,470 hours per slave per year.[535] A typical U.S. work year in 2017 is 2080 hours. When comparing the workload of Northern farmers to that of Southern farmers, we find that the Northern farmer typically worked 3,100 hours per year while the typical Southern farmer worked only 1,800 hours per year.[536] It should be pointed out that these calculations do not include the hours per year worked by the plain folk of the old South. They were primarily herdsmen who engaged in relatively very little commercial farming. A review of the workload of four, typical, plain folk families revealed that "each of the twenty-three working age family members ... would have had to work only about 423 hours or approximately eleven forty-hour weeks, per year."[537] Working eleven weeks in a 52-week year leaves a lot of leisure time. A materialistic nation, such as the Yankee Empire, values work because it produces greater acquisition of material goods (wealth for wealth's sake), whereas a spiritual or a leisure-oriented society, such as the antebellum South, values work only as far as it provides for leisure. The spiritual South worked to enjoy life while the materialistic North worked to acquire wealth. The wealth of the South that provided for a leisurely lifestyle vanished with the advent of Yankee invasion, conquest, occupation, and exploitation.

---

[535] *Ibid.*, 1098.

[536] *Ibid.*, 1100.

[537] *Ibid.*, 1103.

The Yankee Empire's Destructive Reign of Terror

As a result of the Yankee Empire's invasion of the Confederate States of America, the people of the South suffered (excluding the value of slaves) between $1 Billion and $1.5 Billion of private and public property destroyed by marauding Yankee armies.[538] This estimation of property value destroyed by the invader does not include the investment value of slaves—to be addressed later. The Southern property destroyed by Lincoln's war of conquest would be equal to between $27 Billion to $41 Billion in 2015 dollars.[539] During the Yankee Empire's campaign to "free the slaves and save the Union," over 10,000 miles of Southern railroads were destroyed.[540] It just so happened that these emerging Southern railroads had been a key competitor of Northern railroads, especially as it relates to the location of the transcontinental railroad.[541] In any area of the South where potential industrial competitors to Northern industry were found, those factories or industries were destroyed entirely—thus assuring complete Yankee monopoly of textile, iron, railroad, and other commercial activities after their conquest of the South. Prior to the war, a major textile industry was emerging in parts of the South which posed a competitive threat to New England textile mills. It must be pointed out

---

[538] Hummel, *Emancipating Slaves, Enslaving Free Men*, 322.

[539] Calculated at CPI Inflation Calculator, www.in2013dollars.com/1860-dollars-in-2015?amount=1 (Accessed 12/24/2016). Note: This takes into consideration only the inflation factor over time. It does not take into consideration of the opportunity cost suffered had the same amount of capital been invested and allowed to grow over an equal period of time.

[540] Kennedy & Kennedy, *Punished With Poverty*, 98.

[541] *Ibid.*, 97-8; also see, Graham, John R., *Principles of Confederacy* (Salt Lake City, UT: Northwest Publishing, 1990), 657, fn. 14.

that these New England textile mills were financed in part or completely by the capital gained from the New England states' participation in the nefarious, international, African slave trade. Yankees were also made rich by protective tariffs and the milling of slave-grown cotton. But the Yankee Empire never allows free competition if it can destroy it by military or other despicable means. As noted previously, profit is the only enduring principle of Yankeedom.

In Roswell, Georgia, Yankees not only destroyed the mills but depopulated the area by capturing the civilian population and sending them out of the Confederacy to be sold as indentured servants! Family members were separated, and most were never reunited.542 Such are the workings of empires. They do not invade a peaceful country to improve the life of the people of the invaded nation—the Yankee Empire is no different than any other empire—empires invade in order to exploit coveted resources and to create a new group of subjects

Yankee invaders destroying Southern railroads | Courtesy LOC

---

542 Kennedy & Kennedy, *The South Was Right!*, 122-124.

that the empire can use as a base of taxes, tribute, and eventually the sons of the impoverished captive nation will volunteer to become cannon fodder for the Empire's imperial armies. Armies that in modern times engage in endless "no-win" wars that achieve death and destruction, leaving wounded soldiers to return home who are quickly forgotten by those politicians that sent them to war. This scenario has often been described as "rich man's war, poor man's fight."

Confederate General Patrick Cleburne, an Irish-born Southerner, understood how subjugation by an empire would cause the sons of the captive nation to join the empire's military. With subjugation comes poverty. To escape the poverty of his native land, Ireland, Cleburne joined the British 41st Regiment of Foot at the age of 18. Starvation was rampant in Ireland at the time. In the winter of 1845-1846, there were 5,000 beggars in County Cork, Ireland, suffering a death rate of 100 per week.[543] Serving in the empire's military is often one of the few options for the impoverished sons of a captive nation. The private soldiers in Cleburne's British Regiment were composed of poor Irish lads.[544] Confederate General Patrick Cleburne learned by personal experience the reality of being subjugated by an empire. This is why he warned the Southern people:

> Every man should endeavor to understand the meaning of subjugation before it is too late.... It is said slavery is all we are fighting for.... Even if this were true, which we deny, slavery is not all our enemies are fighting for. It is merely the pretense to establish sectional superiority and a more centralized form of

---

[543] Symonds, Craig L., *Stonewall of the West-Patrick Cleburne and the Civil War*, (Lawrence, KS: University of Kansas Press, 1997), 20.

[544] *Ibid.*, 21.

government, and to deprive us of our rights and liberties.⁵⁴⁵ [Emphasis added]

Unfortunately, his prediction has become the modern-day Southern reality. Today pacified Southerners willingly accept their assigned place as subjects of the Yankee Empire—as a result of generations of subjugation and anti-South Yankee propaganda pacified Southerners have learned to love their chains. Pacified Southerners have fulfilled Rousseau's description of the docile slave:

> Force made the first slaves, and their cowardice perpetuated the condition…. Slaves lose everything in their chains, even the desire of escaping from them: they love their servitude.⁵⁴⁶

Pacified Southerners have learned to accept their second-class political, economic, and social standing in the Yankee Empire. To the pacified Southerner, the South's poverty and political domination are "normal." But it is not normal; it is the result of the plundering, the destruction, and the continuing exploitation of the occupied South by Lincoln's Yankee Empire.

Attempts to Exterminate Black and White Southerners

From the very beginning of the Yankee Empire's quest to conquer the Confederate States of America, it was openly proclaimed by many Yankee leaders that they aimed to "exterminate" the troublesome people of the South. Representative Thaddeus Stevens (Republican from

---

⁵⁴⁵ *War of the Rebellion*: Serial 110 Page 0587 Chapter LXIV, ehistory.osu.edu/books/official-records/110/0587 (Accessed 8/10/2015).

⁵⁴⁶ From *The Social Contract* by Jean-Jacques Rousseau: https://www.bartleby.com/168/102.html (Accessed 01/21/2017).

Pennsylvania) announced their intention to "exterminate or drive out the present rebels as exiles," while military officials such as Brigadier General James H. Lane (a personal friend of Lincoln) announced, "We believe in a war of extermination."[547] Yankee Colonel Marc Mundy testified that:

> A vigorous war policy, as generally understood in the army ... means the adoption of all means not only to crush out the rebellion but *to punish indiscriminately all persons who live in a rebellious territory*.[548] [Emphasis added]

Nor was it merely junior-grade Yankee military officers who endorsed the concept of a "vigorous" war policy. Yankee General Grant declared that to accomplish the "subjugation" of the Southern people it would be necessary to destroy "their means of subsistence, withdrawing their means of cultivating their fields and in every other way possible."[549] Yankee General Sherman promised that he would retaliate against Southern civilians at a ratio of 5 to 1 for every Union man killed.[550] Both the military and political leadership at the highest level in Washington, D.C., not only endorsed but actively encouraged this genocidal warfare against innocent Southern civilians.[551]

As a result of attacks against Southern civilians and the destruction of their homes, thousands of innocent Southerners, the old, the sick, women, children, and infants, were left homeless. In the Southern States of Alabama, Mississippi, and Georgia in late 1865, there were five

---

[547] As cited in Kennedy & Kennedy, *Punished With Poverty*, 69.

[548] *Ibid.*, 76.

[549] *Ibid.*, 78.

[550] Hummel, *Emancipating Slaves, Enslaving Free Men*, 277.

[551] Kennedy & Kennedy, *The South Was Right!*, 278-294.

hundred thousand Southerners without the necessities to maintain life. Many died that winter.552 But this was part of the Yankee's plan for a "vigorous" war policy. The intention was to create a vast burden of homelessness of the South's civilian population that would require support from the Confederate government. The support provided to Southern civilians by the Confederate government would take away from resources available to the Confederate army. Lincoln and his cronies also hoped that when Southern civilians saw the fate of those who resisted Yankee invasion, it would lower their morale and willingness to continue their struggle for freedom. Homelessness and starvation became so bad that Confederate President Jefferson Davis was forced to recommend the eating of rats to avoid starvation.553 By the end of the war, there were over 200,000 homeless civilians in the South.554 It has been estimated that, if normalized for 2010 population, the total number of black and white Southern civilians who died as a result of the Yankee invasion of the Confederate States of America, would be 3.5 million deaths. These Southern deaths were the result of an aggressive "vigorous war policy" carried out by the Yankee Empire.555 This vigorous war policy was nothing less than a Southern Holocaust engineered and carried out by the Yankee Empire! But such data is seldom, if ever, fairly presented in

---

552 Fleming, *The Sequel of Appomattox*, 14.

553 Hummel, *Emancipating Slaves, Enslaving Free Men*, 279

554 *Ibid.*

555 DiLorenzo, Thomas, "The Founding Fathers of Constitutional Subversion," *Rethinking The American Union*, Donald Livingston, ed. (Gretna, LA: Pelican Publishing Co., 2013), 80. The number of civilian deaths due to direct military action is minor as compared to the civilian death due to malnutrition and disease that resulted from the intentional destruction of non-military private property and food production equipment and supplies. See Kennedy, *Uncle Seth Fought the Yankees*, 90-93.

contemporary history texts. For those who know the truth about Yankee propaganda, this is not surprising. In reality, "What passes as standard American history is really Yankee history written by New Englanders or their puppets to glorify Yankee heroes and ideals." [556]

Financial Loss Due to Yankee-imposed Emancipation of Southern Slaves

When a Southerner complains about the huge financial loss of capital investments in "slave property," he is immediately censured and branded as a greedy proponent of human bondage. And with that rebuke, the discussion is supposed to end! (This is another example of "soft" censorship the Yankee Empire imposes upon the South). But before looking at the huge capital loss suffered as a result of Yankee-imposed emancipation down South, let us first look at the manner in which the thrifty Yankees removed slavery from their fair—as in white—Northern states.

When the Thirteen American Colonies seceded from the British Empire (1776), every Colony allowed for the ownership of slaves. Indeed, the New England states became a major factor in the nefarious, international, African slave trade, while the capital they gained from this nefarious African slave trade became the very basis for their vast industrial, commercial, and financial economy. Shortly after the founding of the United States, the Northern states began seeking ways to eliminate black people from their "fair" states. Removing its black population from Northern states is an embarrassing point for Yankee propagandists, also known as establishment historians, therefore it is

---

[556] Dr. Grady McWhiney, as cited in Kennedy & Kennedy, *The South Was Right!*, 15.

seldom if ever discussed in their "official" history. One of the major reasons that Yankee propagandists fixate on slavery down South is to distract from the Yankee Empire's hideous record of slavery and racism. President John Adams, from the New England (Yankee) state of Massachusetts, plainly declared this truth. He stated that moral arguments "might" have had "some" impact on the Yankee's desire to abolish slavery in their states:

> But the *real cause* was the multiplication of laboring white people, who would no longer suffer the rich to employ these sable rivals so much to their [white people] injury.... The common people would not suffer the labor by which alone they [white people] could obtain a subsistence, to be done by slaves.[557] [Emphasis added]

John Adams, a New England Yankee and major political leader of New England, clearly states the reason for which Yankees wanted to abolish slavery *in their states*—slavery threatens the livelihood of white workers. He even admitted that if slavery had remained in their states, the whites would "have put the slaves to death, and their masters too perhaps."[558] From this freely offered confession, we see the true nature of Yankees who like to claim that they freed their slaves because slavery was immoral—implying that Southerners were immoral and therefore, required the chastening rod of Yankee invasion to correct and redeem the sinful South. Such is the hypocrisy of Yankee self-professed morality, but such hypocrisy remains concealed by the work of well-paid and rewarded Yankee propagandists.

---

[557] Adams, as cited in Kennedy & Kennedy, *Punished With Poverty*, 42.

[558] *Ibid.*, 43.

In all of the self-righteous talk of how they (Yankees) freely abolished slavery, they fail to inform the world that no law was ever passed in the North that granted freedom to a person already in slavery. The thrifty Yankee passed laws declaring children of slaves, born *after* the "freedom" legislation was passed, to be freed upon reaching a certain age—usually eighteen or twenty-one years old. In 1850, there were still over 200 slaves for life in the Yankee state of New Jersey. Under their system of emancipation, the thrifty Yankee slave owner would never lose his financial investment in a slave. Under Yankee emancipation, he would enjoy the service of all slave-born children up to the age of adulthood. The Yankee slave owner had total control of slaves born to him by his "slaves for life." Before a slave reached the age of emancipation, his owner could take him to a border state and sell him to a slave trader. The slave then would be transferred down the Ohio River to the Mississippi River to be sold to plantations down the river. Thus, the term, indicating betrayal, often used in the South of being "sold down the river."

Some Yankee states even passed laws allowing for the flogging of free blacks if they remained in their state too long.[559] Also, states such as Lincoln's home state of Illinois enacted exclusion laws to prevent free blacks from entering their states. The idea that the North was motivated by its love of the black slave is one of many Yankee myths used to hide his true love—profits! It is also used to hide his true hatred for black people.[560] This early hatred toward black people continued and was endorsed by Lincoln. Lincoln, during his seventh debate with Senator Stephen Douglas speaking in Illinois and discussing the new lands acquired by the removal of Native Americans from western lands,

---

[559] Kennedy & Kennedy, *The South Was Right!*, 75-76.

[560] Kennedy & Kennedy, *Punished With Poverty*, 80-85.

declared that "our new Territories being in such condition that white men may find a home ... as an outlet for free white people..." Lincoln received loud applause from the gathered crowd of Northerners.[561] Yet today, it is the flag and symbols of our captive nation, the Confederate States of America, that are viciously slandered by the Yankee Empire's propagandists in the press, Hollywood, and academia as being the symbol of racial hatred.

Instead of gradual or compensated[562] emancipation as practiced in the North, the Yankee Empire imposed immediate, uncompensated emancipation upon the defeated and occupied South. In so doing it caused approximately $2 Billion of capital investments in slave property to disappear overnight![563] This 1860 investment would be equal to $55 Billion in 2015.[564] No nation in the entire history of the world has been forced to endure such an instantaneous and dramatic destruction of its capital resources! The impact on the Southern economy already devastated by the Yankee Empire's illegal invasion was so pernicious that the South would never recover—to be precise—*the South will never recover as long as the South remains a captive nation.*

The Yankee Empire justifies or ignores the devastating impact of its actions by claiming that "slave owners and rebels" do not deserve

---

[561] *Ibid.*, 96, fn. 299.

[562] The United States Congress during the war emancipated all slaves in Washington, D.C., and compensated the slave owners. They also provided a cash bonus to all freed slaves, BUT in order to get the bonus, the newly freed slave had to agree to leave the United States! Kennedy & Kennedy, *Punished With Poverty*, 92.

[563] Fleming, *The Sequel of Appomattox*, 2.

[564] Calculated at CPI Inflation Calculator, www.in2013dollars.com/1860-dollars-in-2015?amount=1 (Accessed 01/21/2017).

economic consideration. But as pointed out in *Punished With Poverty—the Suffering South,* the individuals who suffered the greatest from these Yankee policies were the newly freed slaves! These were the very people whom the Yankee Empire claims it waged an aggressive war to free. The manner in which the Yankee Empire treated its newly created black clientele is evidence of the Empire's true motive for waging aggressive war. The newly freed slaves owned no real property—land. If the Yankee Empire truly loved those blacks who were formerly held in slavery, then they would have provided them with real estate rights in America by giving them ownership to land that they could cultivate and create a new life for themselves and their families. The Yankee Empire owned thousands of square miles of land in the western territories. But instead of providing it to landless former slaves, the Yankee Empire gave it to railroad companies that were busy building the transcontinental railroad. A railroad that, thanks to the Empire's extermination of the South's political power, had a very northern route! Besides, Northerners had already made it clear that they did not want blacks in their pure white states. As *New York Tribune* correspondent Shepherd Pike declared regarding what to do with blacks down South: "hem him in and coop him up" down South thereby leaving the rest of the Yankee Empire for "the white man."[565] While the Yankee nation took care to pass laws removing slavery from their state, their real aims were to reclaim their capital investments in their slaves while removing from their white society a people (blacks) with whom Northerners did not want to associate. Profit and racial hatred were the North's primary motives for wanting to remove slavery from their states—yet it is the South that is universally slandered because of "slavery and racism." It is an unfair accusation conducted with

---

[565] Pike, as cited in Kennedy & Kennedy, *Punished With Poverty*, 74.

impunity by the Yankee Empire. Why? Because captive nations have no official way to defend their people, their history and their right to be free.

The Yankee Empire's Exploitation of its Captive Nation

As soon as Southern military resistance to the Yankee Empire ended, Yankee Treasury Agents moved to the South under the pretense of confiscating "Confederate" cotton. Essentially, agents of the Yankee Empire claimed any cotton it could find as spoils of war. At least $34,000,000 worth of "Confederate" cotton was confiscated from the Southern people and shipped north as payment to the Yankee Empire for the cost of war. But in addition to the cotton confiscated and shipped to the Yankee Treasury, an even greater amount was stolen by the Yankee Empire's "Treasury Agents." The Yankee Empire's Secretary of the Treasury, Hugh McCulloch, admitted this fact when he declared, "I am sure I sent some honest cotton agents South; doubtful whether any of them remained honest long ... lawless men ... engaged in general plunder; every species of intrigue and theft were resorted to."[566] This "general plunder" represents Southern capital extorted and stolen from the beleaguered, war-weary people of the South—money that could have been used to rebuild the Southern economy. But the Yankee Empire was only interested in helping itself and its cronies—it certainly was not interested in helping Southerners who they had so recently conquered. Beginning with its conquest of the Confederate States of America and continuing today, the unacknowledged motto of the Yankee Empire is: "*Vae Victis*, Woe to the Vanquished!"

---

[566] McCulloch, as cited in Fleming, *The Sequel of Appomattox*, 9-10.

The immediate exploitation continued even after all the "Confederate" cotton was confiscated. The Yankee Empire's Congress, under Republican control, passed a cotton tax that extorted another $68,000,000 from the Southern people in three years following the South's defeat. No doubt the Republican-controlled Congress was following up on the Yankee Empire's President Johnson's declaration that "Treason is a crime and crime must be punished. Treason must be made infamous and traitors must be *impoverished*"[567] [emphasis added]. The people of the South have indeed been "punished with poverty." This "punishment" is a sad fact that the pacified South's social and political leaders cowardly ignore.

Exploitation Under the South's Bayonet Constitutions

The term "bayonet constitution" was first applied to the government the Yankee Empire imposed upon the native people of Hawaii. After agents of the Yankee Empire invaded and overthrew the legitimate government of the Kingdom of Hawaii, they imposed a new government on the people of Hawaii, one favorable to the Yankee Empire. Native Hawaiians referred to the Yankee imposed constitution as the bayonet constitution. As we have already discussed in chapter 3, this is the model the Yankee Empire first used in the South and has followed ever since. In the states of the former Confederate States of America, the Yankee Empire, via an aggressive war, denied the Southern people the right to live under a government ordered upon their free and unfettered consent. Post-war, the only way the veneer of "normal" relations could be gained was to form new state governments that would agree to be subservient to

---

[567] Johnson, as cited *Ibid.*, 73.

the ruling elite in Washington, D.C. These new state governments[568] ratified the Thirteenth Amendment that abolished slavery. Their ratifications were accepted by the Yankee Empire's Congress. The Republicans in Congress then wanted to complete its revolution by enacting the Fourteenth and Fifteenth Amendments. These amendments, for the first time in American history, were designed to place state government under federal authority. The Southern states, plus several Northern states, refused to ratify these amendments. The Republicans who controlled Congress then passed the Reconstruction Act which nullified the existence of Southern states, divided the South into five military districts, and began a military rule of their conquered Southern nation. One of the many requirements for readmission to the Union was for the state to ratify the Fourteenth and Fifteenth Amendments.[569] Thus, every Southern State would exist, henceforth, at the sufferance of the federal government (the Yankee Empire), and Southern state and federal constitutions would be the product of Yankee bayonets. Contemporary Yankee Constitutional scholars admit that these amendments "consolidated the North's victory."[570]

The complete political conversion of the United States Federal government from a Republic to a supreme, centralized federal

---

[568] All Southern state governments formed subsequent to the conquest of the Confederate States of America are in fact *illegitimate* governments, because they violate the right of the people to form a government based upon their free and unfettered consent. All subsequent state and federal governments are based not on consent but upon military and political coercion and therefore, according to the Declaration of Independence, are *illegitimate* governments.

[569] Kennedy & Kennedy, *The South Was Right!*, 167-81.

[570] Orth, John V., *The Oxford Companion to the Supreme Court of the United States*, 361.

government (the Yankee Empire) was accomplished by these two amendments and subsequent Federal Supreme Court "interpretations" incorporating their application to the once sovereign states. States are now mere provinces subservient to the central government. While the evolution of the *political* "rationale" for a supreme federal government was occurring, there was also a *social* evolution being promoted by those who supported a supreme centralized federal government—an American government similar to the authoritarian centralized nation/state of Prussia as expounded by Otto von Bismarck. Eventually, it was a successful effort to convince the American people that "their" federal government was supreme, *indivisible*, and one to which the people owed unquestioned allegiance. The most successful effort to promote this idea was led by Francis Bellamy. Bellamy, a defrocked Baptist minister from New York, who with the aid of the Grand Army of the Republic—an association composed of Union war veterans—wrote and convinced public schools to require children to recite his pledge of allegiance. He noted that his efforts to have school children repeat the pledge of allegiance was intended to reinforce everything "Lincoln and the Civil War" had accomplished.[571] In other words, the pledge of allegiance is a public affirmation of a subject's willing obedience to the newly created Yankee Empire. All of this was and is accomplished under the pretext of "patriotism." Any American who questions the "Pledge of Allegiance" is automatically branded as being "un-American" or "unpatriotic." Pacified Southerners are the most zealous defenders of the pledge to a nation (empire) that is now "indivisible." They become extremely angry when asked to point out in the Constitution or even the Declaration of Independence where it is written that the "Union" or "nation" would be

---

[571] Kennedy & Kennedy, *Was Jefferson Davis Right?*, 275.

"indivisible." Their inability to find such rationale for the pledge of allegiance only makes them angrier! They then retreat to the position of hysteria by proclaiming that anyone who rejects the vain repetition of the pledge of allegiance is "un-American, unpatriotic" and "not supporting our troops!" But again, they can cite no authority to validate their hysterical claims. Their false sense of patriotism has turned them into the Yankee Empire's "useful fools."

The Yankee Empire's imposed Reconstruction brought in a decade of state government fraud, corruption, and criminality never before or since seen on the North American continent. Great amounts of Southern state debt were amassed that had to be paid by impoverished, mostly white, Southern landowners. In one month alone, half a million acres in Mississippi were offered at tax-collectors' sales and four-fifths of the town of Greenville, Mississippi, was offered for sale due to unpaid taxes.[572] During Reconstruction, the Republicans took control of Southern state legislatures and passed huge tax increases to pay for their wasteful and corrupt spending. Republican-imposed Reconstruction in the South created a dramatic increase in the tax burden for the people of the South. During Reconstruction, the tax burden on the defeated people of the South increased 200% for Alabama and Florida; 500% for Louisiana; and 1500% for Arkansas.[573] In Louisiana, the Republican Reconstruction Governor H.C. Warmoth openly admitted that he was dishonest but "Corruption is the fashion. I do not pretend to be honest, but only as honest as anybody in politics."[574] The load of debt born by Southern

---

[572] Bowers, Claude, *The Tragic Era*, 452.

[573] Fleming, *The Sequel of Appomattox*, 231.

[574] Warmoth, as cited *Ibid.*, 225.

states as a result of Republican-inflicted Reconstruction is demonstrated by the fact that South Carolina did not repay all of its Reconstruction debt until 1952! Almost a century after the beginning of the so-called Civil War! While the impoverished people of the South were busy paying off their Reconstruction debt, the people in the rest of the Empire were busy enjoying the fruits of victory. In the meanwhile, the people of the South, both black and white, continued to suffer the Yankee Empire's punishment of poverty.

Sharecropping—a New Form of Slavery

Self-congratulating Yankees are quick to tell the world that they had to fight the "Civil War" to rid the nation of slavery. Propagandists for the Yankee Empire faithfully parrot this Yankee "truism" for public consumption all the world over. But the startling and purposely hidden truth is that the so-called "Civil War" did not end slavery! As a result of Yankee invasion and conquest of the Confederate States of America, chattel slavery morphed into a new form of bondage—one that in many ways was even harsher than antebellum chattel slavery. Pre-war chattel slavery was exchanged for post-war sharecropping slavery. Sharecropping was a form of debt peonage (debt slavery) in which landless black and white Southerners were forced to live for almost a century after the end of the war. Pre-war there were approximately 4.5 million chattel slaves in the South. Post-war there were approximately 8.5 million black *and* white sharecroppers in the South. Approximately 60% of these sharecroppers were white. Most of the whites were plain folks whose pre-war open-range, livestock-herding lifestyle had been destroyed during the war by roaming Yankee soldiers and new "enclosure" laws passed by the Yankee-imposed Republican state legislatures which ended the open range grazing in most of the South. The Yankee Empire created a system of economic stagnation and depression in the conquered South. The war had left a large percentage of

Southerners homeless. This new "peasant class"[575] had to depend upon landlords for housing and food supplies. The South's landlords also suffered economically due to the South's lack of capital. To furnish "croppers" most landlords had to borrow at high interest rates from banks. Most local banks were indebted to Northern finance houses who earned substantial profits as a result of the South's lack of capital.[576] The system of sharecropping lasted until the mid-1960s. The Yankee Empire ignored the plight of these "slaves" even when it was well known that many were suffering malnutrition and an almost entirely South-only disease associated with poor nutrition—Pellagra.[577] *Vae Victis*, Woe to the Vanquished!

---

[575] Louisiana Governor Sam Houston Jones, "The Plundered South," The Abbeville Blog, www.abbevilleinstitute.org/blog/the-plundered-south (Accessed 01/31/2018) Reprint of his speech made in 1943.

[576] Kennedy & Kennedy, *Punished With Poverty*, 179-180.

[577] For a more complete explanation of post-war sharecropping slavery, see Kennedy & Kennedy, *Punished With Poverty*, 105-119; 173-195.

Sharecropper's cabin Missouri circa 1935 | Courtesy LOC

Chapter 11: Occupation of a Once Free People

DESPITE POPULAR OPINION typically espoused by pacified Southerners, there was no Kumbaya moment when General Lee surrendered to General Grant at Appomattox Courthouse in 1865. There was no "all is forgiven, now surrender your slaves, let us have a quick group hug, and then everything will go back to normal." It did not happen! Those who controlled the Yankee Empire never intended to "go back to *normal*" after they conquered the South, and their fake issue of slavery was exhausted and no longer useful. If freeing the slaves had been the Yankee Empire's true motive for the war, then once slavery was officially abolished, going back to a *normal* American political condition would have occurred. But notice that after the "false issue" of slavery had been dealt with, *normal* business-as-usual (pre-war) government did not return to the United States. That "*normal*" would have been a return to the constitutionally limited republic with real states' rights and a constitutional amendment abolishing slavery. The political status of sovereign states would have been the same as it had been from the beginning of the United States. The fact that this did not happen is yet another important piece of evidence that supports the South's claim that the war was not about slavery but about Yankee political, economic, and social domination of the Southern people. The North's War to Prevent Southern Independence was about empire—the Yankee Empire!

The Sovereign States in 1776

When the Thirteen American colonies broke (seceded) from the British Empire, they did so as thirteen individual colonies each independent of the other. Each independent colony acted for itself. There was no mass meeting in which the aggregate American people met and voted *en masse* to establish the United States as a sovereign nation. For example, Virginia declared the "union" between Virginia and Great Britain to be "dissolved"[578] in May of 1776—well before the Joint Declaration of Independence was issued July 4, 1776.

This important point was acknowledged by Justice Samuel Chase when discussing a case before the Supreme Court.[579] He noted that "In *June*, 1776, the Convention of *Virginia formally* declared, that *Virginia* was a free, sovereign, and independent state ... [possessing] ALL the *rights* of *public* war (and all other rights of an independent nation) attached to the government of *Virginia*,"[580] [emphasis in original]. Note that this Federalist Justice acknowledged the fact that the state of Virginia was, in fact, an "independent nation," thus demonstrating the 1776 origin of State Sovereignty.

The Joint Declaration of Independence issued July 4, 1776, declared "We, therefore, the Representatives of the united States of America..." Note that while "States" is capitalized, the word "united" is in lower case. Also, note that they specifically selected the word "States" to represent the newly freed Colonies. If they had intended to create an *indivisible* Union or government that would be supreme and to which the colonies would owe their allegiance, then the word would not have been "States" but "provinces." The word "State" as used and understood in the 1700s (and in most of the world today) was synonymous with "nation." Nations are sovereign, and so are states! The fact that they used the plural "States" is also important. If they were creating a unitary nation/state—the United States of America—then the correct term would have been "united State

---

[578] Kennedy & Kennedy, *Was Jefferson Davis Right?*, 258.

[579] *Ware v. Hylton*, 3 Dallas, 199, 224 (1796).

[580] *The Debates In The Federal Convention of 1787 Which Framed The Constitution of the United States of America*, Hunt & Scott ed. (Union, NJ: The Lawbook Exchange, LTD, 1999), xxvii.

of America." The government they were creating would have been a "State" in the singular not "States" in the plural. The Declaration of Independence declares these colonies to now be "Free and Independent States." While the plural "United States" remains in vogue today, it is merely an efficient pacifier, used to calm "conservatives" and pacified Southerners. The name remains the same, the flag is essentially the same, and all the other trappings (window dressings) of the original Constitutionally limited Republic of Republics remain, but they remain for show only—to be seen and admired by the unknowing and therefore gullible. While the trappings of the old Republic remain—the essence of the original constitutionally limited republic of sovereign states is dead. The refusal of pacified Southerners to acknowledge this brutal fact is the major reason the Yankee Empire still exists and spreads its pernicious influence around the world. Pacified Southerners are actually facilitating the fulfillment of General Robert E. Lee's prediction that if the United States federal government becomes a supreme authority in the United States, then the country would become "aggressive abroad and despotic at home."[581]

Before the government of the United States under the Constitution adopted in 1787-1788 was established, the United States government existed under the Articles of Confederation (1781-1788). The very language of the Articles of Confederation (1781-1788) declares that the States of the Union (the United States of America) were "free, independent and sovereign states."[582] At no time in American history have the sovereign states voluntarily surrendered to the federal

---

[581] Gen. Lee's letter to Lord Acton, 1866 as cited in Kennedy & Kennedy, *The South Was Right!*, 41.

[582] Article II, Articles of Confederation, United States of America.

government of the United States their freedom, independence, and sovereignty. During the debates surrounding the writing of the Constitution (the Constitutional Convention of 1787) it was made clear that the states were jealously guarding their status as sovereign states. One measure proposed by the High Federalists was to give the federal government the ability to nullify state laws. In response to this High Federalist proposal, one delegate warned, "The National Legislature with such a power may enslave the States. Such an idea will never be accepted..."[583] After a vigorous debate, a vote was held on the proposal. The proposal to give the federal government the power to nullify state laws was defeated: seven states voting against, three states voting in favor, and one state divided therefore, could not cast its vote.[584] After the Constitutional Convention completed its work, the Constitution (at this point it was a mere proposal having no legal authority) was then submitted to the States for their acceptance or rejection. Again, each "free, independent, and sovereign" state acted upon its own accord. No force outside of that specific state could compel it to accept or reject the proposed Constitution. Great concern was expressed regarding the potential for the consolidation of power into the proposed federal

---

[583] *The Anti-Federalist Papers and the Constitutional Convention Debates*, Ralph Ketcham, ed. (New York: Penguin Books USA Inc., 1986), 60.

[584] *The Anti-Federalist Papers and the Constitutional Convention Debates*, 58. At the Constitutional Convention (1787) each State had one vote regardless of its size. This State equality is expressed today in the U.S. Senate where each state has two votes regardless of population. This reflects the general understanding held by America's Founding Fathers that each state was free, independent and sovereign. In international relations, unless otherwise mutually agreed upon, all nations, regardless of size, are treated as equals.

government and thereby destroying the sovereign states. One anti-Federalist noted in "Letters from the Federal Farmer," October 8, 1787:

> This consolidation of the states has been the object of several men in this country for some time past. Whether such a change can ever be effected in any manner: whether it can be effected without convulsions and civil wars; whether such a change will not totally destroy the liberties of their country time can only determine.[585]

The only way the anti-Federalists, and moderate Federalists who were in the majority in most of the states could be persuaded to vote for the adoption of the new Constitution was with the assurance of an immediate addition to the new Constitution of ten amendments. These ten, especially the Ninth and Tenth Amendments, were to become the major guarantees of State Sovereignty. These ten amendments, also known as the Bill of Rights, applied ONLY to the federal government (until the illegal, fraudulent, and unconstitutional enactment of the Fourteenth and Fifteenth amendments and subsequent Federal Supreme Court decisions). Post-war, the Federal Supreme Court used the illegitimate Fourteenth and Fifteenth amendments to apply (incorporate) the limitations of the Constitution to the once sovereign states. It was, in fact, a revolution in which the federal government (the Yankee Empire) finally gained the power to nullify state legislation—something soundly rejected by America's founding fathers in 1787 at the Constitutional Convention; in the ratification debates in various state legislatures; and, by Southerners in 1861. But today the illegitimate (unconstitutional) use of federal power is accepted as "normal" by pacified Southerners and so-called conservatives.

---

[585] *The Anti-Federalist Papers and the Constitutional Convention Debates*, 260.

Post-war, the ability of the once sovereign states to use its sovereign authority to protect its citizens from an unconstitutional exercise of federal power was lost. States' Rights—which were based on the fact that each state was sovereign and could decide for itself whether or not the federal government was functioning within the limitations of the Constitution—no longer exist. This basic American political principle of States' Rights died at Appomattox with the defeat and surrender of the South's military resistance to federal tyranny. States' Rights as espoused by Thomas Jefferson and James Madison in the Kentucky and Virginia Resolves of 1798 were replaced with states' privileges. States' privileges are exercised only with the permission of the supreme federal government. The once sovereign states kept the title "state" but lost all its meaning as the former state became a mere province of an unacknowledged empire. The state (actually a mere province) was now subservient to and answered to the central government in Washington, D.C. As the old Republic slowly faded into ancient memory, a new "indivisible" supreme federal government emerged to replace it. And in the occupied and impoverished South, pacified and docile Southerners dutifully pledged their allegiance to Lincoln's newly created, supreme federal government. The legitimate Republic was removed and, in its place, now stood an *illegitimate* [586] supreme federal government. The new supreme federal government had usurped all sovereign authority from the states and assumed unto itself the sole authority to determine the extent of its "constitutional" powers. With the victory of federal supremacy, the Yankee Empire then controlled the North American continent and began to look for other worlds, nations, and people to

---

[586] Illegitimate because it was and is a "bayonet constitution" forced upon the people of the South against their will, void of consent, a creature of brute force in its inception and its maintenance.

conquer and exploit. Simply stated, the "aggressive abroad" empire that Confederate General Robert E. Lee predicted became, and remains today, a reality. One would think that pacified Southerners would negotiate something more than the mere "bowl of pottage" in exchange for their birthright of Freedom.[587]

A strategic failure—the South's Refusal to Maintain its Right to be Free

As pointed out in *Dixie Rising-Rules for Rebels,* there have been numerous nations that were invaded by an aggressive empire and held in captivity for many years, even for generations. Yet, these captive nations managed to regain their freedom.[588] If other captive nations have been able to regain their freedom, then why has the South sunk into docile acceptance of its second-class status in the Yankee Empire? Why do Southerners apparently no longer yearn to be free? The unfortunate truth is that the defeated South took the surrender at Appomattox too literally. Southern leaders, since Appomattox, have never dared to mention the subject of the Southern people's right of self-determination. This has been a major strategic failure. *The South's rejection of its right to have a government of its own raises significant questions regarding its motive for fighting the so-called "Civil War."* The South's enemies and detractors can now reduce the struggle for Southern Independence to a struggle between the virtuous North seeking to abolish slavery against an evil, racist South seeking to maintain black people in slavery. The South's

---

[587] "Bowl of pottage" refers to the Old Testament record of Esau exchanging his inheritance for a mere bowl of pottage; see, Genesis, 25: 27-34, *Holy Bible.*

[588] Kennedy, *Dixie Rising-Rules for Rebels*, 117-134.

detractors can claim to prove their position by simply asking: "If the South was fighting for its freedom in 1861-1865, then why did it abandon the struggle for freedom after they lost their slaves?" It appears to the world that the Yankees were right—that is, the South was not fighting for its independence but fighting to keep its slaves. Once slavery was forcefully removed, then there was no reason to keep fighting and demanding freedom—or that is what is inferred by the pacified South's continued inaction. Thus, the Yankee lie, that the South was actually fighting for slavery, has been reinforced by pacified Southerners meekly accepting the war's unfortunate outcome. As is often stated in an old Southern truism, "Silence gives consent." By remaining silent about its right to be free of the Yankee Empire, pacified Southerners in effect gave and continue to give their consent to Yankee domination. By never again declaring its right to be a free and independent people governed by a government established by the free and unfettered consent of the people—Southern leaders made it easy for the Yankee Empire to claim legitimacy for its criminal invasion and tyrannical rule. With its Southern conquest docile and pacified, the Yankee Empire was free to conduct its campaign of genocide against Native Americans in the West; use gunboat diplomacy to deprive the Native Hawaiians of their legitimate government; invade Cuba and make it a protectorate of the Yankee Empire; invade the Philippines and make it a protectorate of the Yankee Empire; used military force or threats of force to compel nations in Central and South America to subordinate their national interests to the commercial interest of the Yankee Empire; and, in modern times, use economic hit men to establish "our kind of guys" as puppet dictators around the world.

The impact of this strategic failure[589] resulted in a distortion of the social conditions in the South. The cultural distortion was a result of a once free people surrendering their right to be a free people and attempting, as a subjugated people, to negotiate the best possible arrangement that the federal government would allow between the conquered Southern people and their Yankee Empire masters. Anytime a formerly free society is invaded, defeated, and occupied by a foreign power the natural or normal social relations between the native inhabitants of the captive nation will be distorted.[590] In the South, this distortion is evidenced by the unnatural divide between black and white Southerners. It is a political divide that was intentionally created by the Yankee Empire in order to "divide and rule" the conquered South.[591] The *initial* efforts of post-war Confederate leaders to establish a political linkage between black and white Southerners[592] was defeated by Republican-imposed Reconstruction. The intentional distortion of Southern society, especially in reference to race relations, produced a divide that would provide the Republican Party guaranteed votes from black Southerners during Reconstruction and then, guaranteed votes to the Democratic Party from white Southerners after Reconstruction and up to the late 1960s. The cultural distortion produced by the Republican

---

[589] The South's post-war strategic failure: The failure of Southern leaders to keep alive in the heart of every Southerner the desire to be a free people; to have a government based upon their free and unfettered consent; to have a government that protects the social, political, and economic interest of the Southern people; and, never allow the people of the South to learn to love the chains of bondage that keep them enslaved to the *indivisible* Yankee Empire.

[590] Kennedy & Kennedy, *Punished With Poverty*, 127-132.

[591] *Ibid.*, 13.

[592] *Ibid.*, 64-66.

Party's "divide and rule" policy was a "win-win" for both national political parties. As a result, both black and white Southerners remained mired in poverty while an unnatural black vs white political divide was fastened upon the South. While both national political parties claimed, at different times, to be the champion of black or white Southerners, in reality the only ones to benefit were and are the ruling elites of both national political parties and their crony capitalist allies.

By abandoning the struggle for Southern freedom, Southern leaders allowed and encouraged cultural distortion, which resulted in continuing poverty, and the imposition of "white supremacy" ideology in the late 1890s, which cemented the racial divide so necessary for the continuation of the Yankee Empire's domination of the South.[593] The "virus of Northern racism"[594] was a "gift" from Republican politicians who inflicted Reconstruction upon the conquered people, black and white, of the South. A people who have much more in common with each other than either has with the ruling elite of both national political parties or their crony capitalists, donor class allies on Wall Street in New York City or K Street in Washington, D.C.

---

[593] Kennedy & Kennedy, *Punished With Poverty*, 131-137.

[594] *Ibid.*, 44.

Chapter 12: Cultural Genocide — the Destruction of a Proud Heritage

SCALLYWAG GOVERNOR NIKKI HALEY, Republican of South Carolina, used the tragic shooting at an African American church in Charleston, S.C., to promote her political career. Her efforts helped to initiate the current round of anti-South cultural genocide. The Republican Party rewarded her with a prestigious post as Ambassador to the United Nations.

Photo courtesy of *Times Examiner*, Greenville, SC

Yankee efforts to slander the South are not new. The Empire's prior and ongoing efforts to slander its first victim are necessary for the Yankee Empire's survival. The ongoing campaign of anti-South bigotry must be maintained IF the Yankee Empire is to maintain its façade of legitimacy! Worldwide recognition of the truth about the War for Southern Independence would destroy the Yankee Empire.

The ongoing efforts of the Yankee Empire, not only to vilify the Cause of Southern Freedom with slanderous lies disguised as "history" but also to remove all monuments to Southern heroes and other reminders of the

South's struggle for freedom, was pointed out in 1994 by these authors.[595] Unfortunately, most of the 130,000 plus people, who purchased and read our warning thought we were engaging in hyperbole at best or "overkill" at worst. We were constantly being accused of being "totally unrealistic and extreme." National officers in well-known Southern heritage organizations chastised us for putting too much emphasis on the need of the South to establish a political response to Yankee cultural genocide. Today, 2018, the realization of our warning, issued 24 years ago, is reality. This reality is evidenced by headlines in mainline media celebrating the destruction of monuments to General Lee, President Davis, and other Confederate leaders across the South. The Yankee Empire's campaign of cultural genocide is not new, it did not develop in our lifetime or in response to the horrific act of a lone, crazed gunman in Charleston, South Carolina, who had no direct or indirect connection to the Southern heritage movement. The Yankee Empire's campaign of anti-South cultural genocide is a permanent part of its continuing efforts to pacify rising generations of Southerners. Nor is the Yankee Empire the first empire to use the technique of cultural genocide against the people of a captive nation.

Every empire must dehumanize the people of the invaded nation. This is made easy in modern America in which the mainline media, educational institutions and political parties are all supporters of the Yankee Empire. The Empire's propagandists dehumanize the targeted population and brand them as being "outside the moral universe." For instance, they constantly imply that any Southerner flying a Confederate flag is an evil racist and/or a neo-Nazi. The implication is that moral

---

[595] Kennedy & Kennedy, *The South Was Right!*, Chapter 13, "The Yankee Campaign of Cultural Genocide," 271-303.

Americans are not racist, and therefore, the individual flying the Confederate flag is not part of "our" (Yankee America's) moral universe. Once such Yankee "truisms" become generally accepted, then it is a small step to take whatever action is necessary to silence or remove the offending "immoral" individual. This "dehumanizing" of the invaded people is done before, during, and after the invasion and conquest of the once free nation. The invader's efforts to dehumanize the invaded population serves an important function. Understanding the important role played by the Yankee Empire's propagandist who continue to dehumanize the once free people of the South gives insight as to why the post-Reconstruction South abandoned its struggle for freedom.

Tennessee's Republican Scallywag Governor William Brownlow wanted to "exterminate" all Confederates and their families. Brownlow was a Methodist minister. (Courtesy of LOC)

Harsh use of power by the invader intimidates and subdues the invaded survivors. William Brownlow, the Post-War Scallywag Governor of Tennessee and former Methodist minister, advocated the "extermination" of all former Confederates and their families.[596] Yankee General Butler and Illinois Governor Yates both recommended that the

---

[596] "William G. Brownlow, American Journalist and Politician," *Encyclopedia Britannica*, www.britannica.com/biography/William-G-Brownlow (Accessed 10/14/2017).

United States initiate a second war against the South in order to "finish the good work."[597] Fear of death will cause an invaded and occupied people to become submissive when faced with the power of their conquerors. The empire's aim during invasion goes beyond overcoming military resistance and putting down resistance to its rule by untrustworthy local leaders. Empires will also set in motion events that result in the maximum death of survivors *after* the end of military invasion via malnutrition, starvation, and disease, thereby gaining a smaller, more sedate, pacified, and docile population. This will make those who survive the post-invasion phase more compliant and obedient subjects of the empire. Those lucky enough to survive both invasion and post-invasion starvation will be a more subservient folk who, out of fear, would never again challenge the empire's illegitimate rule, or so the empire hopes. This docile and passive acceptance of the invader's *illegitimate* rule by the people of the invaded nation sets the stage for ongoing cultural genocide.

Cultural genocide[598] is a key feature of an empire's occupation of a conquered people. When the British Empire defeated Scotland, it subsequently passed the Act of Proscription of 1746. This Act banned major aspects of the Gaelic (Scottish) culture especially as it dealt with the Scottish clan system. The Act prohibited the wearing of "Highland Clothes" such as tartans, plaid, shoulder belts, or anything that could be

---

[597] Mitcham, *Bust Hell Wide Open*, 302.

[598] Genocide includes acts in addition to killing people. It has been described as: "Generally speaking, genocide does not necessarily mean the immediate destruction of a nation.... It is intended rather to signify a coordinated plan of different actions aiming at the DESTRUCTION OF ESSENTIAL FOUNDATIONS of the life of national groups, with the aim of annihilating the groups themselves." Rummel, R. J., *Death by Government*, 32. Rummel also states that it could mean the "absorption of one culture by another."

associated with traditional highland dress. It has often been claimed that Scots were arrested for playing "outlawed tunes on outlawed pipes," although bagpipes were not specifically mentioned in the Act. Violation of the Act could result in the individual being sentenced to "transportation to any of his Majesty's plantations beyond the seas and there to remain for a space of seven years."[599] The British Empire knew that as long as the Scottish people held to their traditional belief, values, and social system, they would never become good pacified subjects of the British Empire. The British Empire's solution was to destroy all symbols and traditions that would remind the conquered people of their former days as a free people. Monuments matter, local traditions matter, local heroes matter. Why do they matter? They matter because they serve as a reminder of the evil forces that destroyed the people's right to live under a government ordered upon their free and unfettered consent. Monuments and such matter to the empire because they pose a potential threat to the empire's continued occupation of the captive nation. Therefore, monuments and other local traditions must be removed and replaced with false history and false heroes to assure the proper assimilation of the conquered people—to make sure the conquered people accept their status as docile subjects of the empire. Eventually, the empire's pacified subjects will learn to "love their chains."

As has already been pointed out, the Yankee Empire used the technique of cultural genocide against Native Americans. The passage of the Dawes Act of 1887 was a major assault against Native American traditions and social structure. Just as the British Empire wanted to destroy the clan system and the authority of local clan leaders, which was

---

[599] "The Act of Proscription," Scottish Tartans Authority, www.tartansauthority.com/tartan/the-growth-of-tartan/the-act-of-proscription-1747 (Accessed 8/15/2017).

the mainstay of local government in Scotland, the Yankee Empire desired the destruction of the tribal system and the authority of Native American tribal Chiefs—two different empires, two different defeated people, but cultural genocide was used for the same purpose.

During Reconstruction, Southern soldiers coming home were often accosted by Yankee soldiers or newly installed carpetbag or scalawag political leaders and made to remove their gray coats, military buttons, or any other item that could possibly represent the defeated Confederacy. In many towns and cities across the South, the occupying Yankee military forces would post guards around local cemeteries where Confederate soldiers were buried to prevent bereaved loved ones from putting flowers on the graves of their slain Confederate veterans. The London *Telegraph* in its November 24, 1866, edition informed its readers that the United States may still *claim* to be a Republic but "some eight million of the people are subjects, not citizens."[600] Nothing has changed since Reconstruction except that today pacified Southerners are now the most ardent defenders of that "one nation indivisible" that destroyed the free and prosperous South. Pacified Southerners are the Yankee Empire's "useful fools" helping the Yankee Empire to maintain its rule over its conquered and occupied captive nation—the Confederate States of America.

The current wave of anti-Southern cultural genocide is being accomplished with the full support of the South's political leadership. Because Southern politicians will not defend the true cause of the war— an effort to assert the South's unalienable right to self-government—the agents and sycophants of the Yankee Empire have had a free hand in promoting the destruction of these last physical reminders of that great

---

[600] Bowers, *The Tragic Era*, 146-147.

struggle for Southern freedom. To understand why Southern politicians will not rise to the occasion and vigorously defend their Southern heritage, one must first understand that the current governments, both state and national, are *illegitimate*. They are bayonet governments imposed upon a defeated people. The primary role of bayonet governments is NOT to serve the best interest of the local population but, first and foremost, to assure the continuation of the *illegitimate* occupation and exploitation of the captive nation—everything else is secondary.

Under the current bayonet constitutions—state and federal—local governments operate at the pleasure of the ruling elite in Washington, D.C., better described as the Yankee Empire. The Yankee Empire can rely upon its propagandists to vilify any Southerner who dares to defend the South; it can rely upon its crazed mobs, such as Antifa,[601] to silence the voice of anyone who dares to publicly speak out on behalf of the South's right to be free; it can rely upon its crony capitalists (the donor class) to punish any worker or employee who openly displays love for his Southern heritage; and it can count on its deep state bureaucrats in the Internal Revenue Service or other such state or federal bureaucracies to harass any outspoken Southern leader. Any politician who challenges the authority of the "deep state" or the ruling elite of the Yankee Empire will face an

---

[601] Antifa is an anarchist, leftist, neo-Communist mob that practices violence against conservative or pro-South groups. It claims to be anti-fascists, but in fact, they use the very same tactics of Nazi Storm Troopers. According to one report, they have been listed by the federal government as a terrorist organization. See Connell, Seth, "FBI and DHS Documents Classify Antifa Activities As Domestic Terrorism – Warn of More Attacks," *The Federalist Papers*, thefederalistpapers.org/us/fbi-dhs-documents-classify-antifa-activities-domestic-terrorism-warn-attacks?utm_source=FBLC&utm_medium=FB&utm_campaign=LC (Accessed 09/01/2017).

almost insurmountable obstacle when he seeks re-election. In the current system of *illegitimate* government, election and re-election are more important to the South's politicians than any abstract idea such as freedom for the people of a captive nation.

This system of control is used for the benefit of both national political parties. Therefore, Southerners cannot look to their favorite political party for aid in the defense of their heritage—much less for a fair hearing regarding the right of the people to live under a government based upon their free and unfettered consent. As has been demonstrated in other books, both political parties are responsible for inflicting "bad" and "ugly" political policies and leadership upon the conquered South.[602] The current campaign to remove Confederate monuments is being conducted with the actual or implicit support of local Southern political leaders. And yet, pacified Southerners still think that they can defend their Southern heritage by an appeal to the goodwill of local elected officials, electing "good" conservatives to national political offices or by taking their appeal to local, state, or federal courts—courts that were established and are maintained via bayonet constitutions!

Another aspect of the current campaign of anti-South cultural genocide is the role of taxpayer-funded educational institutions. These institutions, funded by taxes paid by "conservative" Southerners, are in reality brainwashing centers used to "re-educate" successive generations of Southern young people. These "re-education" centers are operated by left-wing-oriented, anti-Southern "educators" and "administrators." The vast majority of the faculty of these institutions are registered Democrats, which explains their anti-South political orientation. But even the few who are registered Republicans are not any better! They generally are

---

[602] Kennedy & Kennedy, *Punished With Poverty*, 122-146.

extreme neoconservatives and "one nation indivisible" Lincoln worshipers. These are the Republicans who leap at any opportunity to "bomb them back to the stone age" when the Empire rattles the war sabers and initiates another no-win war. These brainwashing stations turn out the educators who will then gain employment as elementary, middle, or high school instructors. Even those who come from traditional, conservative, Southern homes are influenced and brainwashed during the time they spend in these universities, better described as brainwashing or indoctrination centers. Generations of Southern students have been brainwashed successfully in taxpayer-funded public schools across the South. Ask a high school graduate from any Southern state, "Why was the Civil War fought?" The answer you will get will be one centered on the Yankee Empire's narrative about the War: "It was fought over slavery," or "It was fought to save the Union," or "It was fought because the South tried to destroy the Union in order to keep their slaves." Re-educating Southern children in order to make them compliant, mind-numbed sycophants of the Yankee myth of history was predicted by Confederate leaders.

President Jefferson Davis predicted that if the South lost the war, the victorious Yankees would write and enforce their version of the war. He knew that the Yankee invaders would attempt to crush the truth to hide their many crimes against the people of the South. He foresaw a future in which every new Southern generation would be denied the opportunity to understand the righteousness of the South's struggle for freedom. His prediction has sadly become a reality in classrooms all across the South. His wife, Varina, lamented the "startling absence of truth and fact in many of the tales that stand forth as history."[603] Men like former Confederate

---

[603] Varina Davis, as cited in Kennedy & Kennedy, *The South Was Right!*, 17.

General Stephen D. Lee understood the dangers posed by an evil enemy that was writing the official history of the war. He instructed young men who were sons of Confederate veterans that they had a duty to "see that the true history of the South is presented to future generations."[604] Writing in 1894, an Alabama educator, J.L.M. Curry, bemoaned the sad fact that "History as written if accepted in future years will consign the South to infamy."[605] Another Southerner writing shortly after the close of World War I openly declared:

> These attacks and untruthful presentations of so-called history demand refutation, for the South cannot surrender its birthright and we pray the day may never dawn when it will be willing to abandon the truth in a cowardly or sluggish spirit of pacifism.... Nor has this defamation ceased—it still goes on unabated, and there is a constant and strong stream of misrepresentation and false historical statement flowing from the North ... false history almost overwhelms us.[606]

Writing in 1930, distinguished historian and author, Frank Lawrence Owsley, declared that the purpose of Yankee history was to:

> ...write error across the pages of Southern history ... and set the rising and unborn generations [of Southerners] upon stools of everlasting repentance.... Northern text books were used in Southern schools.... There was for the Southern child very little choice. They had to accept the Northern version of history with all its condemnations and carping criticisms of Southern

---

[604] S. D. Lee as cited *Ibid*.

[605] J. L. M. Curry as cited *Ibid*.

[606] A. H. Jennings as cited *Ibid*, 18.

institutions.... Lincoln was the real Southern hero because Lincoln saved the Union. So, they were told![607]

In 1950, *The Gray Book,* which had first been published in 1920, was republished. The preface of the republication is indicative of the continuing campaign of cultural genocide being waged against the South:

> Falsehood is still spewed forth in the United States.... It is hoped that this re-published book may serve to inform those who wish to know the facts and to shame those who still wish to spread falsehood and engage in the defamation.[608]

Note how in 1950, almost a century after the so-called "Civil War" had ended, the vicious slandering of the South continued! The sad truth—something pacified Southerners both then and now cannot comprehend—is that the war is not over! The war to destroy the truth that the South was fighting for freedom must continue in order to assure that the people of the South will remain docile and pacified—good "patriotic" subjects of the "one nation indivisible" Yankee Empire.

Censorship is a necessary practice in any empire. In an authoritarian empire, the state organizes and conducts the censorship to assure that only its version of history and current events are allowed for public consumption. But in a "democratic" empire, such as the Yankee Empire, the government does not engage in direct censorship—such acts would be undemocratic! But censorship does occur. Censorship in the Yankee Empire is not conducted in the Orwellian[609] style of Big Brother

---

[607] Owsley, Frank Lawrence, "The Irrepressible Conflict," *I'll Take My Stand,* 63.

[608] A. H. Jennings as cited in Kennedy & Kennedy, *The South Was Right!,* 23.

[609] George Orwell's description of the total thought control accomplished by the authoritarian state in his novel, *1984.*

government; censorship in the Yankee Empire is accomplished in the Orwellian style, but it is "soft censorship" conducted by richly rewarded, private agents of the government in the media, education, and Hollywood. This fact and its impact on society, especially young people in college, was noted by Russian dissident Aleksandr Solzhenitsyn (1918-2008) in an address at Harvard University in 1978:

> Without any censorship in the West, fashionable trends of thought are carefully separated from those that are not fashionable. Nothing is forbidden [by law], but what is not fashionable will hardly ever find its way into periodicals or books or be heard in colleges.[610]

Thus, the Orwellian censorship of any idea that might put the South in a favorable light continues today. It has produced and continues to produce deadly results for the heritage of a people who have borne the afflictions of Job,[611] and still, there remains a courageous few who refuse to surrender their belief in the goodness of God and the righteousness of their Southern homeland.

All across the South today (2018), Confederate monuments are being defaced, destroyed, and removed. This work of cultural genocide is being done by mobs and various local Southern governments. Even though numerous opinion polls have demonstrated that the majority of Americans, as well as Southerners, do not want to remove these

---

[610] Aleksandr Solzhenitsyn speaking at Harvard University in 1978. Cited in *Why the South Will Survive*, Clyde Wilson, ed. (The University of Georgia Press, Athens, Georgia: 1981), 121.

[611] God allowed Satan to test Job's faith by afflicting him with numerous personal disasters. Yet, through it all, Job refused to take the world's advice to "Curse God and die." See *Book of Job* in the Old Testament of the Christian Bible.

monuments "our" elected leaders still joyfully remove them. A poll conducted in August of 2017 for PBS Newshour in conjunction with NPR and Marist Poll discovered that 62% of Americans do not want Confederate monuments to be removed! Only 27% were in favor of removal.[612] Yet our Confederate monuments are being removed—democracy and fairness has never stood in the way of the Yankee Empire. Majority rule and other inconvenient facts makes no difference to the agents of the Yankee Empire. Why? Because the Yankee Empire does not believe in the right of consent—the Yankee Empire and its bayonet governments are founded on the principle of compulsion! Subjects must obey—and today pacified Southern subjects are meekly watching (or ignoring) the Yankee Empire's campaign to destroy the last physical vestige of the Confederate States of America. This is occurring because the South opted to forgo the continued struggle for freedom. Because it abandoned the morally correct struggle for freedom, it allowed the invader to assume the moral high ground—"we fought to free the slaves," the descendants and sycophants of the invaders falsely claim. Instead of taking the morally right but politically difficult task of continuing the struggle for freedom, the South conceded the moral high ground to the Yankee Empire. Perhaps without realizing it, they sold their birthright of freedom for the promise of an undisturbed life as subjects of the Yankee Empire. And just like most Yankee promises—the Yankee Empire never intended to keep its promise. If the South had continued to demand the

---

[612] "NPR/PBS NewsHour/Marist Poll of 1,125 National Adults," maristpoll.marist.edu/wp-content/misc/usapolls/us170814_PBS/NPR_PBS%20NewsHour_Marist%20Poll_National%20Nature%20of%20the%20Sample%20and%20Tables_August%2017,%202017.pdf (Accessed 12/2/2017), p. 9.

The words of Yankee General Sherman demonstrate the Yankee hatred of the Southern people: "There is a class of people men, women, and children, who must be killed or banished before you can hope for peace." (Courtesy of LOC)

unalienable right of self-determination, the right to throw off *illegitimate* bayonet constitutions and institute a new government that would protect the interests of the people of the South, it would at least have placed itself in a strong negotiating or bargaining position. As Gandhi demonstrated during India's struggle for freedom, even a powerful empire cannot hold a people forever in political slavery against their will—especially when such evil is demonstrated to the world.[613] "A 'no' uttered from deepest conviction is better than a 'yes' merely uttered to please, or worse, to avoid trouble."[614] Every Southern student should have been taught the simple truth that the South was fighting for freedom and that the war is not over until freedom is won! But even in this dark hour—all is not lost! The war is not over until freedom is won!

---

[613] Kennedy, *Dixie Rising*, 117-120.

[614] Mahatma Gandhi, cited in Gandhi, Arun, *The Gift of Anger and Other Lessons From My Grandfather Mahatma Gandhi* (New York: Gallery Books, 2017), 35.

Chapter 13: Globalism—Yankee International Crony Capitalism

Globalism served as a euphemism for soft or informal empire.
—Andrew J. Bacevich[615]

THE FIRST THREE PRESIDENTS of the United States made it clear that the new nation would not be like European nations and attempt to establish itself as an empire. President George Washington, in his Farewell Address after serving two terms as President, clearly expressed his vision for the new nation's role in international affairs:

> The great rule of conduct for us in regard to foreign nations is in extending our commercial relations, to have with them as little political connection as possible.[616]

President John Adams, President of the United States who, even as a High Federalist favoring a powerful central government, held similar views and declared the U.S.A. is the well-wisher of freedom and independence of all, "But she goes not abroad, in search of monsters to destroy."[617]

Thomas Jefferson, the third U.S. President, in a letter written to T. Pinckney in 1792, wrote of the United States, "concerning themselves or

---

[615] Bacevich, *The Limits of Power*, 2.

[616] "Washington's Farewell Address 1796," The Avalon Project, avalon.law.yale.edu/18th_century/washing.asp (Accessed 06/27/2017).

[617] Adams, "Warning Against the Search for 'Monsters to Destroy,' 1821," www.mtholyoke.edu/acad/intrel/jqadams.htm (Accessed 06/27/2017).

other nations, we wish not to intermeddle in word or deed."[618] In short, their views regarding international relations were simply that we mind our business and expect others to do the same.

In the early years of the Republic, it was clear that the Hamiltonian vision of an "energetic" federal government that would use its power to assist the development of a commercial / financial empire had not taken over. But with the passing of each year, the demands of the High Federalists—whose political strength was centered in New York and New England—gained more followers and influence in the federal government. Hamilton's victory in persuading President Washington to support the establishment of the first United States Bank was just the beginning. President Thomas Jefferson saw a national bank as merely a pretext by a small elite group to use the centralized power of the federal government to exploit America's workers and farmers. He branded such efforts as an attempt to establish:

> A single and splendid government of an aristocracy, founded on banking institutions and moneyed incorporations...[619]

Thomas Jefferson understood the dangers that commerce imposed and maintained by bayonets and international intrigues would create for the newly established American Republic. But somewhere between Jefferson's time and today, a dramatic change occurred—the United States changed from a Republic to the Yankee Empire, and today, Southerners, other Americans, as well as people worldwide live with the tragic results.

---

[618] Coates, "Foreign Relations & Jeffersonian Principles," eyler.freeservers.com/JeffPers/jefpco30.htm (Accessed 06/29/2017).

[619] Jefferson, as cited in Kennedy & Kennedy, *Was Jefferson Davis Right?*, 219.

This "dramatic change" was predicted in 1861 by Senator Joseph Lane speaking in the United States Senate. He warned that Lincoln's aggressive war against the South would result in the United States becoming an empire while the states would become mere provinces held in the "Union" by military force: "A province of an empire ... is held by the oppressor as an integral part of his dominions."[620] In 1861 Senator Lane foresaw the emerging connection between an aggressive form of American nationalism—masquerading as patriotism—and crony capitalism. He saw it as a connection that would eventually destroy the Republic and create a global American empire.

In 1861, Senator Joseph Lane from Oregon warned that America was becoming an empire. (Courtesy LOC)

The close connection between a few financial institutions and government is the hallmark of crony capitalism. *As such it is not free market capitalism.* It is closer to the national socialist or fascist partnership between big industry and big government. Such political / economic systems are not new but have been developing since the turn of the twentieth century. In 1917, Lenin described such systems thusly:

---

[620] *Ibid., Op cit.*

> Monopolies, oligarchy, the striving for domination instead of the striving for liberty, the exploitation of an increasing number of small or weak nations by an extremely small group of the richest or most powerful nations—all these have given birth to those distinctive characteristics of imperialism which compel us to define it as parasitic or decaying capitalism.[621]

Even in the early 1900s, it was apparent that larger and larger banks supported by larger and larger governments were beginning to present a threat to individuals who were not part of the elite. Marxists, socialists, and anarchists of the early 1900s sought to attack the system—unfortunately, they misdiagnosed the underlying pathology. It was not free market capitalism that was the culprit, it was an emerging global financial elite in conjunction with big governments—crony capitalism. But these left-wing revolutionaries nonetheless understood the dangers presented by concentrated wealth made possible by special government considerations.

> As banking develops and becomes concentrated in a small number of establishments the banks become transformed, and instead of being modest intermediaries they become powerful monopolies having at their command almost the whole of the money capital of all the capitalists and small business men.... The small banks are being pushed aside by the big banks.[622]

Lenin incorrectly saw the evolution of global banking as a natural part of colonialism and eventually, according to the ideology of Marxism, with the death of capitalism, the move toward a utopian communist world order would occur. But even though he mislabeled crony capitalism as

---

[621] Lenin, V. I., *Imperialism: The Highest Stage of Capitalism*, 124.

[622] *Ibid.*, 31-32.

free market capitalism, he was correct regarding the dangers posed by the worldwide rule of a few financial elites in conjunction with a powerful empire—such as the Yankee Empire.

> Capitalism has grown into a world system of colonial oppression and of the financial strangulation of the overwhelming majority of the people of the world by a handful of "advanced" countries.[623]

In reality, late 19th and 20th-century colonialism was financed largely by government-created monopolistic or quasi-monopolistic financial institutions. From the beginning of the 1900s, U.S. banking began to be more and more entangled with the Yankee Empire.[624] As time passed, post-1865, a symbiotic relationship between a supreme federal government and financial / commercial institutions developed—or as we say down South: "one hand washes the other." This of course had been the dream of High Federalists such as Alexander Hamilton from the very beginning of the United States—a dream that was denounced and resisted by Southerners such as Thomas Jefferson and John C. Calhoun. After Appomattox, there was no effective resistance to the Hamiltonian dream of a vast American commercial / financial empire. The Yankee Empire was free to begin the development of its central banking system—later to be called the Federal Reserve (the "Fed"). This federal central banking system (the "Fed") would eventually support the development of

---

[623] *Ibid.*, 10-11.

[624] This entanglement of high finance and big government was something that Southerners such as Thomas Jefferson and John C. Calhoun had warned Americans against. With the *extermination* of Southern political power in the United States after the Yankee's victory in its invasion and conquest of the Confederate States of America, the development of a vast worldwide commercial/financial/military Yankee Empire began in earnest.

worldwide financial organizations such as the World Trade Organization, World Bank, and the International Monetary Fund. All would be centered around elites on Wall Street with close connections with the Federal Reserve and powerful government elites with powerful lobbying offices on K Street in Washington, D.C.

The benefits of having close connections with the Yankee Empire's political and financial elites is demonstrated by the fact that, from 2009 to 2012, those Americans making approximately $400,000 a year or more (the top 1%)[625] enjoyed an income increase of almost 32% while those making less than $400,000 a year (the bottom 99%) saw their income increase by an incrementally small 0.4% which actually did not keep up with inflation.[626] The result was that the top 1% enjoyed 95% of the new wealth created during Obama's so-called "economic recovery."[627] Those with close connections "recovered" from the Great Recession of 2007 to 2009 while the rest of society saw an actual decrease in their purchasing power. Crony capitalism protects the connected, it impoverishes those who are not connected, and it provides anti-free market revolutionaries of the socialist (Occupy Wall Street, Bernie Sanders) school with ammunition to discredit true free market capitalism. They do this by confusing free market capitalism with crony capitalism. Confusing free market capitalism with crony capitalism in the early 1900s was done primarily because no one had made a clear

---

[625] According to some "experts," the top 1% begins at $394,000, not $400,000.

[626] Inflation is a government-created indirect tax upon workers. See, Kennedy, *Reclaiming Liberty*, "Sound Money," 127-145.

[627] Weber, Peter, "CHARTS: How the rich won the Great Recession," *The Week*, theweek.com/articles/460179/charts-how-rich-won-great-recession (Accessed 08/19/2017).

distinction between crony and free market capitalism, but today it is done intentionally.

There were those who, before the current era of Globalism, attempted to make a distinction between free market and crony capitalism, although they used other terms to denote the connection between government and monopolistic business. The idea of crony capitalism was addressed by Ludwig von Mises in chapter 33 of *Human Action-A Treatise on Economics,* published March 5, 1945. In this short chapter of his major Austrian economic treatise, he described crony capitalism as "corporatism."[628] Almost a century earlier, June 1850, a Frenchman, Frederic Bastiat, warned that "the law" or government places:

> The collective force [of government] at the disposal of the unscrupulous who wish, without risk, to exploit the person, liberty, and property of others. It has converted plunder into a right, in order to protect [those who] plunder. And it has converted lawful defense into a crime, in order to punish lawful defense.[629]

The "unscrupulous" elites of the Yankee Empire seized the "collective force" of the supreme federal government and turned it into an agent to develop, defend and expand worldwide the Hamiltonian vision of American (Yankee) crony capitalism. Its impact has been felt ever since the death of America's original constitutionally limited Republic of Republics. Lincoln, the Republican Party, and their crony capitalist allies converted the Jeffersonian Republic of Republics into a supreme Yankee

---

[628] Mises, Ludwig Von, *Human Action-A Treatise on Economics* (1945, Auburn, AL: The Ludwig von Mises Institute, 1998), 808-816.

[629] Bastiat, Frederic, *The Law* (1850, New York: The Foundation for Economic Education, Inc., 1979), 9.

Empire. Today's political parties do not question the legitimacy of Lincoln's Empire but only fight over whose turn it is to hold the reins of power and thereby dispense to their allies the Yankee Empire's perks, privileges, and power.

The years of 2016 and 2017 gave the elites of the international financial world an unexpected shock. With their complete control of the world's financial markets, they never thought that a popular revolt against global financial elites would be possible. These elites have profited from their close connection with various governments—primarily the Yankee Empire. They used their vast financial resources to "purchase" close connections with key government officials, who in turn provided favored treaties, laws, rules, and (cheap labor) immigration regulations that favor and enrich the financial elite. But beyond all of this was the fact that they knew that, regardless of how risky their international investments might be, they would never be compelled to bear the risk—they were "too big to fail." Their losses would be transferred to the general tax-paying public. But the public worldwide was beginning to groan under the continuing impoverishment of the vast majority who were not part of the financial elite.

The disastrous impact of Globalism on working-class families in America can be seen when viewing census data measuring net worth and median household income for American families. In 2000, the median household income (income, not net worth) was $57,790, but ten years later in 2010, the next decennial census, it was discovered that the 2010 median household income had fallen to $52,790.[630] While the well

---

[630] Amadeo, Kimberly, "What Is the Average American Net Worth? Compare Your Wealth to that of the Average American," *The Balance*, www.thebalance.com/american-net-worth-by-state-metropolitan-4135839 (Accessed 08/19/2017).

connected on Wall Street and Washington, D.C. were "making a killing," America's middle-class families were struggling. This was not strictly an American phenomenon, it was occurring worldwide. But a large segment of well-connected globalists and crony capitalists are located in New York or Washington and are a part of the Yankee Empire's elite. It is worth looking at a few of these financial elites who have close connections with the ruling elite of the Yankee Empire. The table below lists examples of some of America's leading crony capitalists—the men who today have taken the place of J. P. Morgan and John D. Rockefeller of the late 1800s and early 1900s.

Crony Capitalist	Educational Institution	Net Worth
Warren Buffett	Columbia Business School	$76.6 B
Carl Icahn	Princeton University	$15.9 B
John Paulson	Harvard Business School	$7.9 B
Jamie Dimon	Harvard Business School	$1.55 B
Ben Bernanke	Massachusetts Institute of Technology	$3 M

These five men have far more influence on the monetary policies of the Yankee Empire than the entire American electorate combined. These men and their comrades in the donor-class are the ones who decide what federal policy will or will not be enacted. They control the purse strings from which elected members of Congress draw their re-election campaign funds. It is often said that in Washington, D.C. "money talks and bull sh-- (bovine fecal matter) walks!" Note also that the five listed above all received their education from "Ivy League" schools of the Northeast. They think alike and they demand the same type of big government policies regardless of what impact it will have on the average working-class American. These are the cronies who supply the money to maintain the "deep state" or ruling elite in power. Also, look at their net worth. In 2013, the average net worth (total value of assets minus total liabilities) for American families was $80,039.[631] How can these five men and the rest of their tribe of financial elites relate to the distress caused by their elitist economic policies? How can they relate to the typical American family as it struggles to send its children to school, pay for a home, and all the other requirements of a typical family? In 2015, the median household income for the Southern State of Louisiana was $45,727, and for the U.S., it was $55,775.[632] If the "poorest" fellow on our list of crony capitalists, Ben Bernanke, were able to invest his entire net worth of $3 million at a paltry 0.016%, he would earn more money in one year than the average Louisiana household makes in the same year! These crony capitalists and their donor-class comrades cannot understand the sufferings that a typical middle-class family endures. But what is worse is that they do not care! Their goal is to make profits—they are the descendants of those thrifty Yankee merchants who only have one guiding moral principle, "profit," regardless of how those profits are obtained. The Yankee Empire's commercial and financial empire has bound the people of the United States and the people of other developed nations, as well as the wretched poor in the third world with the profitable yoke of globalism—profitable for the elite. As we pointed out earlier, the only enduring principle the Yankee follows is the principle of profit—regardless of how crooked or bloody that pathway may be.

Washington, D.C.'s political elite are prospering almost as well as their donor-class allies on Wall Street. The year 2012 was the first time in history in which a majority of the members of the United States Congress

---

[631] Campbell, Todd, "Here's the Average Net Worth in the United States," *The Motley Fool*, www.fool.com/investing/2017/03/17/heres-the-average-net-worth-in-the-united-states.aspx (Accessed 08/19/2017).

[632] "Louisiana Household Income," *Department of Numbers*, www.deptofnumbers.com/income/louisiana (Accessed 8/19/2017).

were millionaires. The average net worth of members of Congress was $1,008,767.[633] The donor-class provides these millionaires with the millions of dollars necessary to win re-election. Donor-class money is the lifeblood of all elected members of Congress. When American voters go to the polls and vote for who they consider to be the best candidate, the one most likely to represent the interest of the voter, all they are doing is selecting the lesser of the evils offered to the voters by the establishment. The ruling elite and their donor-class comrades seldom if ever lose an election—the opposite of that is also true; the average voter seldom, if ever, wins an election. These millionaire politicians may profess loyalty to the workers of America, but in reality, they are owned by the donor-class. Follow the money, and you will discover where America's liberal *or conservative* politicians' true loyalties reside.

The emergence and continued existence of the Yankee Empire made possible the eventual dominance of Globalism. The key element in the existence and growth of the Yankee Empire's financial hegemony was the creation of the Empire's central bank—the Federal Reserve (the Fed). Americans are taught that the Fed was an outgrowth of popular demand for a government bank that would protect them from bank runs, panics, recessions, and depressions. The history of depressions and recessions that have regularly occurred *after* the establishment of the Federal Reserve in 1913 stands as brutal testimony to the failure of the central bank (the Fed) to prevent depressions or recessions. But the Fed has fulfilled its secret function—to use taxpayers to protect and bailout big banks and other Wall Street financial institutions.

---

[633] "Net worth of United States Senators and Representatives," *Ballotpedia*, ballotpedia.org/Net_worth_of_United_States_Senators_and_Representatives (Accessed 08/19/2017).

The truth is that the demand for a central government bank did not come from the American public but from big bankers who wanted a system that would allow them to use the government to "bail out" their bad investments. They also sought a way to rid themselves of competition from small, local banks. Americans, as already pointed out, did not trust government-controlled banks. Not only did Southerners such as Thomas Jefferson and John C. Calhoun oppose a federal banking system, but many Northerners did so as well. In 1819, the Northern State of Ohio even went so far as to nullify Federal Court orders and other federal acts dealing with the Bank of the United States. The Governor of Kentucky in 1825 enthusiastically endorsed Ohio's acts of nullification against the Federal Banking system.[634]

The financial elites understood that the public would resist their efforts to suggest a national or central banking system. The financial elites used their political influence to persuade their friends in Washington to enact their dream of an American central bank. In 1910, big bankers and financiers from the Northeast met in secret on Jekyll Island, Georgia, and drafted the Federal Reserve Act. Note that they drafted this key federal law and then presented it to their allies in Washington. They relied on their friends in Washington and a friendly press to convince Americans to accept central banking—something the people had opposed from the beginning of the Republic. But of course, by 1910, the United States was no longer a Republic but had mutated into an evil Empire. Propagandists for the Yankee Empire use standard history textbooks to teach Americans that these "public-spirited" men met on Jekyll Island to design a banking system that would protect the little people from the hazards of panics and bank runs. One scholar courageously challenged this notion:

---

[634] Kilpatrick, *The Sovereign States*, 151-157.

Now we can either believe that this is the first and only time in history in which an interest group drafted legislation aimed more at the public good than their own benefit, or we can consider the possibility that its interest was to entrench special privileges for one particular industry at the expense of the rest of society.[635]

The Federal Reserve was established by an Act of Congress in 1913. Before the end of the century, it would help to finance the Hamiltonian dream of an American (Yankee) worldwide commercial / financial empire. The Yankee Empire was made possible by the defeat of the Confederate States of America. It will remain in place as long as pacified Southerners accept the Yankee Empire as a legitimate government and refuse to demand the right to live under a legitimate government—one based upon the free and unfettered consent of the Southern people.[636]

---

[635] Woods, Thomas E., *Meltdown-A free market look at why the Stock Market collapsed* (Washington, DC: Regnery Publishing, Inc., 2009), 120.

[636] For a definition of what the authors mean by "Southern freedom" see Kennedy, *Dixie Rising*, 11-12.

"There are only two reasons why you [Americans] should ever be asked to give your youngsters [to the American military]. One is defense of our homes. The other is the defense of our Bill of Rights and particularly the right to worship God as we see fit. Every other reason advanced for the murder of young men is a racket, pure and simple." General Smedley Butler circa 1940, author *War is a Racket*. | Courtesy LOC

Chapter 14: Do Slave-owners or Their Descendants Deserve Freedom?

IF ONE WERE TO ASK A TYPICAL, conservative Southerner why the South fought the "Civil War," the likely answer would be "States' Rights." Most conservative Southerners believe the South fought for the right of local self-government under the Constitution. But if you ask the typical Northerner (liberal or conservative) the same question, the answer would be "slavery." In their view, the North was fighting to force the South to remove the institution of slavery from America. From the Southern point of view, Southerners were fighting for their freedom—the right to live under a government ordered upon the American principle of the "consent of the governed." Sycophants of the Yankee Empire respond to the allegation that the South was fighting for freedom with pretended, incredulous shock. Their self-righteous and condescending response is, "How could you fight for freedom when your society owned slaves?" And with that, the conversation automatically ends—no further discussion—case closed.

The assumption or "official narrative" advanced by the sycophants of the Yankee Empire is that a people who were trying to secure freedom for themselves while living in a society that sanctions slavery do not deserve to be free. Therefore, any amount of violent aggression used against the slave-owning society is justifiable if the aggressor's intention is to destroy slavery. This narrative is critical to upholding the Yankee Empire's pretense of moral superiority and legitimacy. Actually, it is essential, because it covers with pretended virtue a whole host of genocidal crimes committed by the Yankee aggressor in the War for Southern Independence. The United States of America under the command of Abraham Lincoln, supported by the Republican Party and its crony capitalist allies, established aggression as the Yankee Empire's policy.

As the victor in the War for Southern Independence, the Yankee Empire has the luxury of commanding and enforcing the "official" narrative of the war. It uses its power (political, financial, military, and social) to enforce the teaching of its narrative[637] and to reward its sycophants who dutifully parrot the Empire's narrative. It also uses its power to punish any Southerner who attempts to provide a defense of the South's struggle for freedom. But, nonetheless, there are still those who challenge the Yankee Empire's narrative by asking, "Is the Yankee Empire's narrative about the 'Civil War' historically accurate? Is it true, as alleged by the Yankee Empire, that the presence of slavery in a society nullifies the right of free people in that society to live under a government of their own choosing?" If the Yankee Empire's narrative is historically correct then it certainly would provide some "moral" justification for the successful efforts of the North to "exterminate" the South's political power in the United States as well as its efforts to "exterminate" large numbers of black and white people of the South.[638]

One of the primary reasons why the current round of anti-South cultural genocide is occurring is that the Yankee Empire's narrative is false! All things Confederate must be removed because, during this time of popular revolt against the Yankee Empire's Globalist ruling elite (this ruling elite has been most recently referred to as the "Deep State"), anything that reminds a large portion of the Empire's subjects (Southerners) about their once free and prosperous nation might serve as encouragement for a real revolt. Removing national monuments, expunging the memory of a captive nation's heroes, and rewriting a captive nation's history to conform to the invader's narrative is standard operating procedure for empires trying to pacify and control an occupied people. The Yankee Empire has been very successful during the last 153

---

[637] A visit to any National Civil War Battle site will prove this point. "National" of course meaning U.S.A., *i.e.*, Yankee Empire.

[638] Kennedy, *Punished With Poverty*, 69-87.

years in its efforts to enforce its narrative, but even with overwhelming propaganda power, the Empire still fears the slightest hint that the truth may become common knowledge. What then is the truth regarding the right of a society to be free even if that society tolerates a system of slavery? The Yankee Empire claims that slavery is so evil that it destroys the right of free people in that society to establish a government of their own ("free people" in the South of 1861 would have included whites, Native Americans, and free blacks).

The first fallacy contained in the Yankee Empire's narrative is that it assumes that all Southerners owned slaves, and therefore all Southerners do not deserve the right to establish a government of their own—one based upon their free and unfettered consent. It has been established that approximately 80% of Southerners *did not* own slaves.[639] This puts the Yankee Empire in the absurd position of claiming that it fought a war which resulted in subjugating 80% of the white South to prevent 20% of the South (this 20% were slave owners composed of a multi-racial group of whites, free blacks, and Native Americans) from owning slaves. Southern mothers teach their children that "two wrongs do not make one right." Unfortunately, this truism apparently does not apply to the elite of the Yankee Empire.

The second fallacy contained in the Yankee Empire's narrative is that slavery contaminates any society that allows slavery. This "contamination" caused by the existence of slavery is so evil, according to the Yankee Empire's narrative, that it nullifies (destroys) that society's right to be a free and independent nation. It thereby justifies the Yankee Empire's invasion, conquest, and occupation of the Confederate States of America. If we assume, for the sake of discussion, that this allegation is

---

[639] *Ibid.*, 161, footnote 398.

correct, then we are faced with the stark historical reality that every national democratic movement in the Western world has no right to be a free and independent nation! Ancient Athens, Greece, is known as the "cradle of democracy," yet slavery existed in Athens.[640] If, as the sycophants for the Yankee Empire claim, slavery contaminates a society so thoroughly that the free people of that society have no right to freedom and self-government, then, by this Yankee logic, the ancient "cradle of democracy" was evil and did not deserve to exist. What it also means is that great efforts must be made by the politically correct sycophants of Yankeedom to brand ancient Athens as an evil society that does not deserve any recognition for its contributions to modern civilization. Once the politically correct mob has pulled down the Parthenon, leveled the Acropolis, and rewritten Athenian history, it could then move on to the Roman Republic. According to Yankee logic, Rome could not be a Republic because it was contaminated by the sin of slavery! The same could be said for Great Britain, France, Holland, Spain, and Portugal because they all not only sanctioned slavery but were actively engaged in the nefarious international African slave trade.[641] According to Yankee logic, the English Common Law that established protection for individual liberty is tainted with slavery, and therefore it must be consigned to the trash bin of history. But by this intellectually superior Yankee logic, we must also condemn every New England Colony and State as well as the

---

[640] "The Greeks: Crucible of Empire," www.pbs.org/empires/thegreeks/background/32b.html (Accessed 10/14/2017). It is also interesting to note how mildly, and with great sympathy, politically correct individuals treat slavery in Athens, Greece, as opposed to the harsh treatment they afford slavery in the South.

[641] Paiewonsky, Isidor, *Eyewitness Accounts of Slavery in the Danish West Indies* (New York: Fordham University Press, 1989), vii.

United States that emerged from its victorious fight for freedom in 1781, because all were "contaminated" with the sin of slavery. Quite obviously there is no real logic in "Yankee logic" beyond the "logic" of power, greed and profits.

The third fallacy contained in the Yankee Empire's narrative is that Southerners wanted to maintain in perpetuity the system of chattel slavery. And of course, the claim that the South intended to maintain in perpetuity the system of chattel slavery has become the *casus belli* (justification) for the North's aggressive war against the South. The current removal of monuments to Confederate General Robert E. Lee and other Southern heroes is justified by the Yankee Empire's propagandists by claiming that the South was evil and wanted to maintain slavery. But what was General Lee's attitude toward the institution of slavery?

General Lee, before the war, made clear his view on the institution of slavery by writing, "In this enlightened age, there are few I believe, but will acknowledge, that slavery as an institution, is a moral and political evil in any country."[642] Words could not be clearer, but clarity and truth are of no use to the Yankee Empire's sycophants. General Thomas Jonathan "Stonewall" Jackson was another famous Confederate who had no desire to maintain chattel slavery. General Jackson did not own slaves until late in his life when two slaves came to him and asked him to buy them because their master had died, and his estate was being liquidated. General Jackson agreed but told them that he would keep an account of their services, and when the value of their service was equal to the

---

[642] Kennedy, *Myths of American Slavery*, 167; citing Douglas S. Freeman, *R. E. Lee* (New York: Charles Scribner's Sons, 1947), Vol. I, 372.

purchase price, he would grant them freedom.[643] General Forrest, the most maligned Confederate officer in the entire war, was a slave owner. He armed his slaves and took them with him as he waged war against the Yankee invaders. Stories of armed slaves fighting side by side with—not against—white Southern soldiers will cause politically correct heads to explode. Before the end of the war, General Forrest called his slave troopers together and gave them their freedom. He told them that as free men they could stay with the Confederate army or leave. While a few left and returned "home," the majority freely elected to stay in the Confederate Army and continue the fight! Yet, salacious, false stories of cruel, evil, slave-beating Southerners continue to be a key ingredient in the mixture of slanderous lies about the South that is used by the Yankee Empire to justify its aggressive war against the people of the Confederate States of America.

The fact that slaves were willing to serve in the Confederate military voluntarily demonstrates that the system of chattel slavery as practiced in the South was radically different from the system of slavery as practiced in other parts of the world such as the Caribbean.[644] Slavery in the Caribbean was typically a system of absentee landlords who hired overseers to run their plantations. Southern chattel slavery was practiced by families headed by a patriarch who (for the most part) treated his slaves as part of an extended family very similar to the way Old Testament patriarchs, such as Abraham, treated their slaves. Certainly, there were exceptions, but they were "exceptions" and not the general rule. A reading of the federal government's "Slave Narratives" collected in the late 1930s

---

[643] General Jackson also owned a third servant, a mentally infirmed young black woman that he and his wife had under their care.

[644] Hummel, *Emancipating Slaves, Enslaving Free Men*, 57-58.

from former slaves demonstrates the veracity of the claim that good treatment of slaves in the South was the rule and evil treatment was the exception. Had this not been the case, there would have been a generalized slave revolt in the South, as vicious as the one that occurred in Haiti, as soon as white males of military age left the plantations and entered Confederate military service during the war.

In 1889, former Confederate States President Jefferson Davis passed away in New Orleans, Louisiana. It had been more than two decades since the end of the war and the end of chattel slavery. Yet, many of Jefferson Davis' former slaves came to pay homage to their former master. This outpouring of grief shocked Northern reporters covering Davis' funeral. One of Jefferson Davis' former slaves was seen weeping and was asked by a reporter why he wept. The former slave replied, "That I loved him this shows, and I can say that every colored man whom he ever owned loved him. He was a good and kind master." [645] Thornton Montgomery, a former slave that Davis helped educate, sent the following message of condolence to the Davis family: "I have watched with deep interest and solicitude the illness of Mr. Davis … and I had hoped that with his great willpower to sustain him he would recover…. I appreciate your great loss, and my heart goes out to you in this hour of your deepest affliction…. I beg that you accept my tender sympathy and condolence."[646] Yes, President Davis had owned slaves, but as they testified, he was a "good and kind master." He was a master who believed, as did most Southerners, that slavery must eventually end. He hoped to abolish slavery in a manner that would be beneficial to all parties, especially the

---

[645] Kennedy & Kennedy, *Was Jefferson Davis Right?*, 120.

[646] *Ibid.*

slaves.[647] Yankee invasion, conquest, and occupation prevented the South from developing a good system of emancipation. Instead of a constructive system of emancipation, black and white Southerners received from their Yankee masters a new form of slavery—sharecropping. Post-war sharecropping with over 8.5 million black and white people held in debt peonage (debt slavery or bondage) replaced chattel slavery.[648] *Vae Victis*—Woe to the vanquished.

Do slave owners or their descendants deserve freedom? According to the Yankee Empire's sycophants, the answer is no! Southerners did not have a right to be free of the emerging Yankee Empire in 1861 because of the sin of slavery, and their descendants today have no such right. According to the prevailing Yankee mythology, the people of the South are now the property of the federal government, and henceforth must remain the subjects of the Yankee Empire—forced to remain seated upon the "stools of everlasting repentance."[649] According to this flawed Yankee theory, slavery has tainted all Southerners, and therefore Southerners can never claim the right to remove themselves from a government that was established, not only without their consent, but in violation of their militant desire not to be part of the government subsequently imposed upon them. It is a form of "corruption of blood" by which current Southerners are denied their right to withdraw from the oppressive Yankee Empire, because some (approximately 20%) of their ancestors were contaminated and corrupted by the sin of slavery. Both English Common Law and American Constitutional Law prohibit the theory of

---

[647] *Ibid.*, 38-40.

[648] Kennedy & Kennedy, *Punished With Poverty*, 105-119 & 173-195.

[649] Owsley, "The Irrepressible Conflict," *I'll Take My Stand*, 63.

"Corruption of Blood,"[650] but according to Yankee logic, that is not a valid defense because both English Common Law and American Constitutional Law have been tainted and corrupted by the sin of slavery! As far as the Yankee Empire is concerned, the South entered the Union with the Northern majority and cleverly hidden over the portal to that Union was the Yankee's perpetual union clause. Southerners in 1861 and subsequently are at last allowed to read that hidden Yankee perpetual Union clause: *"Abandon hope all ye who enter here."*[651]

The Altar of Freedom is Bathed in Southern Blood

If the total number of Southern deaths caused by Yankee invasion and occupation were normalized to the South's 2010 population, the total number of Southern deaths would be equal to 3.5 million deaths.[652] Compare Southern deaths caused by Yankee invasion to European and Japanese death rates caused by the war that resulted from German and Japanese attacks during World War II: Approximately 572,000 French

---

[650] "Corruption of Blood" is a theory that the punishment for an act of treason or felony punishable by death—said punishment can be passed on to successive generations. See *West Law Dictionary.*

[651] "All hope abandon ye who enter here" is the inscription over the entrance to hell (Dante's Inferno) as described by the 14th Century author Dante in his epic poem *The Divine Comedy.*

[652] DiLorenzo, "The Founding Fathers of Constitutional Subversion," *Rethinking the American Union*, 80.

people died,[653] 451,000 English people died,[654] 2.9 million Japanese died,[655] 5 million Poles died,[656] while the United States suffered 419,000 mostly military deaths.[657] If the United States had suffered the same casualty rate during the Revolutionary War as the South suffered during the so-called "Civil War," instead of suffering 12,000 casualties, the Thirteen American Colonies would have lost 94,000 men! If the United States had suffered the same casualty rate during World War II as the South suffered during the War for Southern Independence, the American casualties, instead of being 419,000 deaths in World War II—would have been approximately 6 million deaths![658] Very few nations in the world (such as Russia during World War II) have sacrificed a higher percentage of its population in an effort to maintain its freedom—yet slanderous Yankee propaganda continues to claim that Southerners were fighting for slavery while pacified Southerners are too timid to proudly proclaim that while the North was fighting for empire, the South was fighting for Freedom!

---

[653] "France," *World War II Database*, ww2db.com/country/France (Accessed 11/23/2017).

[654] "World War 2 Statistics," *Second World War History*, www.secondworldwarhistory.com/world-war-2-statistics.asp (Accessed 11/23/2017).

[655] *Ibid.*

[656] "Polish Victims," *Holocaust Encyclopedia*, www.ushmm.org/wlc/en/article.php?ModuleId=10005473# (Accessed 11/23/2017).

[657] "World War 2 Statistics," *Second World War History*, www.secondworldwarhistory.com/world-war-2-statistics.asp (Accessed 11/23/2017).

[658] McWhiney, *Attack and Die* (Tuscaloosa, AL: The University of Alabama Press, 1982), 194-195.

"Every man should endeavor to understand the meaning of *subjugation before it is too late*... It means that the history of this heroic struggle will be written by the enemy; that our youth will be trained by Northern school teachers; will learn from Northern school books their version of the war; will be impressed by all the influences of history and education to regard our gallant dead as traitors, our maimed veterans as fit objects for derision
—General Patrick Cleburne, Irish Confederate.

Is it "too late?" Have pacified Southerners learned to accept *subjugation*?

Chapter 15: The Will to be Free?

THE TITLE OF THIS CHAPTER IS NOT a statement but a question. While there are certainly a fair number of Southerners who would vote to form a separate Southern Republic, their percentage out of the total population would be less than a majority. Several recent polls have demonstrated that a significant minority of Americans, including those living in non-Southern states, still believe that a state has the right to secede from the United States and form an independent country. A Rasmussen poll conducted in 2013 documented that 17% of those surveyed stated they believed in the right of secession. A more recent poll conducted by Reuters/Ipsos found that 24% of Americans believed that their state had the right to break away from the United States.[659] The poll was divided into sections of the United States in which Texas, Oklahoma, Maryland, and Missouri were not included in the South—the South being designated Southeast. The results are as follows:

---

[659] Muskal, Michael, "Poll: Nearly one in four in America would favor secession," *Los Angeles Times*, www.latimes.com/nation/nationnow/la-na-nn-secession-poll-america-20140919-story.html (Accessed 8/19/2017).

Geographical Section	Percentage in Favor of Right of Secession	States Included Within Each Section [Note: Section designation for states made by individual who designed the poll. Does not represent traditional designation of Southern States]
New England	19%	ME, NH, VT, MA, RI, CT
Mid Atlantic	21%	NY, PA, DE, MD, NJ
Great Lakes	22%	OH, IN, IL, MI, WI, MN
Southeast	25%	AR, LA, MS, AL, GA, SC, FL, NC, TN, KY, VA, WVA [Note: The traditional South includes TX, OK, MO, & MD but these Southern states were placed in other sections in this poll]
Southwest	34%	TX, OK, AZ, NM
Plains	21%	ND, SD, NE, KS, MO, IA
Rockies	26%	WY, UT, CO, MT, ID
West	22%	CA, OR, WA, AK, HI, NV

The data for the table came from a Reuters/Ipsos poll.[660] Various polls have shown a consistent 20 to 30% of the Southern population in favor of secession.[661]

The interesting thing about the sizable number of Southerners who voiced a favorable attitude toward secession in these polls is that these numbers come from a people who have been subjected to generations of unanswered anti-South, "one nation indivisible," pro-Lincoln, "you guys are bad, evil, racists," slanderous, Yankee propaganda! Added to this is the sad fact that there has been no official [662] response to the Yankee Empire's continuous slandering of the cause of Southern independence. Beginning in the mid-1950s, there was a renewal of the determined effort on the part of the Yankee Empire's propagandists to portray the South as evil. Anyone (then and now) who dared to speak up in defense of the South was and is depicted as an evil, hate-filled, racist. Yet, despite all the negative Yankee propaganda—there still remains a strong sentiment among the Southern people that the South was right in 1861!

---

[660] *Ibid.*

[661] Another report that gave similar results, for a January 2017 poll see: www.vermontindependent.org/secession-poll-do-you-support-your-state-peacefully-withdrawing-from-the-united-states-of-america-and-the-federal-government-reuters (Accessed 8/19/2017).

[662] Southern elected officials have been too busy "kissing up" to the elite of the Yankee Empire as they maneuver for a larger reward for betraying their native land. The recent round (2015-2018) of destruction of Confederate monuments is being accomplished with the active or passive endorsement of the South's elected officials. These same officials continue to be re-elected by pacified Southerners. The vast majority of the South's elected officials do not represent the true South but are playing the Judas role of Vichymen, Quislings, and Scalawags.

The fact that today so many Southerners still believe in the right of secession—even after generations of slanderous Yankee lies masquerading as standard American (Yankee) history—demonstrates an important point. It proves the point that in order for the Yankee Empire's negative, anti-South propaganda to be effective, it must be overwhelming, continuous, and allowing *no effective* reply from the subjugated people. For the Yankee Empire's propaganda to be effective, it must be total—it only takes a relatively small amount of truth to undo the result of the Empire's negative propaganda. A dedicated effort of even a small number of Southerners could awaken, in the hearts of the subjugated people, a desire to be rid of their chains. Such a dedicated effort could awaken the desire to claim for themselves and their children the right to live under a government based upon their free and unfettered consent and to live in a nation where the moral values they cherish are respected and defended.

Imagine what the previously discussed opinion poll results would have been if, for the previous four years, there had been an active, organized effort to challenge the legitimacy of the Yankee Empire's abusive rule of the South! Think about what a difference it would have made, not only in these recent polls but in the Southern society at large. Think about what a difference it would have made if there had been shadow governments established in even half of the Southern states for the past four years! Try to picture in your mind the difference it would have made if the Southern people had just one statewide elected official who would consistently use his office as a "bully pulpit" to encourage the people of the South to defend their moral social values, their Confederate heritage, their Confederate monuments, and their legitimate right to be the master in their own homes—the right of local self-government. This spokesman, occupying a bully pulpit, would be a true unreconstructed Southerner who would travel the South expounding the virtues of regaining the right to live under a legitimate government—a government that answers to the people of the sovereign states—and a leader who exhorts the people of the South to rise again in defense of their freedom. Imagine the difference if the South had a spokesperson who would work for the best interest of the people of the South and not the best interest of crony capitalists on Wall Street and their donor-class running dogs [663] in Washington, D. C. Imagine the difference in the poll results if an elected official had been traveling around the South denouncing the Yankee Empire as an illegitimate governing force! Think about the value of a true Southerner who is elected to high office but whose role in life is NOT to be a successful politician in the Yankee Empire's political apparatus but to help to organize the people of the South and challenge the Yankee Empire on the national and international stage. What a difference it would have made! There would have been no massive movement to remove the Ten Commandments from public display, promote anti-Christian, hedonistic, vulgar lifestyles, nor would there be an ongoing campaign to destroy the last vestige of Southern history—instead, there would have been hundreds of Confederate flags posted on highways all across the South and more going up every month until freedom would be won! [664] And any scalawag[665] politician who betrayed the South would be made to pay politically at the next election or immediately via a recall petition. All of this "could have been," but unfortunately, the South has lacked dreamers, visionaries, and nonviolent revolutionaries. The South's political and Southern heritage leadership preferred to remain docile and pacified rather than risk being labeled "extremists," or "controversial." When faced with the choice of striking for freedom or the safe comfort of bondage, they have

---

[663] The term "running dogs" is a literal translation from a Chinese insult or pejorative—zǒu gǒu. It is similar to "lap dog" or "lackey." It is one of the most demeaning expressions in their language.

[664] The concepts of shadow governments and "bully pulpit" are fully discussed in Kennedy, *Dixie Rising*.

[665] "Scalawag" is a term used during Reconstruction to denote a Southerner who betrays his own people and leagues himself with the Yankee Empire. Today, such Southern elected officials are modern-day running dogs for the Yankee Empire!

consistently made the coward's choice and remained silent and pacified—good "patriotic" subjects and sycophants of the Yankee Empire.

What Price for the South's Soul?

What is the price for a captive nation's soul? What is the price that Southerners must continually pay for the destruction and constant vilification of their democratically elected sovereign nation—the Confederate States of America? What cost must the children of the conquered nation pay just for the privilege of remaining second-class citizens (actually subjects) in the Yankee Empire? What is the Judas[666] payment that pacified Southerners receive for sacrificing the dream of freedom and licking the boots of their political, social, and economic masters—the Yankee Empire's ruling elite? What value should we place upon the soul of a subjugated people? What is the worth of being pacified Southerners that make it more valuable than being free men living in a country of their own? Are there no dreamers left in the South? Are there no old men to dream dreams, or young men to see visions? [667] If there are no such men and women, then the chains that bind pacified Southerners to the illegitimate Yankee Empire shall forever remain "indivisible!"

The Southern people are a religious people who place a high value on social morality. One of the principal reasons for the victory and overwhelming acceptance and even embracing of the Civil Rights movement of the 1960s was that it caused the average white Southerner

---

[666] Judas was the Disciple who betrayed Jesus for thirty pieces of silver; Matthew 26:14-16, 47-50, *Holy Bible*.

[667] Joel 2: 28 & Acts 2: 17, *Holy Bible*.

to question the morality of imposing discriminatory laws upon black Southerners. It caused white Southerners to ask themselves whether or not these "Jim Crow laws"[668] were consistent with the commandment that Jesus gave his followers to "Do unto others as you would have them do unto you."[669] While the federal government could forcefully remove discriminatory laws, it was the white South's sense of morality that removed the support for these laws and the rationale used to justify their initial enactment. This same sense of Southern morality has been used by the Yankee Empire to convince pacified Southerners that it would be wrong for "patriotic" Southerners to refuse to freely give their allegiance to the federal government as currently constituted. The Yankee Empire's ruling elite intuitively understand that Southerners will not be easily persuaded to violate their sense of morality especially when that morality is unknowingly based on a false premise. This "false premise" asserts that the current status quo, the current federal government, is a legitimate government—a logical and legitimate outgrowth of the original Republic as established by America's founding fathers 1776-87.[670] Pacified

---

[668] "Jim Crow laws" was the term applied to laws passed to enforce racial segregation. Racial segregation was a matter of law (*de jure*) in the South and a matter of tradition (*de facto*) in the North. It was made "legal" by the U. S. Supreme Court in its infamous 1896 *Plessy vs Ferguson* case.

Note: it was the Federal Empire that gave Jim Crow laws official sanction. The majority of Justices who voted in favor were Northerners, while the only vote against it was from a Southerner from Kentucky whose family had owned slaves prior to the war. See Kennedy & Kennedy, *Punished With Poverty*, 132.

[669] "And as ye would that men should do to you, do ye also to them," Luke 6: 31, *Holy Bible*.

[670] These dates reflect the announcement of the Independence of the Thirteen American Colonies (1776) and the adoption by the sovereign states of the Constitution of the United States (1787-1788).

Southerners think that the current federal government (the Yankee Empire) is a legitimate government, therefore, according to the thinking of pacified Southerners, it would be socially immoral to be disloyal to "their" government. This is not the first time that an empire has used a captured people's sense of morality against the captive nation and thereby kept the captive people enslaved to the empire.

By the time Mahatma Gandhi arrived on the political stage in India, the people of India had suffered generations of rule by the British Empire. Gandhi noted that the people were held in captivity by the British Empire because they had no faith in themselves. They had no moral imperative to seek a better life of freedom for themselves and their children. India's people clung to the old ways of subjugation under British rule while feeling no moral outrage at being a subjugated people. They had no faith in their ability to successfully resist British rule but worse still—they felt no moral need to resist the British Empire.[671] Yet Gandhi taught them that "physical force is nothing compared to moral force and that moral force never fails."[672] Gandhi's efforts renewed the peoples' faith in themselves and produced a sense of the moral superiority for their cause. Their sense of moral justification for the cause of India's independence produced a movement that was recognized worldwide as being just, while it caused the world to begin viewing the British Empire's rule as unjust

---

[671] This is a very simplistic view because there always have been a few in India who suffered and died in numerous, unsuccessful attempts to resist the British Empire's rule. But in general, the population of occupied India, just like the population of the occupied South today, did not see any benefit or need to engage in a massive revolt against the status quo. Being subjects of the British Empire and second-class citizens in their own country did not produce moral outrage among the majority of India's people.

[672] As cited by Fisher, Louis, *The Life of Mahatma Gandhi* (New York: Harper & Row Publishers, 1950), 177.

and illegitimate. The victory for independence would not have been possible as long as the people felt no moral outrage at being ruled by outside forces. Indeed, before Gandhi's movement the people felt a moral obligation to remain loyal to the status quo. Gandhi's non-violent movement destroyed any sense of morality on the part of the British Empire and gave the people of India a sense of being morally right in their demand for independence. Their moral outrage allowed them to challenge the status quo—British Imperial rule.

Today, the people of the South are in the same position as the people of India before they became passionately aware of the immorality of the British Empire's rule. Currently, the Yankee Empire can count on pacified Southerners to support the status quo—the Empire's international struggle to expand and maintain its commercial, financial, and military, worldwide domination.[673] A typical pacified Southerner would think that to do less would seem "unpatriotic," a failure to "support our troops," and therefore immoral. Pacified Southerners feel they owe unquestioned allegiance to the Yankee Empire's "one nation indivisible." As far as pacified Southerners are concerned, morality is on the side of those who give their unquestioned allegiance to the United States of America—never realizing that they are actually pledging their allegiance to the very Yankee Empire that denied their ancestors the right of self-government and today denies them the right to live in a true American Republic. This status quo will remain as long as the Yankee Empire's propagandists maintain their

---

[673] Although it is never explained in such accurate and precise terms. It is usually explained as a "police action" or as an invasion to remove "weapons of mass destruction," or a "war on drugs," or a "war against terrorists." Such excuses for Yankee military action were begun by Lincoln with the excuse that "the South fired on the flag" at Fort Sumter in 1861 and is maintained today by Yankee propagandists who claim the South was "fighting for slavery."

unanswered slanderous attack against the truth about the South's struggle for freedom and independence.

Defining Southern Freedom

The following definition of Southern Freedom is taken from *Dixie Rising-Rules for Rebels*:

> The ultimate goal of this movement is to gain a free and prosperous South. A South where we the people of sovereign states are the masters in our own homes, where we enjoy the right of local self-government enforced by *real* states' rights inclusive of the rights of state nullification and secession. This can be accomplished within the geographical limits of the current United States *provided* a constitutional majority of the states ratify our Sovereign State Amendment and provide reparations to the South for the poverty imposed upon the Southern people as a consequence of the Federal Empire's invasion, conquest, continuing occupation and exploitation of the Confederate States of America. The alternative to the proposed radical restoration of America's original constitutionally limited Republic of Republics is for we the people of the South (as well as all other Americans who are not a part of the Empire's ruling elite or one of the elite's crony capitalists allies) to accept our status as subjects of the secular humanist Federal Empire or strike for independence. For those who love liberty there is but one choice—Freedom![674]

---

[674] Kennedy, *Dixie Rising*, 11-12.

A copy of the proposed Sovereign State Amendment can be found in other Kennedy books.[675]

"Had I foreseen these results of subjugation, I would have preferred to die at Appomattox with my brave men, my sword in this right hand," General Robert E. Lee, C.S.A., August 1870.
| Courtesy LOC

"Where there is no vision, the people perish."[676]

Summary—If the South had Won

What would the world be like today if the South had won its war for independence? There is no real way of knowing, and usually, if such a discussion is attempted, it is cut short by an apologist of the Yankee Empire crying out that "African Americans would still be in slavery!"[677] With that unsubstantiated and absurd declaration, all hope of having a public and civil discussion ends. "Slavery" is a magic wand used by Yankee propagandists to cast a spell of silence (soft censorship) on

---

[675] See Kennedy, *Reclaiming Liberty*, 76-79; Kennedy & Kennedy, *Why Not Freedom!*, 294-297; or , *Nullification: Why and How*, 93-96. [Free pdf at: http://www.kennedytwins.com/Nullification_Book_2012.pdf]

[676] Proverbs 29:18a, *Holy Bible*.

[677] The ruling elite are not above using code words and phrases to incite its base. For example, Vice President Biden told a predominately black crowd in Virginia that "they want to put you all back in chains." Although he denied any association with a return of slavery—the message was clear nonetheless. See abcnews.go.com/blogs/politics/2012/08/vp-biden-says-republicans-are-going-to-put-yall-back-in-chains (Accessed 09/18/2012).

any pro-South discussion. It is imperative for the Yankee Empire to constantly maintain this "soft censorship," because they understand that Yankee propaganda, when appropriately challenged, will utterly fail the test of truth and logic.

A review of the post-war condition of the newly freed slaves demonstrates that slavery did not end with the victory of the Yankee Empire in its war to prevent Southern independence. After the war, the old form of slavery (chattel slavery) morphed into a new form of slavery—debt peonage, commonly referred to as sharecropping. The Yankee Empire's imposed system of sharecropping was described by Louisiana Governor Sam H. Jones in 1943 as, "a system of peasantry."[678] No efforts were made by the victorious Yankee Empire to emancipate these newly "freed" slaves from Yankee-imposed debt peonage—not to mention an even larger number of white Southerners who were also forced into debt peonage after being conquered by the Yankee Empire. Sharecropping continued until it died a natural death in the late 1950s and mid-1960s. It died the same way chattel slavery would have died—due to mechanization. Even if no Southern movements were seeking to abolish slavery—as there had been up to the 1830s—the force of economics would have compelled the peaceful abolition of slavery. If the South had won, the process of the peaceful abolition of slavery would have occurred in a manner in which black and white Southerners would have maintained a sense of mutual respect, a sense of community and kith and kin. Instead, the victors imposed upon the defeated people of the South a system of racial distrust and hatred. This post-war unnatural system of racial mistrust and animosity was a result of the Yankee Empire's divide and

---

[678] Governor Sam Houston Jones, "The Plundered South," The Abbeville Blog, www.abbevilleinstitute.org/blog/the-plundered-south (Accessed 01/31/2018).

rule policy in which black Southerners were used by the Yankee Empire's Republican politicians as a weapon against white (Democrat) Southerners. Post-Reconstruction it was used by Democratic politicians as a way to garner white Southern votes for the Democratic Party.

Racial hatred continues today as a result of the Yankee Empire's propagandists who work diligently to maintain the sense of victimhood in the black community. This sense of victimhood conveniently diverts black attention away from the real culprits who are responsible for rank, social, and economic poverty suffered by black Southerners while helping to maintain a strong liberal, black voting bloc. This victimhood propaganda has resulted in hate crimes committed against whites by blacks who are motivated by a misguided and misdirected sense of outrage and revenge.[679] This sense of black victimhood and hatred for conservative white Southerners is needed to keep black Southerners voting for liberal candidates.[680] Yankee Empire officials and sycophants warn black Southerners to vote the liberal Democratic ticket or else, according to Yankee propaganda as declared by Democratic Vice President Joe Biden, Southern conservatives will "put y'all (you all) back

---

[679] Examples of black hate crimes against whites: Hawkins, Awr, "50 'Teens' Beat White Man to a Pulp For Asking Brawling Girls to Get Off His Car," *Breitbart*, www.breitbart.com/big-government/2015/05/12/50-teens-beat-white-man-to-a-pulp-for-asking-brawling-girls-to-get-off-his-car (Accessed 09/21/2017); Rodriguez, Katherine, "Louisiana Man Arrested for Allegedly Threatening to Kill White People," Breitbart, www.breitbart.com/big-government/2017/09/16/louisiana-man-arrested-allegedly-threatening-kill-white-people (Accessed 09/17/2017); Rocha, Veronica, et al., "Hate crime is suspected after a gunman kills 3 white men in downtown Fresno," *Los Angeles Times*, www.latimes.com/local/lanow/la-me-fresno-shooting-20170418-story.html (Accessed 04/18/2017); "Woman who allegedly attacked man at VA gas station arrested," wtvr.com/2017/04/05/angela-jones-arrest-1 (Accessed 04/07/2017).

[680] Kennedy & Kennedy, *Punished With Poverty* South, 7-13.

in chains." This false claim that white Southerners want to put black Southerners back in some form of slavery is not new. It was also used very effectively by the Republicans during Reconstruction as a means of helping to create a black/white racial divide in the South.[681] It was and still is part of the Yankee Empire's campaign to divide and rule the South.

If the South had won its independence, instead of racial hatred created by the post-war Republican policy of divide and rule, the South could have followed a system of gradual emancipation, integration of freed slaves into society,[682] and mutually sharing in the governance of Southern society. Confederate General Beauregard was a post-war advocate of political power sharing and civil rights for the former slaves. But Yankee economic and political greed enforced by Yankee military power would not allow such a system to arise in the Yankee Empire's newly conquered Southern territories. The reason was that such a system would have destroyed Republican dreams of ruling Lincoln's newly created Yankee Empire.

If the South had won its independence, instead of having a massive Yankee Empire dominating the North American continent, there would have been two democratically elected republics in North America—the United States of America and the Confederate States of America. The likelihood of the post-war United States developing into an aggressive empire would have been greatly reduced, if not wholly eliminated, with the military defeat of Lincoln and his Republican co-conspirators. For example; during the debate on ratifying the 1898 Treaty of Paris ending

---

[681] Fleming, Walter L., *Documented History or Reconstruction* (Cleveland, OH: The Arthur H. Clark Co., 1907), 23.

[682] See, Livingston, Donald W., "Confederate Emancipation Without War," *To Live and Die in Dixie*, 455-489.

the Spanish-American War, there was considerable dissension on whether to ratify the Treaty. Ratification would mean that the United States would take control of vast overseas Spanish territories. Many Americans were opposed to the United States becoming an international power with overseas possessions. Republicans voted 41 out of 46 in favor of the Treaty while the Democrats voted 21 out of 32 against the Treaty.[683] The Spanish-American War, let alone this vote, would not have occurred if the South had been an independent democracy. The reason is that post-war, the big government, Hamiltonian Republican Party would have fallen out of favor and most likely disbanded—just like the failed Hamiltonian Federalist and Whig Parties that preceded the Republican Party. The demise of the Republican Party would have sharply limited the Hamiltonian dreams of New York's crony capitalists. The Kingdom of Hawaii would have remained an independent nation, the Spanish-American War would not have occurred, the Philippines would not have become an American protectorate, the United States would not have been involved in the Boxer Rebellion—all of which would have prevented the death of thousands of (1) United States troops and (2) hundreds of thousands of foreign troops and civilians. God only knows how many "modern day" wars would not have occurred if the world had not been blessed with Lincoln's aggressive Yankee Empire.

Detractors argue that even if the South were an independent nation, it would have become an aggressor in the Caribbean. Detractors would note that the South, prior to the war, had harbored long-lasting desires to bring Cuba under Southern control. While it is true that there was some discussion before the war of gaining control of Cuba, it does not follow

---

[683] Gibson & Castel, *The Yeas and the Nays: Key Congressional Decisions* (Kalamazoo, MI: 1975), 117.

that the Confederate government would have contrived an excuse to initiate a war with Spain over Cuba. The South has a tradition of fighting against foreign domination in 1776 and again in 1861. Cuba had been a major staging point for blockade runners during the war, and a Cuban Revolutionary, Colonel Ambrosio Jose Gonzales, served on General Beauregard's staff during the war. Before the war and while taking his summer vacation in Warrenton Springs, Virginia, Gonzales composed *Manifesto on Cuban Affairs Addressed to the People of the United States* in an effort to give the American people the correct understanding of the Cuban Revolution that was an attempt to gain independence from Spain.[684] Gonzales proudly proclaimed that "the blood of Cubans has mingled with the American ... bring forth the aspiring tree of liberty."[685] It is hard to believe that two peoples, Cuban and Confederate, would not have been able to establish friendly and mutually beneficial relations. But thanks to the overwhelming power of Lincoln's Yankee Empire, the opportunity never materialized.

The vital point to remember is that the Yankee Empire used its victory against the Confederate States of America as a means to establish itself as the supreme economic and military master of the North American continent. One successful military adventure is never enough for an expanding empire. The defeat of the South provided the Yankee Empire with impoverished young Southern men to fill its future military needs, an immense source of raw resources, a captive marketplace for its finished

---

[684] De la Cova, Antonio Rafael, *Cuban Confederate Colonel: The Life of Ambrosio Jose Gonzales* (Columbia, SC: University of South Carolina Press, 2003), 104-105.

[685] *Ibid.*, 104.

products, and it gave the general Yankee public a Yankee version of the British jingoistic[686] spirit of aggressive nationalism.

International Consequences of an Independent Confederate States of America

As already noted throughout this book, Confederate General Robert E. Lee warned that with the victory of the Yankee invader, their subsequent rejection of State Sovereignty and the centralization of political power in Washington, D.C., the United States of America would become "aggressive abroad and despotic at home." Since the unconstitutional, illegal, and immoral war upon the South, the self-righteous Yankee has always felt that he is endowed from on high with the right to meddle and intervene in the affairs of any nation and people—said meddling and interventions are typically motivated by the Yankee's desire to maintain or increase Yankee profits.

Before the defeat of the Confederate States of America, the United States influenced the world via missionaries and merchants—after the defeat of the Confederate States of America, the United States influenced the world via its military, its gunboats and, more recently, its missiles and drones. Why did this change take place, and why did it occur after the *extermination* of the South's pre-war political power in the United States Congress? This change took place because the one thing that stood in the way of Yankee self-aggrandizement from the very beginning of the United

---

[686] "Jingoism" a British term meaning "an extreme chauvinism or nationalism marked especially by a belligerent foreign policy," www.merriam-webster.com/dictionary/jingoism (Accessed 10/21/2017). Some sources claim the term was first used in the U.S. by opponents to the U.S. invasion and occupation of the Kingdom of Hawaii; "Jingoism pure and simple," *Kansas City Times*, 14 February 1893, 4.

States was the conservative, Constitution-loving South. With defeat and "reconstruction" the *New* South's political and educational leaders became little more than the Yankee Empire's lapdogs. The war brought about a radical but unacknowledged change in the relationship of the United States government not only with the people of the United States but also the people of the world. Southern author Andrew Nelson Lytle, writing in the 1930s, was one of the very few who recognized this change. He wrote:

> The mercy of God did not bring independence. Nor was the war over. One phase was done...The avowed purpose [of Northern policy] was the destruction of Southern civilization.[687]

The "destruction of Southern civilization" was and is essential to the Yankee Empire, because the Empire's elite understands that today the South contains the only real possibility of destroying the power of America's ruling elite, its crony capitalists on Wall Street, and its "Deep State" donor class on K Street. While the enemies of the South understand this—unfortunately, pacified Southerners as of yet do not have the ability or perhaps the courage to envision a day in which "the South shall rise again!"

The potential for Southern freedom exists. The strategy has been detailed.[688] All that is lacking is a people with the vision and courage to strike for freedom. If Southerners and other freedom-loving Americans are successful in amending the Federal Constitution to restore to "we the people" of the sovereign States, the ability to force the federal government to abide by the Constitution, crony capitalism and Washington elitism will

---

[687] Kennedy & Kennedy, *The South Was Right!*, 303.

[688] Kennedy, *Dixie Rising*.

be given a deathblow. The military-industrial complex which feeds on no-win wars and international intrigue can be brought under control and forced to work for the protection of the borders of the New United States of America. With the tools of REAL States' Rights in their strong right hand, the people of the sovereign states can nullify the meddling influence of the arrogant Yankee—the REAL "Ugly American!"

If it proves impossible to amend the United States Constitution to protect "we the people" of the sovereign states from federal tyranny, then like India, Ireland, and numerous other captive nations that were faced with domination by an arrogant and uncompromising empire, the struggle for Southern independence will commence. Once the Confederate States of America is free again, the worldwide community will have in the Confederacy an American nation that will be a friend of liberty everywhere but the defender of liberty *only* in the Confederate States of America. In other words, the Confederate States of America will not pursue an aggressive and interventionist foreign policy. The Southern way of government and social structure will be mutually beneficial for the people of the South, but that does not mean that the South has the right to impose its system of government upon other nations—many of whom have a longer and more diverse history than the South. This concept of leaving things alone and keeping one's nose out of other people's business is foreign to the Yankee (Ugly American) character. With the re-establishment of a free and prosperous Confederate States of America on the North American Continent, the wings of the Imperial Yankee Eagle will have been "clipped!" While Yankee Imperialists and pacified Southerners may bemoan this new reality, the people of the world as well as the people of a free and prosperous South will rejoice!

Deo Vindice!

Jefferson Davis, President, Confederate States of America. Flag on President Davis' right is the thirteen-star U.S. flag of the 1776-81 Revolutionary War; to his left is the Confederate Battle Flag | Painting from author's collection—Arbury Hadden, artist)

The lust of *empire* impelled them [Yankees] to wage against their weaker neighbors [the South] a war of subjugation.
—President Jefferson Davis, CSA.[689]

This book is a captive nation's plea for Freedom!

---

[689] Davis, Jefferson, *Rise and Fall of the Confederate Government*, Vol. 1, (1881, William Mayes Coats, Nashville, TN: circa 1980), 229.

Terms and Phrases

The following list will assist those who are unfamiliar with some commonly used American words and phrases which relate to the so-called American Civil War. Some such words and phrases are commonly used in everyday language in the United States while others are more often used in what is known today as the South—the former Confederate States of America.

Anti-Federalist: In the history of the United States, anti-federalists were American Founding Fathers who desired a very limited central (federal) government with all power not delegated to the central government remaining in the hands of the people of each sovereign state of the United States (also see Federalists).

Appomattox: A reference to Appomattox Courthouse, Virginia, where the major portion of the Confederate Army, under the command of General Robert E. Lee, was compelled to surrender. For the people of the South, this word conjures up all the evil that the Yankee victory caused in the South.

Articles of Confederation: The Articles of Confederation was the first "constitution" or plan of common government for the original thirteen American states shortly after declaring their independence from Great Britain. This system of government existed from 1781, the date when the last of the thirteen states ratified it, until 1787, the time when nine states seceded from that government by acceding (ratifying) a new system of government under the Constitution of the United States. It should be noted that, under the Articles of Confederation, each state was recognized as a free, independent, and sovereign state. Nothing in the new system of government under the Constitution voided this claim of state sovereignty.

Bayonet Constitution: A constitution or government that is forced upon a people by military force, therefore it is said to be a government made at the point of a bayonet. It is a government not based on a people's free and unfettered consent but upon compulsion. Such governments, according to the American Declaration of Independence, are illegitimate governments. The mere passage of time does not bestow legitimacy upon an illegitimate government.

Bipartisan or Bipartisanship: Terms used in the United States to denote the cooperation of two major American political parties (the ruling elite) to achieve a common goal. Bipartisanship is often lauded as "working together." This "working together" is usually done for the benefit of the financial elites on Wall Street in New York and corporate lobbyists of the "donor class" on K Street in Washington, D.C. Seldom do the benefits of bipartisanship reach the average American.

Bunker mentality: A hyper-defensiveness usually of a group of individuals or society that feels it is being attacked unfairly by a much stronger adversary.

Carpetbagger: A Yankee who came to the Confederate States of America after its defeat to plunder the already improvised and devastated South. These Yankees often came down south with all they owned in one small bag made of carpet material. They left the South even more improvised, but they had gained much wealth in the process. Their Southern turncoat assistants were known as scalawags.

Circle the Wagons: An effort of self-defense when facing an attack or criticism from a superior force. Taken from the American West when a wagon train was under attack, the wagons were put placed in a circle from which a reasonable defense could be made.

Clipped Wings: Referring to the process of "clipping" or cutting the feathers on the wing of a bird, thus hindering its ability to fly.

Confederate States of America: A sovereign, democratically elected nation formed by thirteen sovereign states of the American Republic of Republics (U.S.A.) in 1861, also known as the "Confederacy." The Confederate States of America was founded upon the American principles as declared by the Founding Fathers in the Joint Declaration of Independence (1776). The Confederacy was established in response to the perceived financial looting and aggressive meddling of Yankees in the life of the Southern people—an agrarian people who only asked to be left alone.

Cultural Distortion: [Cultural Distortion exists] when the natural social relations of a people within a specific culture are radically changed due to the imposition of outside force. It describes the occurrence of adverse social changes that generally would not have occurred without some unnatural or external force. For example; the cooperation of the French in Vichy France with the Nazi forces during World War II.

Cultural Genocide: Cultural genocide is an attempt by an aggressor nation or empire to eliminate the native culture of an occupied people to reduce their natural pride and thereby limit the conquered people's desires to reclaim their right to self-government. It is a subset of genocide and, as such, does not require the immediate extermination of the occupied people, but rather it is a coordinated effort aimed at the destruction of the native population's values, history, and consciousness of national identity. The occupying power's aim is the ultimate destruction of the group and their assimilation into a vast mass of subjects with little or no memory of national freedom.

Divide and Rule: A technique used by empires to help the empire efficiently control the people of the empire's newly conquered nation. The British Empire used it against the Clans of Scotland and the Muslim and Hindu population of India. The Yankee Empire used it against the South by injecting the virus of Northern racism into Southern society, thereby causing black and white Southerners to become political enemies. Post-war Republicans initiated divide and rule during Reconstruction and reaped the benefit of black votes while the National Democratic Party reaped the benefit of Southern white votes during the era of Jim Crow/white supremacy.

Dixie: A name often applied to the American Southland, the Confederate States of America. The name is taken from a famous song by the same title. One portion of that song states: "In Dixie's land I'll take my stand, to live and die in Dixie." This song is the unofficial national anthem of the South but is virtually unsung in the United States today—even in the South (see Cultural Genocide).

Federal Empire: The system of government which replaced the original American Republic of Republics (the Compound Republic or Republic of Sovereign States) in 1861. Under the Federal Empire, states of the old republic were stripped of their sovereignty, and the federal government was thereafter the sovereign agent in the United States. The will of the supreme federal government cannot be successfully questioned or limited by the once sovereign states. Upon completion of its first act of aggressive imperialism (1865) on the North American continent the Federal Empire turned its attention internationally as it morphed into the globalist Yankee Empire. (See Yankee Empire).

Federalists: In the history of the United States, Federalists were American Founding Fathers who desired a stronger central government than the one which existed under the Articles of Confederation. Federalists were divided into two groups: Moderate Federalists who sought to establish a central government that would be capable of defending the United States from foreign attack and ensuring a free trade zone among the sovereign states of the United States and High Federalists who desired the establishment of a supreme central (federal) government whose actions and rules could not be questioned or ignored. Moderate Federalists composed the largest segment of Federalists. The work of Moderate Federalists and Anti-Federalists produced the Constitution and Bill of Rights which became the foundation of the American Republic of Republics known as these United States of America.

High Federalists: American founding fathers who wanted to establish a supreme federal (central) government. Such a government would have the power to nullify the acts of the states of the United States, determine how much power the federal government could exercise, and promote various forms of industry, commerce, and banking as the supreme federal government deemed necessary. The principles of the High Federalists were promoted first by the Federalist Party, and after its demise, by the Whig Party, and finally by the Republican Party. Today in the United States, all major political parties support this form of government-business relationship, often referred to as "crony capitalism or fascism."

Jim Crow Laws: Jim Crow is (was) a derogatory name for African-Americans. Jim Crow Laws restricted the Civil Rights of African-Americans within American society. Contrary to Yankee propaganda, these laws did not originate in the slave society of the South but rather in New England and the North (see Cultural Distortion and Divide and Rule).

Judas Payment: The sum of money (30 pieces of silver) paid to Judas Iscariot to betray Jesus. Judas had been a follower of Jesus but betrayed him for the price usually paid for the wrongful death of a slave. Judas Payment is the price given to a traitor to turn against a friend.

Kith and Kin: An old term brought to North America from the Celtic areas of Britain during the Colonial era. It refers to relatives, friends, and neighbors who are allied by blood and/or neighborly association. It denotes a socially accepted sense of the responsibility to provide mutual aid or defense in times of distress or danger.

Kumbaya Moment: A sense of camaraderie, friendship, or mutual agreement occurring after a friendly or mutually agreed to resolution of a dispute.

Making a Killing: Gaining great profits with little effort or risks.

Middle Class: An economic classification of people also known as the "working class." These people are neither economically poor nor rich but exist somewhere between these two extremes, thus the term "middle class." In the United States, these people comprise the bulk of citizens. The middle class depends upon their labor to earn a livelihood, and their most extensive investment and store of wealth is in their homes.

Neo-Conservative: While all conservatives in the United States proclaim they believe in limited government, neo-conservatives hold to the High Federalist view of a supreme federal government. Neo-conservatives fully support the high federalist view of an imperial government that works hand in hand with business both inside and outside the borders of the United States. Thus, neo-conservatives will be very active in supporting American foreign entanglements which America's Founding Fathers warned against.

New South: The Confederate States of America became known as the "New South" after Reconstruction, and pacified sycophants of the Yankee Empire had filled all elected offices in the defeated South. This New South had to pledge its unquestioned allegiance to the new order in Washington, that is, the "indivisible" Yankee Empire—although it was still called the federal government or the United States of America.

Our Kind of Guy: A foreign leader who willingly supports American (Yankee) interests in their own country. When Our Kind of Guy no longer supports the Yankee Empires' goals, they tend to be overthrown, killed, or both.

Pacified Southerners: Southerners who maintain unquestioned allegiance to the current "indivisible" federal government out of a false sense of patriotism. Pacified Southerners honestly think they are being loyal to America's original Constitutional Republic of Republics as created by America's Founding Fathers in 1776. They intentionally ignore and mentally repress the fact that the original republic was destroyed by Lincoln and was replaced by a supreme federal government. Their blind allegiance to the symbols and name of the old Republic—an allegiance that borders on idolatry—assures the continuation of the Yankee Empire (see Useful Fools).

Plain Folk: The non-plantation whites of the old South. They were mostly herdsmen following the tradition of their Celtic ancestors who practiced low-intensity agriculture while gaining their living from vast herds of cattle, sheep, and hogs. The Plain Folk of the old South composed the clear majority of the white population. Yankee propagandists often disparagingly refer to the plain folk as "poor white trash." They were not poor as evidenced by the fact that the value of their cattle and hogs rivaled the value of the South's cotton and other "plantation" crops in 1860.

Post-War Strategic Failure: The failure of post-war Southern leaders to keep alive in the heart of every Southerner the desire to be a free people; to have a government based upon their free and unfettered consent; and to have a government that protects the social, political, and economic interest of the Southern people. The ultimate result of this strategic failure was that the Southern people were taught to love the chains of bondage that keep them enslaved to the "indivisible" Yankee Empire.

Republic of Republics: A federal republic which is established by a number of smaller republics. Many of the Founding Fathers of the United States referred to the United States as a "compound republic." The motto of these United States is *E Pluribus Unum* which is translated as "Out of many, one." The "many" were the states that created the Federal Republic, each state being a sovereign state at the time of the American Revolution and retained that status as they entered the union under the Constitution. The Constitution clearly states that republican institutions must be maintained to be a member of the union. A supreme federal government is the extreme opposite of a Republic of Republics, a compound republic or a Republic of Sovereign States.

Reconstruction: That portion of time after the defeat of the Armies of the Confederate States of America while the South was under direct or active military rule (1865-75). During this time, it became the object of the Yankee Empire to prevent the South from ever becoming a threat to their political and economic stranglehold on the federal government. Although called "Reconstruction," the theme of the era was to finish the work of deconstruction of a once prosperous and free Southern people. The effort of "reconstruction" saw a prosperous people reduced into rank poverty and the mutation of chattel slavery into debt peonage, also known as sharecropping. This system of debt peonage enslaved twice as many people as did chattel slavery and included white as well as black slaves—the majority being white. This form of slavery flourished almost a century after Appomattox. In circa 1875, direct or active reconstruction was exchanged for indirect or passive reconstruction. Yankee military occupation forces were removed and puppet state governments loyal to the Yankee Empire were established in the conquered South. Thereafter the Yankee Empire held supreme authority in the so-called "New South."

Scalawag: A term of derision and contempt applied to Southerners who willingly became lackeys of the occupying forces of the Yankee Empire. After the defeat of the Confederate States of America by the Yankee Empire, some Southerners sought to enrich themselves by turning their backs upon their defeated nation and people. Presently in the South, this same attitude is seen by the bulk of elected officials in Dixie.

South: Geographically, the South is a term generally referring to that portion of the United States south of the Potomac River extending from the southeast U.S. coast to as far west as Texas, Oklahoma, and Missouri. The South is the most religious section of the U.S.A. and is often referred to as the "Bible-Belt." Politically, the South is the most conservative section of the United States historically insisting upon interpreting the Constitution in such a way as to maintain the sovereignty of each state—this concept of Sovereign States is the foundational principle of States' Rights, as opposed to states' privileges as exercised under the current Yankee Empire. As long as real States' Rights were maintained, the creation of a supreme federal government, that is, the Yankee Empire was impossible. The South is populated by a very diverse group of European, African, Latin American, and Oriental citizens. These people are often referred to as "Southerners." The South is also known as "Dixie." During the War for Southern Independence, Southerners united in their effort to maintain their independence under a government - The Confederate States of America.

Southern Heritage Movement: Even though conquered over 150 years in the past, Southerners have, up until the last 50 years, been free to display pride for their history and ancestors. Freely showing pride in their Southern heritage gradually came to an end and has been replaced with antagonistic displays of anti-South cultural genocide. In response to these attacks, many groups of Southerners attempted to respond but unfortunately have failed to reverse this anti-South tide. The collective efforts of these different and separate groups are often referred to as the Southern Heritage Movement. One main reason for this "movement's" failure is the lack of many Southerners to come to grips with the fact that they are a defeated people living in a conquered country—a captive nation. Not only are they defeated, but the victor also intends to keep them and their children's children equally subdued.

Southerner: See South.

States' Rights: The right of a Sovereign State to be the final judge as to whether or not the federal government is acting within limits imposed upon the federal government by the Constitution. It includes, but is not limited to, the States' Rights of nullification and secession. In contemporary America, the states have become provinces of the central government and no longer have "rights" but merely exercise "privileges" at the discretion of the supreme federal government.

Tar Brush: Originally this phrase was related to race mixing. Today, in the South, it usually means something or someone who has been unfairly vilified or socially denigrated, generally by one's opponent. For example, enemies of Southern freedom use the "tar brush of racism" to stigmatize Southerners who advocate pride in their Southern heritage. It is a tool used by progressives/liberals to chill free speech and silence advocates of Southern heritage and freedom—it is a form of soft censorship.

Tow the Line: To conform to or obey rules even if one does not necessarily agree with said rules. Compliance with unreasonable regulations is the hallmark of a person who "tows the line."

Too Big to Fail: A scare term used to justify the use of taxpayer funds to "bailout" large financial firms—firms that have close connections with the Yankee Empire's ruling elite.

Useful Fools: "Useful fools" is derived from "useful idiots" attributed to Lenin describing capitalists who were willing to help the communist revolution even though it would ultimately mean the destruction of capitalism. Pacified Southerners are the Yankee Empire's "useful fools." Their unquestioning allegiance to the "indivisible" Yankee Empire assures the ultimate destruction of all Southern traditional, conservative, social, political and religious values.

Yankee Empire: A vast global commercial/financial empire backed by the Empire's military power. Its origin is traceable to the invasion, conquest, and continued occupation of the Confederate States of America. The Yankee Empire has usurped the name and symbols of the Republic of Sovereign States established by America's Founding Fathers in 1776 and replaced it with a supreme federal government which is the sole judge of its Imperial powers (see Federal Empire). The Yankee Empire uses the name "United States of America" but that nation no longer exists—the constitutionally limited Republic of Sovereign States as established by the founding fathers and titled the "United States of America" was replaced with a supreme federal government which quickly morphed into the Yankee Empire.

Select Bibliography

Books & Articles

Bacevich, Andrew J., *The Limits of Power* (New York: Metropolitan Books, 2008)

Bastiat, Frederic, *The Law* (1850) (New York: The Foundation For Economic Education, Inc., 1979)

Berendse & Lucas, *The Act of Abjuration, the Dutch Declaration of Independence (1581)* (Amsterdam: Elsevier-Boeken, 2014)

Bettersworth, John K., *Mississippi: A History* (Austin, TX: The Steck Co., 1959)

Bowers, Claude, *The Tragic Era* (New York: Halcyon House, 1929)

Bradford, M. E., *Against the Barbarians* (University of Missouri Press, 1992)

Butler, Smedley D., *War is a Racket* (1935, Townsend, WA: Feral House Publishers, Port 2003)

Chappell, Paul K., *The Art of Waging Peace* (Westport, CT: Prospecta Press, 2013)

Chomsky, Noam, *Rouge States* (Chicago: Haymarket Books, 2000)

Clark & Kirwan, *The South Since Appomattox* (New York: Oxford University Press, 1961)

Cooper, Jr, William J., *Jefferson Davis—American* (New York: Alfred A. Knopf, 2000)

Evans, Eli N., *Judah P. Benjamin-the Jewish Confederate* (New York: The Free Press, 1988)

De la Cova, Antonio Rafael, *Cuban Confederate Colonel: The Life of Ambrosio Jose Gonzales* (Columbia, SC: University of South Carolina Press: 2003), 104-5

Denoon, Donald, *The Cambridge History of The Pacific Islanders* (Cambridge, UK: Cambridge University Press, 1997)

DiLorenzo, Thomas J., *Hamilton's Curse-How Jefferson's archenemy betrayed the American Revolution and what it means for Americans today* (New York: Crown Forum, 2008)

DiLorenzo, Thomas, J., *The Real Lincoln* (New York: Three Rivers Press, 2002)

Downs, Jim, *Sick from Freedom* (Oxford University Press: 2012)

Dubois, W. E. B., *The Suppression of the African Slave Trade 1638-1870* (1896, New York: Russell and Russell, 1965)

Ewing, E.W.R., *Northern Rebellion and Southern Secession* (Richmond, VA: J.L. Hill Co., 1904)

Fisher, Louis, *The Life of Mahatma Gandhi* (New York: Harper & Row Publishers, 1950)

Fleming, Walter Lynwood, *The Sequel of Appomattox* (New York: Glasgow, Brook & Co., 1970)

Fogel & Engerman, *Time on the Cross-The Economics of American Negro Slavery* (1974, New York: W.W. Norton & Company, 1989)

Forbes, David W., *Hawaiian national bibliography, 1780-1900* (University of Hawaii Press: 2003)

Gabriel Cardona, Juan Carlos Losada Malvárez, *Weyler, Nuestro Hombre En La Habana* (Barcelona, Spain: Planeta, 1988)

Gandhi, Arun, *The Gift of Anger and other lessons from my grandfather Mahatma Gandhi* (New York: Gallery Books, 2017)

Gibson & Castel, *The Years and the Nays: Key Congressional Decisions* (Kalamazoo, Michigan: 1975)

Graham, John R., *Principles of Confederacy* (Salt Lake, UT: Northwest Publishing, 1990)

Hoppe, Hans-Hermann, *Democracy; The God That Failed* (New Brunswick and London: Transaction Publishers, 2001)

Howard, Helen Addison, *Saga of Chief Joseph* (1941, Lincoln, NE: University of Nebraska Press, 1978)

Hummel, Jeffrey Rogers, *Emancipating Slaves, Enslaving Free Men* (Chicago: Open Court Publishing, 1996)

Johnson, Chalmers, *The Sorrows of Empire* (New York: Henry Holt and Company, 2004)

Johnson, Ludwell H., *North Against the South* (Columbia, SC: Foundation for American Education, 1978)

Kennedy, James Ronald, *Dixie Rising-Rules for Rebels* (Columbia, SC: Shotwell Publishing, 2017)

Kennedy, James Ronald, *Nullification! Why and How* (Wake Forest, NC: The Scuppernong Press, 2014)

Kennedy, James Ronald, *Reclaiming Liberty* (Gretna, LA: Pelican Publishing Co., 2005)

Kennedy, James Ronald, *Uncle Seth Fought the Yankees* (Gretna, LA: Pelican Publishing Co, 2015)

Kennedy, Walter D., *Myths of American Slavery* (Gretna, LA: Pelican Publishing Co., 2003)

Kennedy, Walter D., *Rekilling Lincoln* (Gretna, LA: Pelican Publishing Co., 2015)

Kennedy & Benson, *Lincoln's Marxists* (Gretna, LA: Pelican Publishing Co., 2012)

Kennedy & Kennedy, *Punished With Poverty—the Suffering South* (Columbia, SC: Shotwell Publishing, 2016)

Kennedy & Kennedy, *The South Was Right!* (Gretna, LA: Pelican Publishing Co., 1994)

Kennedy & Kennedy, *Was Jefferson Davis Right?* (Gretna, LA: Pelican Publishing Co., 1998)

Kennedy & Kennedy, *Why Not Freedom?* (Gretna, LA: Pelican Publishing Co., 1995)

Kilpatrick, James Jackson, *The Sovereign States* (Chicago: Henry Regnery Co., 1957)

Kinzer, Stephen, *Overthrow—America's Century of Regime Change From Hawaii to Iraq* (New York: Times Books, 2006)

Lenin, V. I., *Imperialism; The Highest Stage of Capitalism* (1917, New York: International Publishers, 1939)

Limerick, Patricia Nelson, *The Legacy of Conquest: The Unbroken Past of The American West* (New York: W. W. Norton & Company, 1987)

Livingston, Donald, "Why the War Was Not About Slavery," *To Live or Die in Dixie*, Powell, Frank, ed. (Columbia, TN: Sons of Confederate Veterans, 2014)

Lytle, Andrew Nelson, *Bedford Forrest and His Critter Company* (1931) (Nashville, TN: J.S. Sanders Co., 1992)

Lytle, Andrew Nelson, "The Hind Tit," *I'll Take My Stand* (1930) (Baton Rouge, LA: Louisiana State University Press, 1983)

Mahan, A. T., *The Influence of Sea Power Upon History* (Boston, MA: Little, Brow & Co.,1890)

Masters, Edgar Lee, *Lincoln the Man*, (1931) (Columbia, SC: The Foundation for American Education, 1997)

McKenney, Tom C., *Jack Hinson's One-Man War* (Gretna, LA: Pelican Publishing Co., 2009)

McDonald & McWhiney, "The South from Self-Sufficiency to Peonage: An Interpretation," *The American Historical Review* (Vol. 85, No. 5. Dec. 1980)

McWhiney, Grady, *Cracker Culture-Celtic Ways in the Old South* (Tuscaloosa, AL: University of Alabama Press, 1988)

Milton, John, *Paradise Lost*, Book IV, *John Milton Complete Poems and Major Prose*, Merritt Y. Hughes, ed. (Indianapolis & New York: The Odyssey Press, 1957)

Mises, Ludwig Von, *Human Action-A Treatise on Economics* (1945, Auburn, AL: The Ludwig von Mises Institute, 1998)

Mitcham, Samuel W., *Bust Hell Wide Open-the Life of Nathan Bedford Forrest* (Washington, DC: Regnery History, 2016)

Moore, George H., *Notes on the History of Slavery in Massachusetts* (New York: D. Appleton and Company, 1866)

Northern Opposition to Mr. Lincoln's War, Jonathan D. White, ed. (Waynesboro, VA: Abbeville Institute Press, 2014)

Orth, John V., *The Oxford Companion to the Supreme Court of the United States*, Kermit L. Hall, ed. (New York: Oxford University Press, 1992.)

Owsley, Frank L., *Plain Folk of the Old South* (1949) (Baton Rouge, LA: LSU Press, 1982)

Paiewonsky, Isidor, *Eyewitness Accounts of Slavery in the Danish West Indies* (New York: Fordham University Press, 1989)

Patrick Henry: Life, Correspondence and Speeches, Vol. III, W.W. Henry, ed. (Harrisonburg, VA: Sprinkle Publishing, 1993),

Perkins, John, *The New Confessions of an Economic Hit Man* (Oakland, CA: Berrett-Koehler Publishers, Inc., 2016)

Pollard, E. A., *Southern History of the War*, Vol. I (1866) (New York: The Fairfax Press, 1977)

Queen Lili'uokalani, *Hawaii's Story by Hawaii's Queen* (Honolulu, HI: Hui Hanai, 2013)

Rawle, William, *A View of the Constitution*, Kennedy & Kennedy, eds. (1825) (Baton Rouge, LA: Land & Land Publishing, 1993)

Rethinking The American Union, Donald Livingston, ed. (Gretna, LA: Pelican Publishing Co., 2013)

Robertson, Henry O., *"In the Habit of Acting Together"—The Emergence of the Whig Party in Louisiana, 1828-1840* (Lafayette, LA: Center for Louisiana Studies, University of Louisiana 2007)

Rummel, R. J., *Death By Government* (Transaction Publishers, 1994)

Semmes, Raphael, *Memoirs of Service Afloat* (1868) (Secaucus, NJ: The Blue & Grey Press, 1987)

Seabrook, Lochlainn, *A Rebel Born, A defense of Nathan Bedford Forrest* (Franklin, TN: Sea Raven Press, 2010)

Simkins, Francis Butler, *A History of the South* (New York: Alfred A. Knopf, 1959)

Ste. Claire, Dana, *Cracker-The Cracker Culture in Florida History* (University of Florida Press: 1998)

Stevens, Thaddeus, "Reconstruction," *A Just and Lasting Peace*, Smith, John D., ed. (New York: Signet Classics, 2013)

Stokes, Karen, "Fort Sumter and the Siege of Charleston," *To Live or Die in Dixie*, Powell, Frank, ed. (Columbia, TN: Sons of Confederate Veterans, 2014)

Symonds, Craig L., *Stonewall of the West-Patrick Cleburne and the Civil War* (Lawrence, KS: University of Kansas Press, 1997)

The Anti-Federalist Papers and the Constitutional Convention Debates, Ralph Ketcham, ed. (New York: Penguin Books USA Inc., 1986)

The Debates In The Federal Convention of 1787 Which Framed The Constitution of the United States of America, Hunt & Scott ed. (Union, NJ: The Lawbook Exchange, LTD, 1999)

Weaver, Richard, *The Southern Tradition at Bay* (New York: Arlington House, 1968)

Why the South Will Survive, Clyde Wilson, ed. (Athens, Georgia: The University of Georgia Press, 1981)

Wills, Gary, *Lincoln at Gettysburg: The Words that Remade America*, (New York: Simon & Schuster, 1992)

Wilson, Clyde N., *The Essential Calhoun* (New Brunswick, NJ: Transaction Publishers, 1992)

Wilson, Clyde N., *The Yankee Problem: An American Dilemma* (Columbia, SC: Shotwell Publishing, 2016)

Wisniewski, Richard A., *The Rise and Fall of the Hawaiian Kingdom* (Honolulu, HI: Pacific Basin Enterprise, 1979)

Woods, Thomas E., *Meltdown-A free market look at why the Stock Market collapsed* (Washington, DC: Regnery Publishing, Inc., 2009

Court Cases

Carter v. Carter Coal Company, 298 U. S. 238 (1936)
Baldwin v. Missouri, 281 U.S. 312, (1921)
Plessey v. Ferguson, 163 U.S. 537, (1896)
Ware v. Hylton, 3 Dallas, 199, 224, (1796)

About the Authors

James Ronald (Ron) and Walter Donald (Donnie) Kennedy were born and reared in Mississippi. Each received his Bachelor's degree from the University of Louisiana, Monroe, Louisiana. Ron holds a Master's degree in Health Administration (MHA) from Tulane University, New Orleans and a Master's of Jurisprudence in Health Law (MJ) from Loyola University Chicago. Donnie is a graduate of Charlotte Memorial Medical Center School of Anesthesia, Charlotte, North Carolina.

The Kennedy Twins are best known for their bestselling book *The South Was Right!,* which has sold over 140,000 copies as of 2018. Following the success of *The South Was Right!,* the Kennedy Twins have written eleven other books and edited, annotated, and republished an 1825 textbook on the United States Constitution by William Rawle. Books by the Kennedy Twins include the following: *Why Not Freedom! America's Revolt Against Big Government, Was Jefferson Davis Right?, Reclaiming Liberty, Myths of American Slavery, Lincoln's Marxists* (Donnie and Al Benson), *A View of the Constitution* (William Rawle, 1825), *Nullifying Tyranny, Rekilling Lincoln, Nullification: Why and How, Uncle Seth Fought the Yankees, Punished With Poverty,* and *Dixie Rising: Rules for Rebels.*

Many in the media have noted the Kennedy Twins advocacy of limited government, that is, real States' Rights, which have led to several interviews and TV appearances. The Kennedy Twins have been interviewed by numerous local and national talk radio shows including Col. Oliver North's radio show, Alan Comes's radio show, Bill Maher's show Politically Incorrect, BBC, French National TV, Louisiana Public Broadcasting TV and Mississippi Public Broadcasting radio and TV.

Both have served as Commander of the Louisiana Division Sons of Confederate Veterans. They have received special recognition awards from the National Commander of the Sons of Confederate Veterans, the Jefferson Davis Historical Gold Medal from the United Daughters of the

Confederacy and numerous other awards from various Southern Heritage organizations.

The Kennedy Twins are frequent speakers at civic associations, church groups, patriotic groups, and Southern Heritage conferences.

INDEX

A

Abolitionist, 108, 181, 244

Acton, Lord, ix, 65-66, 175, 180

Adams, John Quincy, 139, 297

Adams, 261

Afghanistan, 90

African slave trade, 180, 183-185, 187, 192-193, 237, 244, 255, 260, 314

"Almighty dollar," 161

Anaconda Plan, 232, 235

Anti-Federalists, 135, 277, 343, 346

Appomattox, 5, 11, 76, 80-81, 273, 278-279, 301, 343, 349

Arab Spring, 28

Arbenz, Jocobo, 44-45

Arthur, Chester A., 68

Articles of Confederation, 134, 201, 275, 343, 346

Austro-Hungary, 38

B

Bailouts, 307, 351

Bancroft, Charles, 246

Batista y Zaldívar, 100

Bay of Pigs, 47

Bayard, James A., 120

"Bayonet Constitution," 266

Beecher, Henry Ward, 82

"Benevolent Empire," 86

Benjamin, Judah P., 105

Benton, Senator Thomas H., 158

Bible-Belt, 1, 350

Blaine, James G., 59, 68

Boxer Rebellion, 33-36, 39, 85, 337

British Petroleum, 18, 27

Brownlow, William, 285

Buchanan, James, 227-228

"Bully Pulpit," 326-327

Bush Administration, 31, 143

Bush, George W., 90, 144

C

Calhoun, John C., 77-81, 301, 308

California, 107, 194

Capitalism, Free Market (see also, Crony Capitalism) 110, 174, 212-213, 242, 300, 302-303, 351

Captive Nation, ix-x, xii, 2, 5-6, 11-12, 94, 111, 118, 126, 156, 176, 184, 192, 217, 231, 244, 246, 256, 263, 281, 284, 287-290, 312, 328, 330, 342, 350

Caribbean, 46, 90, 149, 192, 214, 252, 316, 337

Castro, Fidel, 99-100

Censorship, 118, 123, 159, 165, 260, 293, 294, 333-334, 351

Central America, 1, 81, 124, 214

Central Bank, 170, 307-308

Central Intelligence Agency (CIA), 18, 20, 21-22, 24, 27, 30, 47, 163, 215

Chad, 27

Chaffee, General Adna R., 35-36

Chattel Slavery (see also, Slavery), 4, 7, 136, 180, 192-193, 270, 315-317, 334, 349

China, 33-37, 56, 85, 87, 89, 91, 214-215

Chinese Nationalists, 34, 37

Chomsky, Noam, xi

"City on a Hill," 196-197

Clay, Henry, 209-210

Cleburne, General Patrick, 256

Clemens, Samuel (Mark Twain), 93

Cleveland, Grover, 63, 68

Clinton, Hillary, 28

Clinton, Bill, 20, 26, 31

Cold War, 15, 19, 23, 27, 175, 213

Collateral Damage, xii, 47, 100, 122, 129, 214, 217

Colombia, 41, 45

Commercial empire, 41, 43

Compound Republic, 66, 346

Confederate Peace Commissioners, 147

Connecticut, 46, 67, 82, 99, 183

Constitutional Convention, 133, 205, 276-277

"Copperheads," 165, 245

Crony Capitalism (see also, Capitalis, Free Market), 77, 96, 110, 138, 164, 209-210, 212-213, 299-300, 302-303, 340, 346

CSS Alabama, 104, 149, 175

CSS Shenandoah, 51

Cuba, 45-47, 69, 84, 89-90, 97, 99, 121, 122, 124, 128, 280, 337

Cultural genocide, 10, 108, 125-126, 220, 241, 283-284, 286, 287-288, 290, 293-294, 312, 350

D

Damn Yankee, 2

Davis, Jefferson, 17, 41, 70, 150, 152, 164-165, 196, 203, 229, 259, 284, 291, 317, 361

Dawes Act, 125-126, 287

Debt peonage, 7, 44, 198, 270, 318, 334, 349

Declaration of Independence, 17, 52, 69, 78, 202, 215, 267-268, 274, 344

Deep State, 289, 305

DeRosa, Marshall, 142

Divide and rule, 94, 115, 124, 195, 281, 334, 336, 345

Dixie, 1, 345, 350

Dole, Stanford B., 57, 61, 67-68

Dollar Diplomacy, 43, 90, 123

Dollar worshipping, 91, 103, 205

Dominican Republic, 46-47

Donor class, 45, 282, 289, 340, 344

Douglas, Stephen A., 106, 262

Drug Cartels, 23

Dulles, John Foster, 216

Dutch Declaration of Independence, 78

E

East Timor, 20, 25-26, 31

Economic Hit Men (EHM), 22-23, 25, 31, 43, 85, 90, 141, 163, 280

Eisenhower, Dwight D., 21, 45, 139, 216-217, 236

Emerson, Ralph Waldo, 53-54, 151

European Union Parliament, 32

Exclusion laws, 262

F

"Fake News," 149, 165, 184, 225, 237, 240

Fascism, 189

Federal Reserve ("The Fed"), 22, 29, 79-80, 170, 212, 301, 307-309

Fifteenth Amendment, 95, 115, 117, 267, 277

Foreign interventions, 23, 133

Fort Sumter, 19, 82, 111, 119-121, 145, 147-148, 229-231, 331

Founding Fathers, x, 75, 77, 168, 202, 206, 242, 277, 329, 343-344, 346, 347-349, 352

Fourteenth Amendment, 95-96, 115, 117, 208, 267, 277

France, 18, 38, 84, 113, 314, 345

G

Gaddafi, Muammar, 26-29

Gandhi, 99, 296, 330-331

García, Somoza, 47

Garrison, William Lloyd, 194

Germany, 38

Gettysburg Address, 141

Globalism, 297, 303-304, 306-307

Gonzales, Jose Ambrosio, 338

Granada, 47

Grant, U.S., 195, 225, 235, 258, 273

Great Britain, 17, 27, 38, 52, 59, 133, 184, 186, 273, 314, 343

Guam, 69

Guatemala, 44-47

H

Habeas Corpus, 168, 169, 210

Haitian slave revolt, 182-183, 244, 317

Haley, Nikki, 283

Hamilton, Alexander, vii, 77, 133, 135, 205-209, 298, 301

Harrison, Benjamin, 63, 68

Hawaii, 51-52, 55-56, 58-64, 66-71, 86-87, 89, 99, 121, 127, 163, 266, 337

Hay, John, 35

Hay-Bunau-Varilla Treaty, 46

Hearst, William Randolph, 97

Henry, Patrick, 156, 157, 184, 201-202

High Federalists, 77, 133, 135-136, 205-206, 276, 298, 301, 346

Ho Chi Minh, 215

Holmes, Justice Oliver H., 96

Honduras, 42-43, 47

Hussein, Saddam, 26-27, 29, 32

I

Imperial Glory, 89, 207

Imperialism, 2-3, 10, 38, 41, 51, 69, 90, 118, 123, 180, 207, 300, 346

Indians, American (see also, Native Americans), 35, 89, 102-103, 105-108, 194, 197

Indonesia, 25-26, 29, 31

Inflation, 169-170, 302

Internal improvements, 16, 22, 158, 209

International Monetary Fund (IMF), 22, 26, 29, 80, 212, 302

Iran, 18, 21, 30

Iraq, 27, 29-32, 90, 175

Ireland, 150-152, 155, 256, 341

Islamic Revolution, 21, 30

Italy, 28, 38, 189

J

Jamaica, 45

Japan, 37-38, 56, 59, 88

Jay, Chief Justice John, 206

Jefferson, Thomas, 79, 81, 114, 116, 135, 139-141, 181, 202, 207-209, 226, 278, 297-298, 301, 308

Joint Chiefs of Staff, 100

Jones, Sam H., 7, 334

Joseph, Chief, 108

K

K Street, 124, 282, 302, 340, 344

Kamehameha, King, 52

Kentucky and Virginia Resolves, 116, 203, 210, 278

Khomeini, Ayatollah, 30

Kissinger, Henry, 26

Kith and Kin, 3, 334

Kurds, 30

Kuwait, 26, 31

L

Lane, Joseph, 64-66, 70-71, 299

Latin America, 43, 46

Lee, Robert E., ix, 11, 51, 53, 65-66, 69, 71, 84, 96, 126, 141, 175, 180, 273, 275, 279, 284, 315, 339, 343

Lenin, V. I., xi, 212, 242, 299-300, 351

Libya, 26-29, 90

Lili'uokalani, Queen, 51-52, 54-55, 58, 61-62, 70-71

Lincoln, Abraham, x, 2, 9-10, 16, 17-19, 32, 65, 68, 71, 77, 81-88, 96, 100, 105, 108-110, 116, 118-121, 141-145, 147-148, 159-169, 174-175, 194-195, 203-204, 210-213, 215, 217, 225-227, 229231, 234-235, 242-243, 245, 247, 254, 257-259, 262-263, 268, 278, 291, 293, 299, 303-304, 311, 325, 331, 336-338, 348

Long, Huey P., 19

Los Alamos, New Mexico, 101

Lytle, Andrew Nelson, 171, 175, 213, 340

M

Mahan, Alfred T., 86-88

Maine, 67, 68, 172

"Make Georgia howl," 92, 93

"Make Samar howl," 93

Manifest Destiny, 83

Mao Zedong, 216

Marines, 35, 47, 60, 62, 99

Mason, George, 157

Massachusetts, 53-54, 67, 79, 126, 174, 180, 183, 192-193, 226, 246, 261

Materialism, 25, 103, 154

McGrew, Dr. John S., 67

McKinley, William, 63, 69, 98

Mexico, 81, 84, 89, 172-173

Middle East, 28, 90

Military bases, 85, 94

Military industrial complex, 15

Milton, John, 144

Mission accomplished, 4, 110

Missionaries, 54, 56, 67, 339

Missionary Party, 56, 58-59

Moderate Federalists, 135, 277, 346

Money-worshiping, 25, 151, 161, 172

Monopoly, 21, 209, 254

Monroe Doctrine, 42

Morgan, J. P., 88, 305

Morrill Tariff, 243

Morton, Oliver P., 168

Mosaddeq, Mohammad, 19, 20

Muslim, 25, 28, 345

N

Native American (see also Indians, Ameican), vi, 92, 98, 102-109, 117, 125- 126, 156, 262, 280, 287, 313

"Negro Whipper," 193

Neo-conservatives, 347

New England, xi, 1, 24, 46, 54, 56, 79, 82, 99, 126, 134, 139, 150-151, 154, 160-162, 172-173, 180-181, 183-186, 193, 196, 205, 207, 209, 227, 236, 244-245, 254, 260-261, 298, 314, 347

New Hampshire, 164-165, 183

Nez Perce, 103

Nicaragua, 45, 47

Nightingale, 192

Ninth Amendment, 10, 76, 207, 277

Northerners, 2-3, 106, 149, 153, 156, 160-161, 166, 180, 189, 193, 195, 198, 246, 263, 264, 308

O

Oak Ridge, Tennessee, 102

Obama, Barack, 28, 90, 302

Ohio, 35, 53, 63, 67, 69, 88, 92, 98, 108, 160, 186, 210, 244, 262, 308

"One nation indivisible," 10, 174, 288, 291, 293, 325, 331

Open door policy, 35

Operation Guatemala, 47

Operation Northwoods, 100-101

Opium Wars, 34, 37

Oregon, 64-66, 70, 194

Organization of American States (OAS), 23, 32

"Our kind of guy," 20, 25-31, 43, 45, 100, 124, 280, 348

Owsley, Frank Lawrence, 292

P

Pacified Southerner, 10, 16, 31, 37, 48, 85, 99-101, 108, 141, 164, 174, 176, 207, 212,

214, 217, 241-242-243, 257, 268, 273, 275, 277, 279-280, 288, 290, 293, 309, 320, 325, 328-331, 340-341, 348, 351

Panama Canal Zone, 46

Parker, Joel, 198, 247

Peace-Democrats, 120, 162

Pearl Harbor, 57, 60, 148

Pellagra, 153, 271

Pennsylvania, 68, 96, 144, 150, 162-163, 183, 186, 219, 245, 251, 258

Perkins, John, 45

Philippines, 25, 33, 35-36, 69, 84, 89-91, 93-94, 96, 121-122, 124, 128, 149, 214, 280, 337

Pierce, Franklin, 164-165

Pike, Shepherd, 264

Plain folk, 153, 155, 159, 252-253, 270, 348

Platt Amendment, 46, 99

Pledge of Allegiance, 10, 268-269

Profit-driven, 162

Puerto Rico, 46, 69

Puppet governments, x, 16, 31-32, 41, 45, 113-114, 117, 121-123, 128, 216, 349

Puritan, 54, 150

Q

Quislings, 18, 113, 325

R

Radical abolitionists, 148, 171, 181, 183, 185, 188, 190

Radical Republicans, 118

Railroad, 162-163, 171, 254, 264

Randolph, Thomas J., 186

Randolph, John, 201

Rape, 30, 70, 220

Rawle, William, 76, 169, 188

Reconstruction, 20, 84, 90, 95, 107-108, 113-117, 122, 127, 175, 180, 184, 195, 198, 211, 228, 267, 269, 281-282, 285, 288, 335-336, 339, 345, 348-349

Reconstruction Act, 114, 267

Red Army, 37

Republic of Hawaii, 60, 62, 67, 68

Republic of Republics, x, 65, 75-76, 82, 129, 135, 137, 163, 275, 303, 332, 344, 346, 348-349

Republic of Sovereign States, ix, 7, 66, 76-77, 135, 142, 164, 203, 207, 212, 217, 242, 346, 349, 351

Republican Party, x, 2, 65, 70, 96, 100, 110, 115, 141, 170-171, 174, 190, 195, 203, 210-211, 219, 235, 281, 283, 303, 311, 337, 346

Revels, Hiram, 195

Rhode Island, 183, 231

Rockefeller, John D., 88, 305

Roman Empire, 85

Roosevelt, Franklin D., 144

Roosevelt, Kermit, 22

Roosevelt, Theodore "Teddy", 22, 41-42, 46, 88, 91

Ruling elite, xi, 5, 11, 15, 25, 31, 45, 52, 78, 110, 112, 116-117, 126, 129, 137, 144, 153, 169, 207, 211, 214-215, 217, 267, 282, 289, 305, 307, 312, 328-329, 332, 340, 344, 351

Russia, 38, 88, 320

S

Santo Domingo, 45

Scalawag, 20, 219, 288, 325, 327, 344, 349

Scotch-Irish, 150

Semmes, Admiral Raphael, 104, 149, 175-176

Seward, William Henry, 165-166, 210

Shah of Iran, 20-21, 24, 30

Sharecropping, 7-8, 44-45, 198, 270-271, 318, 334, 349

Sherman, General William T., 5, 92, 98, 161, 258

Sherman, John, 211

Shiite, 30

Shoshoni, 107

Silicon Valley, 124

Simkins, Francis B., 174, 179, 205

Sioux Indians, 103, 105, 108

Slave uprising, 183, 244, 317

"Slaveocracy," 185-186, 195

Slavery, 4, 7, 8, 44, 79, 111, 136, 151, 154, 156, 158-159, 162, 171, 175, 179-180, 183-188, 191-192, 194, 198, 205, 207, 229, 241, 243, 252, 256, 260-262, 264, 267, 270, 273, 279, 291, 296, 311-318, 320, 331, 333-335, 349

Smith, Jacob A., 92

"Sold down the river," 262

Solzhenitsyn, Aleksandr, 294

South America, 32, 41, 42-43, 46, 48, 85, 90, 163, 192, 214, 280

Soviet Union, 19, 27, 37

Spain, 46, 84, 99, 121, 314, 337

Spanish American War, 64

Standard Oil, 19, 35, 89

States' Privileges, 116-117, 278, 350, 351

States' Rights, ix, xi, 65-66, 115-117, 135, 162, 164, 203, 207-209, 273, 278, 311, 332, 340, 350-351, 361

Stevens, John L., 59-63, 67-68

Stevens, Thaddeus, 219, 251, 257

Subjugation, 2, 4-5, 36, 38, 53, 55, 71, 86, 245, 251, 256-258, 281, 326, 328, 330

Suharto, General, 20, 25-26, 31

T

Taft, William Howard, 42

Taney, Chief Justice Roger, 166, 168

Tariffs, 5, 7, 160, 171, 207-208, 227-228, 242, 243, 255

Teller Amendment, 99

Tenth Amendment, 10, 76, 207, 277

Texas, 64, 323, 350

Thomas, Justice Clarence, 204

Thurston, Lorrin A., 59, 67

Time Magazine, 19

"Too big to fail," 5, 80, 110, 153, 170, 213, 304, 351

Tuskegee Syphilis Experiment, 101

U

Union League, 114

United Fruit Company, 44, 47

USS Maine, 121

V

Vallandigham, Clement L., 53, 244

Vermont, 68

Vichy, 18, 113, 215, 325, 345

Vietnam, 214-217

Vigorous war policy, 217, 258-259

Virginia, 11, 27, 38, 88, 116, 135-137, 156, 183-187, 201-202, 210, 222, 224, 238, 273-274, 278, 338, 343

W

Wall Street, 11, 22, 29, 35, 77, 79-80, 89, 117, 124, 134, 160, 162, 206-207, 212, 282, 302, 305-307, 326, 340, 344

War for Southern Independence, x, 10, 11, 16, 25, 35, 37-38, 42, 51, 53, 65-66, 68, 77, 81-82, 86, 92, 97-98, 102, 107, 118, 149, 151, 153, 179, 192-193, 195, 211, 214, 219, 221, 223, 232, 236, 241, 283, 311, 320, 350

War to Prevent Southern Independence, x, 219, 273

Warmoth, H. C., 269

Washington, George, 137-138, 181, 206, 297-298

Watie, General Stand, 109

Webster, Daniel, 77, 79, 226

Weyler, Valeriano, 98, 354

Whig Party, xi, 136, 209-210, 357

Wilson, Clyde, 219

Wilson, Woodrow, 144, 211

Wirz, Major Henry, 231, 234-236

World Bank, 22, 80, 212, 302

World Trade Organization, 302

World War I, 144, 220, 292

World War II, 18, 94, 144, 148, 215, 232, 236, 319, 320, 345

Wounded Knee, 108

Y

Yellow Journalist, 97, 148-149, 160, 166, 220-221, 223, 225, 237-239

Z

Zapata Oil, 45

Available From Shotwell Publishing

If you enjoyed this book, perhaps some of our other titles will pique your interest. The following titles are now available at Amazon and all major online retailers. Enjoy!

Joyce Bennett

Maryland, My Maryland: The Cultural Cleansing of a Small Southern State

Jerry Brewer

Dismantling the Republic

Andrew P. Calhoun, Jr.

My Own Darling Wife: Letters From a Confederate Volunteer [John Francis Calhoun]

John Chodes

Segregation: Federal Policy or Racism?

Washington's KKK: The Union League During Southern Reconstruction

Paul C. Graham

Confederaphobia: An American Epidemic

When the Yankees Come: Former South Carolina Slaves Remember Sherman's Invasion

James R. Kennedy

Dixie Rising: Rules for Rebels

JAMES R. & WALTER D. KENNEDY
  Punished with Poverty: The Suffering South
PHILIP LEIGH
  The Devil's Town: Hot Spring During the Gangster Era
MICHAEL MARTIN
  Southern Grit: Sensing the Siege at Petersburg
CHARLES T. PACE
  Lincoln As He Was
  Southern Independence. Why War?
JAMES RUTLEDGE ROESCH
  From Founding Fathers to Fire Eaters: The Constitutional Doctrine of States' Rights in the Old South
KIRKPATRICK SALE
  Emancipation Hell: The Tragedy Wrought By Lincoln's Emancipation Proclamation
KAREN STOKES
  A Legion of Devils: Sherman in South Carolina
  Carolina Love Letters
JOHN VINSON
  Southerner, Take Your Stand!
CLYDE N. WILSON
  Lies My Teacher Told Me: The True History of the War for Southern Independence
  SOUTHERN READER'S GUIDE
  The Old South: 50 Essential Books (I)

THE WILSON FILES
> *The Yankee Problem: An American Dilemma (1)*
> *Nullification: Reclaiming Consent of the Governed (2)*
> *Annals of the Stupid Party: Republicans Before Trump (3)*

Green Altar Books (Literary Imprint)

RANDALL IVEY
> *A New England Romance & Other SOUTHERN Stories*

JAMES EVERETT KIBLER
> *Tiller (Clay Bank County, IV)*

KAREN STOKES
> *Belles: A Carolina Romance*
> *Honor in the Dust*
> *The Immortals*
> *The Soldier's Ghost: A Tale of Charleston*

GOLD-BUG (Mystery & Suspense Imprint)

MICHAEL ANDREW GRISSOM
> *Billie Jo*

BRANDI PERRY
> *Splintered: A New Orleans Tale*

MARTIN L. WILSON
> *To Jekyll and Hide*

FREE BOOK OFFER

Sign-up for new release notification and receive a FREE DOWNLOADABLE EDITION of *Lies My Teacher Told Me: The True History of the War for Southern Independence* by Dr. Clyde N. Wilson by visiting FreeLiesBook.com or by texting the word "Dixie" to 345345. You can always unsubscribe and keep the book, so you've got nothing to lose!

Southern without Apology.

www.ingramcontent.com/pod-product-compliance
Lightning Source LLC
Chambersburg PA
CBHW050310120526
44592CB00014B/1848